Book Four of the Hidden Series

SONG OF SONGS

the book for daughters

Written by
Michael Ben Zehabe

THE HIDDEN SERIES

Esther (Item #1)
Ruth (Item #2)
Ecclesiastes (Item #3)
Song of Songs (Item #4)
Lamentations (Item #5)

SHEMA PUBLISHING COMPANY
LOS ANGELES

SONG OF SONGS:
the book for daughters

Copyright 2012/2024 by Michael Rankin / Agent
Second Edition: Copyright 2019
Third Edition: Copyright 2024

Permission requests should be addressed to:

info@benzehabe.com
or
Attn: Michael Rankin/Agent
917 Springfield St, #B
Upland, California 91786
www.benzehabe.com

Ben Zehabe, Michael,
Song of Songs: the book for daughters / Michael Ben Zehabe

Library of Congress Cataloging-in-Publication Data
p. cm. – (book #4 in Michael Ben Zehabe's, the hidden series)
Hebrew and English
1. Bible. 2. Christian Studies. 3. Wedding.
LCCN: Pending
ISBN: 979-8-9876254-1-5

(6 X 9) This edition printed on acid-free paper.

All rights reserved. No part of this publication may be reproduced, stored in a retrieval system, or transmitted in any form or by any means—electronic, mechanical, photocopy, recording, or any other—except for brief quotations in printed reviews, without the prior permission of the publisher.

Printed in the United States of America

SONG OF SONGS

the book for daughters

(אִישׁוֹן) *ee-shone*: apple-of-the-eye; an affectionate Hebrew term for daughter.

TABLE OF CONTENTS

Dedication...	i
Getting Started	iii
The Shunemite Is Without *Ch 1*.................	2
Shunemite Intercedes For Brothers *Ch 2*...	46
Solomon's Presence *Ch 3*............................	88
This Is The Gate of The Heavens *Ch 4*........	116
She Awakens As A Shulamite *Ch 5*............	154
Solomon Inspects Graveyards *Ch 6*............	180
Final Parade to Heaven *Ch 7*......................	214
Last Shulamite Meets Her Mother *Ch 8*.....	240
Summary...	282
Holy Text Sources...	284
Key Words...	288
Main Characters..	292
Stay In Touch..	302
Endnotes...	303

Unless otherwise indicated, Bible quotations are taken from *The American Standard Version*, © 1929 *The American Standard Version* is now in the public domain.

DEDICATION

Every bride has a plan. That's how her drama starts. A world of so-called experts vie for her attention: blogs, websites, self-help books, magazines, and cable channels. Whether Muslim, Jewish, or Christian, brides are surrounded by an endless barrage of conflicting opinions.

In the immortal words of professional boxer, Mike Tyson, "Everybody's got a plan . . . 'til they get hit." One blow to the ego and too many brides throw in the towel—before reaching the one-year bell.

Every wife will eventually reach her wit's end. The Bible's matriarchs were no exception. Consider just a few examples: "And Sarai said unto Abram, My wrong be upon thee: I gave my handmaid into thy bosom; and when she saw that she had conceived, I was despised in her eyes.'" –*Ge 16:5* Rebekah had her problems. "And Rebekah said to Isaac, I am weary of my life because of the daughters of Heth. If Jacob take a wife of the daughters of Heth, such as these, of the daughters of the land, what good shall my life do me?'" –*Ge 27:46* Leah makes one of the most heart-wrenching wishes I've ever heard. "And Leah conceived, and bare a son, and she called his name Reuben. For she said, 'Because Jehovah hath looked upon my affliction. For now my husband will love me.'" –*Ge 29:32* Apparently, Jacob didn't love Leah—and Leah knew it.

Sarah, Rebekah, Leah, and the Shulamite have all had their turn in the barrel. These matriarchs left modern brides profound lessons for repairing a fractured marriage. The Bible's matriarchs overcame huge problems. You can too.

This book is an opportunity to discover the wit and wisdom that made our matriarchs heroic.

As you read *Song of Songs*, God forces you to quantify your religious tenants by measuring them against the family problems they solve. If your religious beliefs aren't solving family problems, then something is broken, and it can be fixed.

All the wisdom *of* this age is seldom *from* this age. More often than not, ancient wisdom is the best solution for modern problems. Never hesitate to consult these ancient matriarchs. The following pages are packed with their insights.

Few listen, however. It sickens me to admit this, but there is no difference between the divorce rate of the religious and the non-religious. Is it preposterous to expect marriage to last for a lifetime?

Marriage is held together with such flimsy things—lace, vows, and wishes. We humans are so unskilled at sustaining intimacy. We begin with such high hopes, yet lose our way so quickly.

In marriage, those who do persevere are rewarded with the most precious thing earth has to offer: marital love. It takes time, but those who perservere are rewarded with, falling in love with their spouse.

M.B. 11-1-10

*A wedding gift to
my daughter, Heather*

GETTING STARTED

Jules de Goncourt said, "Surely nothing has had to listen to so many stupid remarks as a painting in a museum." He was wrong. This beautiful love song, *Song of Songs*, has endured centuries of one stupid commentary after another.

Song of Songs is easier to understand if you frame it in the context of a national relationship. Israel's messiah (Solomon) is taking wives. His God, on the other hand, is in the throws of a national divorce. As *Lamentations* teaches us, Jehovah divorced unfaithful Israel, because she made ill-considered alliances with foreign kings. (Is 50:1; Jas 4:4)

Not all marriages survive.

From *Genesis* to *Revelation*, holy text is about family. In *Genesis*, Jehovah loses his family. In *Revelation*, He gets them back. A woman has an infinite vocabulary to describe relationships, and man must tap into a woman's talent for nuance. Otherwise, the underpinnings of emotional data, within all 66 books of holy text will elude them.

In fact, the emotional tone of *Song of Songs* is very connected to *Revelation*. Chapter 12 of *Revelation* describes the messiah's heavenly mother (she is also described in chapter eight of *Song of Songs*); chapter 14 of *Revelation* mentions a song that only 144,000 could master (*Song of Songs* is that song); chapter 19 of *Revelation* mentions the marriage of the messiah (the entire book of *Song of Songs* is about this same marriage); chapter 20 of *Revelation* mentions a millennial reign on earth, and a separate group ruling them from Heaven (chapter eight of *Song of Songs* adds more detail); chapter 21 of *Revelation* mentions a repaired earth (chapter eight of *Song of Songs* paints a beautiful picture of the same scene). The book of *Revelation* and the book of *Song of Songs* are eternally bound—emotionally and factually.

Thousands of years from now, when we're all sitting around the campfire, discussing holy text, we'll realize that we were being told the same story, in all 66 books of the Bible. The only difference was . . . perspective.

Sometimes holy text is speaking from the Father's perspective, the son's perspective, angels' perspective, a king's perspective, a widow's perspective, etc. If you doubt this, re-examine the parables of Jesus. He continually expands on the same theme, reconciliation, but from a different angle, with every telling.

This methodology is not uncommon. The prophets did the same thing. Family reunion is woven throughout holy text. *Song of Songs* was written for, and about, the Bride Class, who will help to rule earth, from Heaven, during the 1,000-year reign.

Most religions agree that the Bible speaks of a Bride Class, but after that, each religion branches off into many interpretations. They all teach about a world-to-come. They all teach about a Solomon-like messiah who will lead us into that world-to-come. They all teach about a small group of enlightened disciples who would recognize, and assist, this "coming" messiah.

Since we all agree that *Song of Songs* is holy text, this sacred book seems like a friendly place to begin the dialogue on how that event will take place, how it will re-shape our lives, and marriages.

SONG OF SONGS

Chapter 1:[1]
The Shunemite is Without

1 [HEAVENLY BROTHERS:]
The superlative song to Solomon.

א שיר השירים אשר
לשלמה:

    1 ***The superlative song*** (שיר השירים) literally; "song the-songs."

    With such a grand title, this book has an obligation to answer fundamental questions that bewilder today's lovers. Alan and Marilyn Bergman wrote, *How Do You Keep the Music Playing?* Their song starts by asking, "How do you keep the music playing? How do you make it last? How do you keep the song from fading too fast? How do you lose yourself to someone and never lose your way? How do you not run out of new things to say?"

    Such sad and hopeful questions, but *Song of Songs* is anxious to answer their questions.

    One Hebrew word that sets the tone, for all eight chapters, is *zim-reth* (#H2176 זמרת). Yet, it only appears about three times in holy text: "Jehovah is my strength and my song" –*Ex 15:2* "Jehovah is my strength and my song," –*Ps 118:14* "Jehovah is my strength and my song," –*Is 12:2*[2]

    In each of these instances, this Hebrew word is referring to the essential beat, or rhythm, behind the words. Or more precisely, a life course that keeps us on beat—"*zim-reth*."

    There's a predictable "arrangement" to a life that works.

The best partners find that rhythm. The best partners are great simplifiers. The best partners cut through arguments, doubt, and misinformation. They discover a path (a beat) that everyone can embrace.

This word's root, *zaw-mar* (#H2167 זמר) also appears at So 2:12. The key to mastering *Song of Songs* is connecting to the core rhythm (or steps) that God provides, behind His words. After all, Jehovah's personality is discernable in the lyrics, the tempo, and the *steps* of His song. A dance-step—so to speak.

As a side point, the actual music, taken from the Hebrew letters in *Song of Songs,* is available for download. Please google to find the artists I've collaborated with.

Back to the commentary.

Why should we care? Because you can't get in Heaven unless you master this "new" song. "And they sing as it were a new song before the throne, and before the four living creatures and the elders: And no man could learn the song save the hundred and forty and four thousand, [even] they that had been purchased out of the earth." –Re 14:3

This is no choir tryout. Mastering this symbolic song means adhering, step-by-step, to the full range of God's requirements. It means, conforming to the harmonious teachings of God.

The thematic difference between David's 40-year rule and Solomon's 40-year rule is, David's reign was blessed with victory in war (1Ch 22:7-10), while Solomon's reign was blessed with peace. (1Ki 4:25) The root word of Solomon, Shulamite, and Jerusalem, is: peace.

2 [HEAVENLY SHULAMITE:] He quenches me with the kisses of his mouth—for our principled love is more delightful than wine.	ישקני מנשיקות פיהו כי־טובים דדיך מיין:

2 ***He quenches me*** (יַשְׁקֵנִי) literally; "He-gives-to-drink-me."

The first chapter is a trio of expressions between the Shulamite, Shunemite, and Solomon. Verse two is the Heavenly Shulamite (The Jerusalem Above) speaking. The Shulamite knows what Solomon (Jesus) wants. Our struggling Shunemite does not. No Heaven for her . . . until she finds the theocratic pattern, or rhythm.

The Shulamite has found the spirit of that symbol-laden word, "rhythm." Solomon's family must never be left to whims. The Shulamite does not make life decisions based on feelings, alone. She takes God's point-of-view, despite feeling otherwise. "He that trusteth in his own heart is a fool; But whoso walketh wisely, he shall be delivered." *–Pr 28:26*

Young couples face a hard lesson: their hearts will lie to them. There is an important reason *dod* (דּוֹד) is translated here as "principled love." The Shulamite begins this sacred book explaining what really binds her and Solomon: "principled love." Beware young brides! The cruelest deeds are done in the name of, what the unrighteous label as, "love."

How does he "quench" her? What she needed, he gave. But, how could the Shulamite's thirst be "quenched," unless she, first of all, thirsted?

What did she thirst for? "Blessed are they that hunger and thirst after righteousness: for they shall be filled." *–Mt 5:6* "And the Spirit and the bride say, Come. And he that heareth, let him say, Come. And he that is athirst, let him come: he that will, let him take the water of life freely." *–Re 22:17*

with the kisses of his mouth (מִנְּשִׁיקוֹת פִּיהוּ) literally; "with-kisses-of from-mouth-of-him."

In the Semitic culture, a kiss expresses acceptance. It's not easy being an outsider. Pursuing Solomon means, rejecting, and being rejected, by all the other princes. Note that Solomon is kissing the Shulamite (not the reverse). With a kiss, the Solomon entity has publicly declared his love. He knows her, and celebrates her.

Solomon has an enterprise. With God's help, Solomon is developing the nation of Israel. Even Jesus warned about the Jezebel-like leader who would disrupt the peace of his nation—his enterprise. Solomon prefers a wife who knows how to grow a nation—not take from it, like a parasite. The Shulamite's contribution has won her a special place in Solomon's heart. "Mercy and truth are met together; righteousness and peace have kissed each other." –*Ps 85:10*

"Kiss" has its definition, but what does "mouth" mean, to a Hebrew? *Romans* explains the symbolic meaning: "For with the heart man believeth unto righteousness; and with the mouth confession is made unto salvation." –*Ro 10:10*

Just as a kiss-on-the-mouth demonstrates a vow in a wedding ceremony, this kiss-on-the-mouth publicly declares their covenant. This kiss-on-the-mouth is a public declaration of love, and a proclamation of matrimonial law.

Our unclaimed Shunemite can only look on. No kiss for her. Being the most beautiful woman in Israel isn't enough. Solomon needs partners to help him grow God's nation. Abishag is relegated to wishing Solomon's new wives well, but in the mean time, her life as an outsider is bitter.

> **NUMERICS:** *kiss* (נשק) literally; "catch fire, inflame, kindle." This is the first of three uses. At the *remez* level, the number three is a very significant number. On the third day, God created the seed-within-the-seed, recursive life, life in perpetuity. By the final occurrence (at So 8:1), you will discover what his kiss means to the one receiving it.
>
> **NUMERICS:** *principled love* (דוד) literally; "principled love, family-love, but mostly

translated as, beloved." This is the first of 40 uses. At the *remez* level, 40 is a significant number. When a Hebrew describes gestation, they do so in weeks. It takes 40 weeks to give birth. Therefore, being re-born is conveyed in the subtext—by using the number 40. By the final occurrence (at So 8:14) the Earthly Shunemite's principled love will cause her to be re-born into Heaven.

than wine (מיין) literally; "eventuating-from-wine."
This is the second indicator as to who is speaking. The Earthly Shunemite cannot drink wine at Solomon's table. His table is in Heaven. "But ye are they that have continued with me in my temptations; and I appoint unto you a kingdom, even as my Father appointed unto me, that ye may eat and drink at my table in my kingdom; and ye shall sit on thrones judging the twelve tribes of Israel." –*Lk 22:28-30*

The Festival of Booths took place after the grape harvest (approx. October). That event was a symbolic celebration of family. Abundant fruitage reflects the heavenly Father's blessing. (Le 26:5; Hag 2:19; Zec 8:12; Mal 3:11; Ps 128:3) In the negative sense, ancient Israel became like a rejected vineyard, in the wilderness (Ho 9:10; 10:1), like a foreign vine producing wild grapes. (Is 5:4; Jer 2:21)

Grapes symbolize children, but wine symbolizes highly-developed children. Unlike ancient Israel, the Shulamite carries the positive attribute of a fine "vine." Consider a prophecy found in the book of *Revelation*. An angel gives the command, "Gather the clusters of the vine of the earth, because its grapes have become ripe." Then, the vine of the earth was gathered and hurled into the great winepress. A few faithful Israelites were diligent about refining their children, through holy text, because of God's promise to make Israelites a blessing to the nations. (Ge 28:14) Thus, the connection of a grape harvest to family.

NUMERICS: *wine* (יין) literally; "effervesce, fermenting." This is the first of eight uses. When you reach the final occurrence, at So 8:2, you will understand the purpose of Jesus refusing to drink wine *until* he is in *his new kingdom*.

3 [HEAVENLY SHULAMITE:] Pleasing, is the fragrance of your perfumed oils. Your name is like perfumed oils, poured out. No wonder the virgins love you!	לריח שמניך טובים שמן תורק שמך על־ כן עלמות אהבוך:

3 *Your name is like perfumed oils, poured out* (שמן תורק שמך) literally; "perfumed-oil she-is-poured-out name-of-you."

This is a pivotal text, full of significance. This woman is anxious to take Solomon's name, because she fully recognizes its value.

For instance, the honorable Abishag would not lay with the anointed king David, unless she was his wife—thus protecting his, and her, family name. (Pr 14:1) Yet, not even Abishag exhibited the discretion of the Shulamite.

Solomon understood the importance of a name. He forbade another man to take his *unclaimed* wife, Abishag. To do so would diminish his family name, and his anointed position. This verse also helps Westerners (and young brides) to understand the Hebrew mind, regarding why Christians should pray in the anointed "name" of Jesus.

"Hitherto have ye asked nothing in my name: Ask, and ye shall receive, that your joy may be made full. These things have I spoken unto you in dark sayings: the hour cometh, when I shall no more speak unto you in dark sayings, but shall tell you plainly of the Father." –*Joh 16:24-25*

In Hebrew, the word for anointing is *ma-shach* (#H4886 משח), from which we get the word *ma-shi-ach* (#H4899 משיח), from which "messiah" is derived. In Israel, *anointing* (#H4886 משח) a person with perfumed "oil" (שמך) was an official action that elevated the anointed to a godly position of authority.

Such an anointing allowed them to speak in the "name" of God. Aaron, for example, was anointed when he became high priest. (Le 8:12) David was anointed, by Samuel, as King Designate. "Then Samuel took the horn of oil, and anointed him in the midst of his brethren: And the Spirit of Jehovah came mightily upon David from that day forward." –*1Sa 16:13*

The phrase "poured out" (תורק) is often misunderstood. The divine author is referring to, *filtering*. The more a barrel of perfume is "poured out," and filtered, the cleaner it gets, the more it increases in value. This also tells us how the Father filters potential brides who will assume His son's "pleasing" name. (Mt 20:23)

love (אהבוך) literally; "they-reflect-divine-love-for-you."

Love, and the type of love, will become progressively important in this song. Divine love, like anything else, can be perverted. For example: this same "divine love" (אהבה) gets dangerous in verses such as, So 2:7. Because, divine love delivers those who are deserving, but is deadly for those who misuse it.

Hosea's wife "loved" indiscriminately. "And Jehovah said unto me, Go again, love [אהב] a woman beloved of [her] friend, and an adulteress, even as Jehovah loveth [אהב] the children of Israel, though they turn unto other gods, and love [אהבה] cakes of raisins." –*Ho 3:1-2*

According to God, love [אהבה] is not enough. "Love" must be connected to something worth loving. Married ones: don't squander love the way Israel did!

NUMERICS: *love* (אהבה) literally; "divine love, godly attraction, desired." This is the first of 17 uses. At the *remez* level, 17 is a very significant number. Joseph was sold into bondage, by his brothers, when he was 17. Yet, Joseph's love for God remained unbroken. By the final occurrence (at So 8:7), you will learn why distance never extinguished the Shulamite's godly love (אהבה) for Solomon.

4 [EARTHLY SHUNEMITE:] Take me away with you. Let us hurry! [HEAVENLY SHULAMITE:] The king has brought me into his chambers. You will be our joy and our gladness. We shall celebrate family love through wine. Legitimate members know God's love is exponential.	משכני אחריך נרוצה הביאני המלך חדריו נגילה ונשמחה בך נזכירה דדיך מיין מישרים אהבוך: ס

4 *Take me away* (משכני) literally; "take-away-me."

At a distance from Solomon's chosen women (Shulamites), stands the unchosen Shunemite who calls out to the Heavenly Solomon, but she is ignored. Just as So 5:6 demonstrates, Solomon does not dialogue with an unclaimed Shunemite. He only speaks to Heavenly Shulamites, those chosen by his Father.

Would you marry you? Be the right person before seeking the right person. Solomon's brides are carefully chosen for the benefit of his family—for the benefit of his kingdom.

For commentators who claim that Solomon is "abducting" this unclaimed Shunemite, away from another shepherd, this verse will quickly dispel that myth. She is ignored.

Although the Earthly Shunemite remains un-taken, she pleads to be taken away. In fact, she is wise to beg.

Like the wise Shulamite, put your husband's family first. "And he said unto another, Follow me. But he said, Lord, suffer me first to go and bury my father. But he said unto him, Leave the dead to bury their own dead; but go thou and publish abroad the kingdom of God. And another also said, I will follow thee, Lord; but first suffer me to bid farewell to them that are at my house. But Jesus said unto him, No man, having put his hand to the plow, and looking back, is fit for the kingdom of God.'" –Lk 9:59-62

"And he that doth not take his cross and follow after me, is not worthy of me. He that findeth his life shall lose it; and he that loseth his life for my sake shall find it." –Mt 10:38-39

To erroneously assert that the unclaimed Shunemite does not treasure the opportunity to be with Solomon misses the entire point of this superlative song. *She wants to leave with Solomon—because Solomon is the shepherd.* This Earthly Shunemite would be willing to die to be with Solomon, but until she develops skills to further his kingdom, she will remain unclaimed.

his chambers (חדריו) literally; "chambers-of-him."

This word is to be understood as something more than house. Rather, this is the inner part of his house. "Chambers" symbolize an intimate relationship. "Chambers" are where offspring are produced.

The Songs of the Ascents are prophetic accounts describing the "Bride Class" as they journey to the groom's house. The songs of their ascent consist of 14 psalms, from Ps 120 to Ps 134. Within these 14 psalms, you can gain many prophetic insights—including the definition for "inner rooms." Therein, we find the definitive verse for, "chambers." "Thy wife shall be as a fruitful vine, In the innermost parts of thy house; Thy children like olive plants, round about thy table." –

–Ps 128:3 This also helps to identify who is speaking. The Earthly Shunemite, can't get into the houses the Messiah prepared for his Bride Class, let alone the "innermost parts of thy house." The unclaimed Shunemite is earthbound. The Heavenly Shulamite, however, resides in Heaven.

To get anointed, a Levite had to go through a seven-day anointing process—in the Tabernacle. "And ye shall not go out from the door of the tent of meeting seven days, until the days of your consecration be fulfilled: For he shall consecrate you seven days." *–Le 8:33* To enter the heavenly Temple will require the earthbound Shunemite to die, then go through a seven-day anointing process after entering Heaven.

through wine (מיין) literally; "from-wine."

His children are more than mere grapes. (Mt 7:15-16) There is a reason God uses "wine" to describe His highly refined children. The best grapes come through harsh conditions. Pierre Morlet is famed for his superb champagne. His company boasts, "Our vines must struggle to nourish themselves, resulting in a lower yield, but of the highest quality."[3]

That's the delicious wine the Messiah intends to grow. The Shulamite's struggle was painful, but those trials enhanced and flavored their personality.

Legitimate members know (מישרים) literally; "right-ones/equal ones."

This word (legitimate) disappears in many English translations. It gets folded into the following Hebrew word, אהב (godly love). Legitimate, however, has to do with equity. Heavenly Shulamites are tested as far as death. They have gone through the symbolic "seven-day anointing process." They have been filtered, and made valuable. They have been approved—legitimized. The unclaimed Shunemite, however, has yet to prove herself.

For the unclaimed Shunemite there are still many hazards ahead. She may not make it. Few do. "Whereby he hath granted unto us his precious and exceeding great promises; that through these ye may become partakers of the divine nature, having escaped from the corruption that is in that world by lust." –2Pe 1:4

> *Never grow a wishbone, my daughter, where your backbone ought to be.*
> *–Clementine Paddleford*

Like a ragged beggar tapping at the window, the unclaimed Shunemite pleads, "Take me." Depending on her value to the kingdom, Solomon may, or may not, take her.

5 [EARTHLY SHUNEMITE:] Dark am I, yet lovely, O daughters at Jerusalem, like the tents of Kedar, like the tent cloths of Solomon.	שחורה אני ונאוה בנות ירושלם כאהלי קדר כיריעות שלמה:

5 *dark* (שחורה from the root #H7835) literally; "dawn."

Rejected, she wrings her hands and frets at a distance. It may seem like a small thing, but the understanding of this word ("dark") must be precise. Otherwise, a significant insight of this song will be missed.

In this verse, she is "dark" from the absence of a sun, not from the strength of earth's sun. This verse is describing someone who is unrecognizable, because she lacks advanced light. (Joh 16:24-25)

From what word do we get "dark"? The answer is *shawkhar* (#H7835 שחר). Why is this same Hebrew word translated different, at Ge 19:15 שחר = dawn; at Ge 32:24 שחר = dawn;

at Ge 32:26 שׁחר = dawn; and at Jos 6:15 שׁחר = dawn? She is not African, or Nubian. She is not "black." She is speaking prior to sunrise.

Possibly the most respected lexicon, *Brown Driver Briggs*, makes no mention of color. Instead, שׁחר is defined as "new moon [complete absence of moonlight], make conspicuous, notorious, moon, moon god," etc. A "new moon" is without light. The sun is with light. Again, this respected lexicon leans toward the absence of light. It's the wee hours before sunrise, before most people are awake. Her skin is not "black." She simply lacks illumination. (Am 4:13)

Without understanding her type of "dark," you can't appreciate the poetic progression of advancing light. She starts off (chapter one) in the absence of light. She ends up (chapter eight) in light, more brilliant than the sun. (Ac 26:13)

The shadowy Shunemite makes reference to the tents of Kedar and the tent cloths (curtains) of Solomon. These words convey the idea of being hidden away, or unrealized. 41 of the 48 occurrences of "curtains" in the *Tenakh* are describing the "curtains" in God's tabernacle.

The Shunemite cannot see Solomon, because he is inside his tent. The tents of Kedar can withstand the fierce desert winds (רוח). The occupant is sealed inside, safe from devilish winds (רוח). (Job 1:19) Just as the morning darkness obscures the Shunemite, the curtains of Solomon's litter obscures what reclines behind them—Solomon. (Pr 7:4-7) The Shunemite could walk about (in the darkness of dawn) without being recognized, because the symbolic sun has yet to rise.

EARTHLY SHUNEMITE: The non-Christian Jews were in a quandary as to how to treat these new disciples of Rabboni Jesus. They recognized them as family members, but were in the dark as to what role they played in the Jewish community. "'And now I say unto you, Refrain from these men, and let them alone: for if this counsel or this work be of men, it will be overthrown: But if it is of God, ye will not be able to overthrow them; lest haply ye be found even to be fighting against God. And to him they agreed: And when they had called the apostles unto them, they beat them and charged them not to speak in the name of Jesus, and let them go." –*Ac 5:38-40*

  daughters at Jerusalem (בנות ירושלם) literally; "daughters Jerusalem."
  Song of Songs has just begun (the fifth verse), and God has forced us to make a distinction between Jerusalem and Zion. (Ps 135:21) Zion was known as the city of David. (2Sa 5:7-9) Jerusalem was known as the city of Solomon. (Heb 7:2)
  The apostle Paul provides the Christian definition: "But the Jerusalem that is above is free, which is our mother." –*Gal 4:26* Contrast the Christian "mother" with the "mother" of Judaism, who was killed in 70 A.D. (Ho 6:4-6)

> **NUMERICS:** *Jerusalem* (ירושלם) literally; "two-hills, foundation-of-peace." This is the first of eight uses. At the *remez* level, eight is a very significant number. There are seven days in a week. The eighth day symbolizes the beginning of a new week. By the final occurrence (at So 8:4), Heavenly Jerusalem will be fully populated and becomes fully established as a new "mother."

> **NUMERICS:** *Solomon* (שלמה) literally; "connection-to-peace." This is the first of five uses. At the *remez* level, five hints at judgment, with a view to salvation. By the final occurrence (at So 8:12) you will learn how survivors (judged mankind) connect to peace.

NUMERICS: *Daughter* (בה) literally; "daughter, or apple branch." This is the first of 12 uses. At the *remez* level, 12 locates a specific 3-D position on earth. You need six Cartesian coordinates to mark a starting point, and six to mark an ending point. So, to show a relocation, you need the number 12. By the final occurrence (at So 8:4), God's daughter has relocated to Heaven.

6 [EARTHLY SHUNEMITE:] None fear me, because I'm in an imposed darkness. How [my skin] burns, from having known the sun. My mother's sons were angry with me, and named me to care for their VINEYARDS. My own vineyard I have neglected.	אל־תראוני שאני שחרחרת ששזפתני השמש בני אמי נחרו־ בי שמני נטרה את־ הכרמים כרמי שלי לא נטרתי:

6 *None fear me* (אל־תראוני) literally; "nothing you-fear-me."

The theme of being hard to see continues throughout this chapter. From whatever religious position you are reading from, the Shunemite behaves like a widow (Abishag is David's widow). Too often, liberties are taken with widows, since there is no husband to enforce boundaries.

What a contrast to So 6:4. The Shulamite is *not* a widow, and she does inspire terror. The Shunemite is a widow, and inspires no terror.

Despite the fact that English has paired words (such as: widow and widower), their frequency of use reveals an inherent cultural bias. The word "widow" appears in newspapers up to 15 times more frequently than "widower."

The difference suggests that women are still defined by their relationship to men. The Shunemite has no man, thus wields no authority in the community.

because I am in an imposed darkness (שאני שחרחרת) literally; "because-I dusky-thicket."

The first word (שאני) has the prefix, *shin* (ש). This is a very interesting letter, since it serves many purposes in Hebrew. With a simple mark (') at the *shin* ('ש), the *shin* ('ש) can indicate a year, or an hour. Could this hint at an imposed time-period of darkness?

Generally, as a prefix, *shin* (ש) can be translated as "who." Depending on context, it can also be rendered as, "because." The letter *shin* (ש) is a letter of projection, or emanation. It helps to explain when something is the source of emanation.

The second word is more troubling, for a translator. The first thing you'll notice, *shaw-khar* (#H7835 שחר) is the first part of a compound word. By itself, it's easy to translate as "dusky; dawn; dark; etc." But what's a translator to do with the remaining (untranslated) letters? We are left with חרת, which most translators simply ignore.

These remaining letters, however, do mean something. The Hebrew word *kheh-reth* (#H2802 חרת) means "forest, or thicket." Some farmers plant a thicket as a wind break. This thicket not only blocks wind (רוח), but it also blocks sunlight. Like the picture that introduces this chapter, these human trees cast a shadow over her. So, the divine author continues with His theme of blocked sunlight.

In each circumstance, she not only needs light to find her shepherd (קהולח), but she needs light for others to recognize her. The absence of light is frustrating her. So much so, that the unclaimed Shunemite is compelled to mention it.

You might even detect an element of blame.

Trees symbolize persons. Can tree-like persons create problems for a widow? Yes! Consider the prophecy of Pharaoh's fall. Ezekiel likened this fallen Pharaoh to a lofty cedar. (Ezk 31) At Jude 12, immoral persons who darken the congregation are likened to fruitless trees, in autumn, that have died twice. Also, when the blind man was healed, his vision came back gradually. He tried to describe the men that he saw: "And he looked up, and said, I see men; for I behold [them] as trees, walking.'" –*Mk 8:24*

What changes when a woman marries? What does a woman lose, and what does she gain? For Abishag, marrying king David gave her instant status. As an illuminated wife, impugning Abishag's character meant a swift death. As a wife, she inspired fear.

What changes when a woman is widowed? For Abishag, it meant foreign women came to Jerusalem to marry Solomon—and she was relegated to that of a spectator. In Abishag's widowhood, none feared her.

Her dream identity, as a wife, surrounded by children, was snatched away. Just as some women wear black in their widowhood, Abishag wrapped herself in gloom. When Jesus died, his followers were also wrapped in gloom.

how [my skin] burns from having known the sun

(שֶׁשֱּזָפַתְנִי הַשָּׁמֶשׁ) literally; "how-she-burned-me the-sun."

The first word is, again, a compound Hebrew word. It begins with a prefix. The same prefix as the previous sentence. The first *shin* (שׁ) could mean "emanating," "reaching," "striving," "extending," or "longing." Generally, it's rendered as "who." Because of context, however, I have rendered it as "How" since it goes to the cause. That seems to be what the Earthly Shunemite is trying to convey to those listening to her—that is, the Heavenly Shulamites. They may have discovered her in darkness, but she wants them to know, like them, she once gloried in light.

The next section of this compound word is *shaw-zaf* (#H7805 שׁזף), which means "to tan, by sun burning, (as if by a piercing ray)." Who, what, or how, was her skin burned? By her "Sun." (Ac 26:13-15) Abishag was once married to King David. The apostles once had Jesus in their midst.

Abishag, who represents the promised brides of Christ, before their death and anointing, is a woman wandering in darkness. So, why is she now in darkness? Where is her sun? The Sun (the center of her universe) has died.

Then, this compound Hebrew word is followed by the feminine *tav* (ת). Feminine words are recessive and yielding. The Earthly Shunemite's "sun" has yielded to greater influences—death.

Finally, this compound Hebrew word concludes with, נִי, which is shortened from, אני = I. Now, how do we make the application? How do we put all these components into an intelligible sentence?

Consider the work of O. Schroeder and L. Durr. Their extensive work on the metaphorical implications of, sun (שׁמשׁ), in holy text, is highly regarded among Hebrew scholars. Regarding the prophet Zephaniah, ". . . he mentions the Torah and, in the spirit and language of our psalm, he compares the moral order that governs the world (משׁפט) to the natural order, exemplified by the shining forth of the morning sun: יתן לאור בבקר בבקר משׁפטו."[4]

So, using the sun (or messiah) as a symbol of "moral order that governs the world" is found throughout holy text. It also describes the well-ordered judicial system of the Jerusalem Above. So, what the earth lost, Heaven gained. The cause of her darkness, became the cause of Heaven's new light. "And he had in his right hand seven stars: and out of his mouth proceeded a sharp two-edged sword: and his countenance was as the sun shineth in his strength." –Re 1:16

The *Douay-Rheims Bible* translates this text as: "The sun hath altered my colour:" Yet, this forest, or thicket, has altered her sun. It's important that scholars take a new look at this verse. Hebrew poetry is highly symbolic, and should be read accordingly. The same idea is used by the Bible writer, Luke.

"And it was now about the sixth hour, and a darkness came over the whole land until the ninth hour, the sun's light failing: And the veil of the Temple was rent in the midst. And Jesus, crying with a loud voice, said, Father, into thy hands I commend my spirit: and having said this, he gave up the ghost." –*Lk 23:44-46* Does Luke deliberately connect "the sun's light failing" to So 1:6? It would seem so.

My mother's sons (בני אמי) literally; sons-of mother-me."

Where is the father? The text deliberately puts the feminine mother (ancient Israel) in charge of this unusual family. This became the sad state of affairs at the time of the prophet Hosea and Amos. As Jesus predicted (Mt 24:1-2), in the year 70 C.E., Israel was put to death, and her "sons" scattered to the four corners of the earth.

Since ancient Jerusalem would be dead, by default, the "earth" (the soil above sheol) would become the womb from which mankind would be resurrected.

In *Song of Songs*, however, Israel is still alive, but the Father was gone. This explains why her Brothers are wielding authority. There is no masculine Father (Jehovah). (Jer 3:8) For more detail on who the Earthly Shunemite's current mother is, refer to the commentary at So 3:4 under *"the one who conceived me."*

The loss of any messiah will dim hope and create chaos. After the death of Jesus, the Christian church was run mostly by administrators (Brothers) and political opportunists (non-

Brothers). The same could be said about Barkafkah, for the Jews, and Muhammad, for Muslims. After the death of these non-Christian messiahs, a time of "darkness" ensued—an apt term.

they were angry (נחרו) literally; "they-were-angry."

The Earthly Brother class will always outnumber the Earthly Shunemite class. Both groups attempt to worship the same God, but the prophetic Shunemite is the first to find God, and the last to be consulted. None fear her.

For the stupid, their unexamined lives are always filled with contradictions. Such idiots will always find reasons to be angry with you, and always find reasons to attack you.

Don't let your enemies dictate your values, certainly not the crooked moral order that governs their world. Their attacks are simply the result of misinformation, or their lack of enthusiasm to become informed.

Partnerships thrive on good information. By contrast, misinformed partners can do more damage than a bomb. Since it only takes one thoughtless partner to destroy a marriage, ask your partner, today: "Under what circumstances would you dissolve our marriage?" More importantly, ask yourself! If you can't be specific, you may be on the verge of a love mistake.

named me to care for their VINEYARDS (שמני נטרה את־הכרמים) literally; "they-named-me one-caring-for the-VINEYARDS."

This assignment (like tending the goats, at So 1:8) is not legitimate. How did her Brothers take title to their vineyard? "And the lord of the vineyard said, What shall I do? I will send my beloved son; it may be they will reverence him. But when the husbandmen saw him, they reasoned one with another, saying, This is the heir; let us kill him, that the inheritance may be ours. And they cast him forth out of the vineyard, and killed him. What therefore will the lord of the vineyard do unto them? He will come and destroy these husbandmen, and will give the vineyard unto others. And when they heard it, they said, God forbid!'" –*Lk 20:13-16* Does Luke deliberately connect "beloved" to So 1:6? Apparently.

Abishag, a daughter of Israel, was at first ignored. In fact, she was ignored for so long that Adonijah was emboldened to ask for her. (1Ki 2:21-24)

My own vineyard I have neglected (שֶׁלִּי לֹא נָטָרְתִּי כַּרְמִי) literally; "vineyard-of-me that-to-me not I-cared-for."

Let us not forget what tribe Abishag came from. She came from the tribe of Ephraim. She came from the city of Shunem. (1Ki 1:3)

After marrying David, she no longer walked under the banner of Ephraim. When David died, however, Abishag was stranded somewhere between the banner of David and the banner of Solomon. Solomon had not claimed her—yet.

It's always a clever strategy to treat an adequate husband like a great husband. Life can be cruel, but it's a thorough teacher. Without a single lecture from you, the years will hammer your husband into a better man.

Like Sarah, treat your husband like . . . what he might become. Damn the facts. When it looked like she would never escape her kidnapper, a weak Abraham got her back. When it looked like Sarah would have no children, she became a matriarch to a nation. Sarah behaved like Abraham was her lord and savior . . . and he grew. (1Pe 3:6)

NUMERICS: *vineyard* (כרם) literally; "vineyard." This is the first of nine uses. At the *remez* level, nine is a very significant number. When a Hebrew speaks of lactation, they do so in months. It takes nine months for a mother's milk to come in. It also becomes a numeric marker for motherhood. By the final occurrence (at So 8:12), this Shunemite gets a new mother—"the woman." But, notice at So 8:8 the new Shulamite becomes a "mother" as indicated by her full "breasts" for the benefit of her coming vineyard/children.

EARTHLY BROTHERS: Did time darken the Shunemite's sun? Did the thicket darken the Shunemite's sun? Did her Brothers darken the Shunemite's sun?

The apostle John was a "Shunemite." He tells us, who his sun was, and who darkened his sun. "There was the true light, [even the light] which lighteth every man, coming into the world. He was in the world, and the world was made through him, and the world knew him not. He came unto his own, and they that were his own received him not. But as many as received him, to them gave he the right to become children of God, [even] to them that believe on his name: Who were born, not of blood, nor of the will of the flesh, nor of the will of man, but of God." –*Joh 1:9-13*

| 7 [EARTHLY SHUNEMITE:] Whisper your insights, you whom I love. Where do you pastor your flock and where do you rest your sheep at midday? Why should I be like a skilled hired nurse to your shepherd-like acquaintances? | הגידה לי שאהבה נפשי איכה תרעה איכה תרביץ בצהרים שלמה אהיה כעטיה על עדרי חבריך: |

7 *Whisper your insights* (הגידה) literally; "mutter-your-deductions."

Wisdom, according to Muslim tradition, is connected to Solomon. They refer to him as, "Solomon the Wise." Unwise shepherds can become oppressors by adding unnecessary rules. By contrast, the tone of Solomon's heavenly household is charged with love, limitless possibilities, and service to family.

The unclaimed Shunemite knows the Heavenly Solomon's wisdom is superior to modern social norms. She knows the information he provides will help her to prosper, and is worthy of further meditation.

Where can you find such meditations? Read So 2:9. "What I tell you in the darkness, speak ye in the light; and what ye hear in the ear, proclaim upon the house-tops." –*Mt 10:27*

"And the king said, 'Divide the living child in two, and give half to the one, and half to the other.' Then spake the woman whose the living child was unto the king, for her heart yearned over her son, and she said, 'Oh, my lord, give her the living child, and in no wise slay it.' But the other said, 'It shall be neither mine nor thine; divide it.' Then the king answered and said, 'Give her the living child, and in no wise slay it: She is the mother thereof.' And all Israel heard of the judgment which the king had judged; and they feared the king: for they saw that the wisdom of God was in him, to do justice." –*1Ki 3:25-28*

Solomon (*A.K.A. Shepherd or Ecclesiastes* [קֹהֶלֶת]) is wise, but for this earthbound Shunemite, no such insights will be whispered. Solomon does not dialogue with this widow-like Shunemite. The Heavenly Solomon only speaks with women offering kingdom-building skills. The unclaimed Shunemite must console herself at Zion, with the stories she hears about Solomon, the shepherd of Israel.

like a hired nurse (כעטיה) literally; "like-giving-nipple-of-me-outside."

No known Hebrew dictionary can help us with this mysterious word. We have an advantage, however. Solving language problems is the same as solving relationship problems. They both involve relational thinking.

Let me share some noble efforts by previous translators: כתף #H3802 = covering shoulders and arms; כעס #H3707 = grieve, rage, indignant, anger; טבע #H2883 = sink, settle; תעה #H8582 = reel, vacillate, wander; עטה (not in *Strong's*) = wrapped about; עטה (not in *Strong's*) = to wander; עטה (not in *Strong's*) = snatch at, pick at fleas. Many of these words are vaguely close, but never a match.

By using the principles from *The Meaning of Hebrew Letters*[5] we can take a more effective approach. For "unknown" or "disputed" words, it's possible to resurrect the lost meaning by studying the letters within the word.

The first letter *kuf* (כ), when used as a prefix, is usually translated as "like." The final letter *hay* (ה) usually indicates "feminine," or "something or someone that goes out." So, let us consider the middle three letters (עטי). The next letter (within this 3-letter group) is *ayin* (ע). *Ayin* (ע) alludes to the eyes. The context hints that this is someone who intelligently "looks" after something or someone. The next letter, *tet* (ט), alludes to "nurturing, or nipples." The next letter, *yod* (י), alludes to "a person's profession—the work of their hands, or the mind (our mind directs our hands)." Thus, "like a skilled hired nurse."

This unorthodox explanation may not come from a lexicon, or from something as tidy as a Hebrew dictionary, but I want to be completely transparent with the methods I use. Now, I invite challenge to my work method.

There is a similar word containing different Hebrew letters. The word "nurse" *yaw-nak* (#H3243 ינק) is defined in *Strong's Concordance* as, "to suck; to give milk; nursing; suckling." (Ge 24:59; Ex 2:7; 2Ch 22:11) This word differs from *ka-oot-yah* (כעטיה) in that *yaw-nak* (ינק) is more of a bodily function. Our word, however, (כעטיה) comes closer to Abishag's profession. She intelligently cared for David.

"Why should I be like a hired nurse, for your shepherd-like acquaintances?" This method may not be traditional, but it does resurrect the image of the Abishag, who served as David's nurse (and unconsummated wife). Imagine what passed through Abishag's mind when the old adulteress, Bathsheba, attempted to demean her, by selling her (as a political favor) to Adonijah.

> *From childhood's hour I have not been as others were; I have not seen as others saw; I could not bring my passions from a common spring. From the same source I have not taken my sorrow; I could not awaken my heart to joy at the same tone; and all I loved, I loved alone. Then, in my childhood, in the dawn of a most stormy life, was drawn from every depth of good and ill, the mystery which binds me still.*
> *–Edgar Allan Poe*

Solomon legally inherited this nurse-like wife from his father, David. Unlike Bathsheba, Abishag had always honored her family name. The Shunemite could rightly complain "Why should I be like a hired nurse, for your shepherd-like (leaders; pastors) acquaintances?" (1Ki 2:19-21) She doesn't want someone like Adonijah. This same thought has an oblique connection at So 8:1.

What's wrong with Adonijah? After all, Adonijah is the son of King David.

Adonijah has neither a kingdom, nor an anointing. Why should this widowed Shunemite (Abishag) lose her royal status? If Solomon would summon her, she would come.

shepherd-like friends (עדרי חבריך) literally; "flocks-of friends-of-you."

Why would she protest? Why not settle for a highly-esteemed alternate shepherd? Adonijah could give her more personal attention. He certainly expressed an interest in doing so.

Queen Esther gave a very profound answer when she found herself in a similar circumstance. "For we are sold, I and my people, to be destroyed, to be slain, and to perish. But if we had been sold for bondmen and bondwomen, I would have held my peace, although the adversary could not have compensated for the king's damage." –Es 7:4

As with Esther, the Shunemite (Abishag) knew that if she was taken by any other king, that would be an insult to Solomon. Being sent away, to serve another, would not have sufficiently compensated the king."

You could offer this Earthly Shunemite all the kingdoms of the earth, but no one, except the duly anointed Solomon, would suffice.

Many years later it was prophesied that this same situation would cycle back and face a new royal wife. "Thus saith the Lord Jehovah: Behold, I am against the shepherds; and I will require my sheep at their hand, and cause them to cease from feeding the sheep; neither shall the shepherds feed themselves any more; and I will deliver my sheep from their mouth, that they may not be food for them.'" –Ezk 34:10

There is a predictable theme, as to what upsets our matriarchs. When it comes to kingdom matters, they are willing to drive out Abraham's son. (Ge 21:10) They are willing to reject Isaac's son. (Ge 27:6-13) Even Abishag, the Shunemite, rejected a prince of Israel, Adonijah, because of her loyalty to her king. (1Ki 2:22-23) In other words, matriarchs are not afraid to reject inferior royalty ("shepherd-like acquaintances") to further God's kingdom goals. (Re 20:4-6)

The unclaimed Shunemite intends to intercept her beloved pastor, Solomon, and openly resents being kept in the dark. Her resentment is proper. She wonders if she might locate him—at a later time—in the brightness of midday.

| **8** [HEAVENLY SHULAMITE:] If you cannot distinguish, most beautiful of women, follow the tracks of the sheep. [EARTHLY BROTHERS:] Care [instead] for the KIDS you were given, near the tents of those shepherds. | אִם־לֹא תֵדְעִי לָךְ הַיָּפָה בַּנָּשִׁים צְאִי־לָךְ בְּעִקְבֵי הַצֹּאן וּרְעִי אֶת־גְּדִיֹּתַיִךְ עַל מִשְׁכְּנוֹת הָרֹעִים: ס |

8 ***distinguish*** (תדעי) literally; "boundary-of-understanding-me."

This compound word is constructed on top of *yaw-dah* (#H3045 ידע). "*Yaw-dah*" (ידע) means "knowing." The word in this verse is more than knowing, however. Otherwise, why would the divine author attach the additional letters?

Being able to "distinguish" requires an ability to understand the original text. Rightly dividing the word of God was more than just a suggestion. Jesus spoke and read Hebrew, even when his nation was dominated by the Romans.[6] Jesus knew his worship would be incomplete without the use of the "holy language." Make no mistake, the New Testament is a Jewish book, originally written by Hebrews—in the Hebrew language. (2Tim 2:15)

of women (בנשים) literally; "in-connection-woman-kind."

This comment is addressing the Earthly Shunemite. Whether you are Christian, Muslim, or Jewish, this Earthly Shunemite is yet to be born into Heaven. So, like all pre-heavenly creatures, currently, she remains a struggling earth person—of mankind.

tracks of the sheep (בעקבי הצאן) literally; "after-tracks-of the-sheep."
It's simple. If you want to find the shepherd, find his sheep. However, knowing the way, and following the footsteps, was not always clear to this unclaimed Shunemite. (Ac 15:1-2)
She resents her brothers' lack of cooperation. The Shunemite intends to bring her complaint directly to her shepherd; the way Abishag brought her complaint to Solomon, regarding Adonijah; the way Esther brought her complaint to Ahasuerus.
The Christian apostle Thomas, for instance, was perplexed by some of Jesus' instructions. "'And whither I go, ye know the way. Thomas saith unto him, Lord, we know not whither thou goest; how know we the way? Jesus saith unto him, I am the way, and the truth, and the life: No one cometh unto the Father, but by me.'" *–Joh 14:4-6*
There is no shame in the Shunemite's confusion. King David, himself, needed, and asked for further clarification. "He restoreth my soul: He guideth me in the paths of righteousness for his name's sake." *–Ps 23:3* "For such is God, our God forever and ever; He will guide us until death." *–Ps 48:14*

KIDS you were given (את־גדיתיך) literally; "YOUNG-GOATS-he-gave."
It's important to notice that within the same verse, one person speaks of "sheep" and a different person speaks of "goats." The את, in the Hebrew text, is never translated into English—because you can't. That's because it's not a word, but a directive. The את informs the reader that the following word

is going to be very important—the object. The sheep aren't important in this exchange. The object of the sentence is the KIDS (young goats).

A woman's "given" name is not the same thing as her married name. What the Shunemite was "given" can only be valued depending on *who* gave it to her. The Earthly Shunemite is not the mother of the Brothers, she is their big sister. That allows the Earthly Brothers some unfortunate bursts of disrespect.

Who gave her goats? Not Solomon. The Heavenly Solomon never referred to his followers as "goats." To the contrary: "And before him shall be gathered all the nations: and he shall separate them one from another, as the shepherd separateth the sheep from the goats; and he shall set the sheep on his right hand, but the goats on the left." –*Mt 25:32-33*

As complex as this verse may seem, verse six may resolve this puzzling verse. The unclaimed Shunemite complains of not being able to care for her own vineyards—not goats. Chapter eight will speak of profits coming from Solomon's vineyards—not goats. The Heavenly Solomon expresses love for his sheep—not goats. It appears these "kids" come from an Adonijah-like authority (shepherd)—an authority (shepherd) she does not like.

The divine author presumes you are a Jew, and you know all the related idioms, translated and un-translated.

9 [HEAVENLY SOLOMON:] I liken you, my alpha cosset, to a mare, harnessed to one of the chariots of a Pharaoh.	לסֻסָתִי בְּרִכְבֵי פַרְעֹה דִּמִּיתִיךְ רַעְיָתִי׃

9 *my alpha cosset* (רַעְיָתִי) literally: "herding-love-mine."

Meanwhile, back in Heaven, this Heavenly Solomon extols the virtues of his Heavenly Shulamite. This is the first time Solomon speaks, and he wastes no time teaching husbands a valuable lesson in love. Show you care!

To understand who Solomon is speaking to, you must look ahead, to verse 10. Who has earrings and who doesn't? The Heavenly Shulamite has earrings. So, Solomon can't be speaking to the unclaimed Shunemite. She has no earrings.

This Heavenly Solomon never dialogues with Shunemites. They have yet to complete their symbolic seven-day-anointing process. (So 5:1-4 / Le 8:33)

"My alpha cosset" is a large composite word, with a theme of meanings, bestowing rank on Solomon's valuables. Solomon has been retrieving wives that contribute to the growth of his kingdom. Those heavenly brides had abilities that our poor Earthly Shunemite did not have. The Shunemite does not know how to care for Solomon's valuables—yet.

You may be familiar with the root word *raw-aw* (#H7462 רע) which means "to tend a flock, to rule." It's the root for "Pharaoh" (פרע). As we learned in verse seven ("shepherd-like friends"), there can be a range of applications for this root word. Our word, however, has even more letters.

In addition to being her lord's "cosset," the Heavenly Shulamite also has a leadership title that proclaims, she is also a shepherdess of people (פרעה). Whatever type of "pet" this verse alludes to, we know he is describing a, cosset, a lead pet, the pet the group follows—an alpha pet.

A translator's dilemma is, the English language has no substitute word. Since the English makes it difficult to capture the full meaning of her leadership role, we are left with "alpha cosset."

Such a description (alpha cosset) is a term of endearment for a second-in-command, a loyal sheep dog, a guard dog, a fellow worker who has made their way into your heart. Beyond emotional attachement, he trusts her the way a

Pharaoh trusted the horse drawing his chariot through a battle. He places his life, and heart, in her hands.

If you doubt a Semitic mans' attachment to pets, read 2Sa 12:1-6.

a mare, harnessed to one of the chariots (ברכבי לססתי) literally; "to-mare-of-me in-chariots-of."

The lord Solomon connects the image of a royally decorated mare to his "pet." Why? How is royalty (such as Solomon) presented to citizens?

Consider the case of Joseph: "And Pharaoh took off his signet ring from his hand, and put it upon Joseph's hand, and arrayed him in vestures of fine linen, and put a gold chain about his neck; and he made him to ride in the second chariot which he had; and they cried before him, Bow the knee: and he set him over all the land of Egypt." –Ge 41:42-43

Consider the case of Mordecai: "Then took Haman the apparel and the horse, and arrayed Mordecai, and caused him to ride through the street of the city, and proclaimed before him, Thus shall it be done unto the man whom the king delighteth to honor.'" –Es 6:11

Consider the case of king Jesus: "And I saw, and behold, a white horse, and he that sat thereon had a bow; and there was given unto him a crown: And he came forth conquering, and to conquer." –Re 6:2

The Father will also parade His son, in tandem, with a royally decorated mare. It has always been so.

Notice that the same woman (Heavenly Shulamite) is progressively given a variety of descriptions, "dove, lamb, horse, gazelle," and "doe."

10 [HEAVENLY SOLOMON:] Your cheeks are beautiful, with earrings, your neck in strings of jewels.	נאוו לחייך בתרים צוארך בחרוזים:

10 ***Your cheeks*** (לחייך) literally; "cheeks-of-you."
What a happy contrast to the Israel of *Lamentations*. Compare disloyal Israel's cheeks, with the cheeks of the faithful Shulamite. "She weepeth sore in the night, and her tears are on her cheeks; Among all her lovers she hath none to comfort her: All her friends have dealt treacherously with her; they are become her enemies." –*Lam 1:2* The cheeks of the Shulamite (the Jerusalem Above) are adorned by "earrings."

beautiful (#H3302 יפה) literally; "to be bright, make self fair, beautiful."
What a happy contrast to the gloominess of the Shunemite and the gloominess of ancient Israel. This verse points out the contrast. "Jerusalem hath grievously sinned; therefore she is become as an unclean thing; All that honored her despise her, because they have seen her nakedness: Yea, she sigheth, and turneth backward." –*Lam 1:8*
Solomon's glowing compliment, however, is directed at the Shulamite (the Jerusalem Above), not the shadowy Shunemite (those with a heavenly hope). Unlike the Shunemite, the Heavenly Shulamite's brightness comes from their lord, who stands before them. "The God of Israel said, The Rock of Israel spake to me: One that ruleth over men righteously, That ruleth in the fear of God, [He shall be] as the light of the morning, when the sun riseth, A morning without clouds, [When] the tender grass [springeth] out of the earth, Through clear shining after rain." –*2Sa 23:3-4*
Compare this to the self-described Shunemite, at verse five.

in strings of jewels (בחרוזים) literally; "in-strings-of-precious-stones."
This text also hints at God's transfer of authority from the Jerusalem below to the Jerusalem Above. Below, fleshly Jerusalem was described by God as "the land of decoration."

Verse 10 evolves from the destruction of Jerusalem. Her jewels are now worn by the Jerusalem Above.

"So the king of the north shall come, and cast up a mound, and take a well-fortified city: and the forces of the south shall not stand, neither his chosen people, neither shall there be any strength to stand. But he that cometh against him shall do according to his own will, and none shall stand before him; and he shall stand in the glorious land [*land of the Decoration* צְבִי #H6643], and in his hand shall be destruction." –*Da 11:15-16* Daniel described the death of earthly Jerusalem, by the Babylonians, while the Heavenly Solomon is describing his "decorated" Shulamite.

11 [HEAVENLY SHULAMITE:] We will make you earrings of gold, studded with silver.	תּוֹרֵי זָהָב נַעֲשֶׂה־לָּךְ עִם נְקֻדּוֹת הַכָּסֶף׃

11 *We will make you earrings of gold* (זָהָב נַעֲשֶׂה תּוֹרֵי) literally; "earrings-of gold we-will-make."

As indicated, this is the Heavenly Shulamite speaking to the Shunemite. The Heavenly Shulamite already has her earrings (compare verse 10 with verse 11).

The word, "will" indicates a future event. The Shulamite "will" make earrings for the Earthly Shunemite—if she remains faithful to the end. (Mt 24:13) The (earringed) Shulamite not only assists her (earringless) earthly daughter with her earthly endeavors, but she assists in preparing her for lord Solomon.

If *Song of Songs* is related to the book of *Esther* (and it is), then special note should be taken of the root meaning of "earring" (#H8447 תּוֹר). At Es 2:12 and Es 2:15, the same word (תּוֹר) is used to convey "her turn" to come into the king's presence. Embedded within the definition (earring / תּוֹר) is a clue that the Shunemite's turn is coming.

"Let us rejoice and be exceeding glad, and let us give the glory unto him: for the marriage of the Lamb is come, and his wife hath made herself ready. And it was given unto her that she should array herself in fine linen, bright [and] pure: for the fine linen is the righteous acts of the saints." –*Re 19:7-8*

> *There's something like a line of gold thread running through a man's words when he talks to his daughter, and gradually over the years it gets to be long enough for you to pick up in your hands and weave into a cloth that feels like love itself.*
> *—John Gregory Brown*

The above text also hints at a transfer of authority, away from fleshly Israel. If you recall, ancient Israel decked herself with earrings. "And I will visit upon her the days of the Baalim, unto which she burned incense, when she decked herself with her earrings and her jewels, and went after her lovers, and forgat me, saith Jehovah." –*Ho 2:13*

An ancient Israelite's mother was the nation of Israel. A Christian's mother is the Jerusalem Above (a.k.a. the Shulamites). Have you figured out who the Shunemite is? She is our big sister—not our mother.

The Heavenly Shulamite is our mother and our big sister's mother. Just as Solomon's foreign wives prepared Abishag for Solomon's wedding bed, so too will the Heavenly Shulamites prepare our big sister, the Earthly Shunemite.

12 [HEAVENLY SHULAMITE:] While the king was at his serving table, my perfume spread its fragrance.	עַד־שֶׁהַמֶּלֶךְ בִּמְסִבּוֹ נִרְדִּי נָתַן רֵיחוֹ׃

12 *at his serving table* (במסבו) literally; "at-table-of-him."

There are lots of circles and cycles in these verses, including this "table." The actual Hebrew word *may-sab* (מסב #H4524), appears to be a round table, conveying the idea that a group would be served at such a table. Also, the first letter in this Hebrew word is *mem* (מ), it coveys the idea that whoever sits at that table has come to full term, thoroughly born-again, having gone through an extensive re-education.

The only reason these details are mentioned, the Shulamites' aroma garners more attention than any food on this table. More than food, the Shulamite's aroma is appreciated by her husband—the Solomon-like Jesus.

The unchosen Shunemite, however, is not at this table. She has yet to prove herself faithful to the end. (Mt 24:13) Instead, Abishag, the Shunemite, wears a reminder (a sachet).

Abishag may be Solomon's property, Abishag may be a potential wife-in-waiting, but she cannot be considered a full-wife without Solomon consummating the marriage with the traditional seven-day marital dues. (Ge 29:27-28)

13 [EARTHLY SHUNEMITE:] My beloved is, to me, a sachet of myrrh—resting between my breasts.	צרור המר | דודי לי בין שדי ילין:

13 *My beloved* (דודי) literally; "beloved-of-me."

In this sacred song, the word *dod* (#H1730 דוד) will be used 40 times—for good reason. David reigned for 40 years. Solomon reigned for 40 years. The number 40 symbolizes gestation. The Earthly Shunemite is on the verge of rebirth.

Since Hebrew is numerical, pictorial, and phonetic, it's full of hidden meanings, at many different levels. It's no accident that one of Solomon's names was *Jedidiah* (#H3041 ידידיה) comes from the root *dode* (#H1730 דוד).

Jedidiah means, "he is beloved of Jah." (2Sa 12:25) As mentioned before, Luke uses "beloved" in his gospel. "And the lord of the vineyard said, What shall I do? I will send my *beloved* son; it may be they will reverence him." –*Lk 20:13*

myrrh (#H4753 מר) literally; "myrrh."

The Shunemite's refrain is less elegant than the Shulamite's, because she (the Shunemite) doesn't have Solomon. She has a sachet, a reminder of Solomon.

Inside this sachet is myrrh. Like "gate," myrrh hints at death. One of the gifts brought by the wise men, was myrrh. (Mt 2:11) What did myrrh represent? Myrrh was used for embalming the dead. (Joh 19:39) Myrrh was mixed with wine and offered to Jesus, during his extended death. (Mk 15:23)

Myrrh, as used in embalming, hides the smell of death, but unlike her brothers, Abishag must die. Like myrrh, her life will be bitter. The same root word was used to describe bitter water. "And when they came to Marah (מרא), they could not drink of the waters of Marah (מרא), for they were bitter: therefore the name of it was called Marah (מרא)." –*Ex 15:23*

Notice how Naomi described her bitter life. "And she said unto them, Call me not Naomi, call me Mara (מרא); for the Almighty hath dealt very bitterly (מר) with me.'" –*Ru 1:20*
The Earthly Shunemite's *bitter* life is in stark contrast to the Heavenly Shulamite's *eternal* life.

between my breasts (בין שדי) literally; "between breasts-of-me."

If fragrance is worn to make a personal statement, then the unchosen Abishag has publicly proclaimed her allegiance. She has put on the scent of her lord, for her lord. She belongs to him. If reputation rests on the decisions we make, then Abishag has impeccable taste. Every facet of her character proclaims rejection of other, so-called, "shepherds." Whether Solomon chooses her, or not, she has chosen him.

When the Hebrew word *shad* (#H7699 שד) is applied to a man, it should be translated as "bosom." Since this word is applied to a woman, and "between" is used in the same sentence, "breasts" is the only logical rendering. The person she pines for, however, is not between her breasts. The item that brings him to mind—the "sachet" is between her breasts. The "sachet" is the memorial she keeps. (Lk 22:19)

Jesus used this word (שד) to connect his followers to Abraham. For centuries dimwitted translators have erroneously translated *El Shaddai* (אל שדי) as "God Almighty." The literal translation is "God bosomed me." It's much more accurate: God took Abraham to His bosom—the Father had a connection with Abraham unlike previous sons. (Jas 2:23)

The Shunemite's Abraham-like behaviors will be remembered in Heaven. "And it came to pass, that the beggar died, and that he was carried away by the angels into Abraham's bosom: and the rich man also died, and was buried. And in Hades he lifted up his eyes, being in torments, and seeth Abraham afar off, and Lazarus in his bosom." –*Lk 16:22-23* "God Almighty" is a horrid translation. It fails to convey this intimate-bosom position—an adoption, of sorts.

14 [EARTHLY SHUNEMITE:] My beloved is, to me, a cluster of henna blossoms, from the vineyards of En Gedi.	אשכל הכפר ׀ דודי לי בכרמי עין גדי: ס

14 *cluster of henna blossoms* (אשכל הכפר) literally; "cluster-of the-henna-blossom."

Henna is a shrub that bears clusters of small cream-colored, four-petaled, flowers. We have already discussed what "four" means to a Hebrew. "Four" points to the inner dimension—what hides within us. The number "four" is critical to making sense of all further references to "henna."

This common shrub is never mentioned in holy text, with the exception of *Song of Songs* (So 1:14; 4:13; 7:11). When the henna paste is washed off, a persistent stain (a reddish color) remains. So, henna is also used for non-permanent tattoos, or just to darken, human skin.

It isn't common knowledge, but "red" stained leather played an important role in the construction of the tabernacle. "And they brought the tabernacle unto Moses, the Tent, and its furniture, its clasps, its boards, it bars, and its pillars, and it sockets; and the covering of rams' skins dyed *red*, and the covering of sealskins, and the veil of the screen; the ark of the testimony, and the staves thereof, and the mercy-seat." –*Ex 39:33-34* This same *red* tabernacle symbolized the body of the future Messiah.

The Hebrew word *ko-fer* (#H3724 כפר), in this sentence, is also used for "covering," possibly because of the henna's use as a *red* dye. (Ge 6:14) The dye "covers" your natural color. This definition is of special interest, since a future messiah will serve as mankind's covering (כפר = covering/atonement).

That Hebrew word was the basis for the holy day of, Yom Kippur (יוֹם כפר), known to Westerners as "Day of Atonement," or "Day of Covering." The Muslim "Day of Atonement" is *Shab-I-Barat* (salvation from guilts).

15 [HEAVENLY SOLOMON:] How beautiful you are, my darling! Oh, how beautiful! Your eyes are doves.	הנך יפה רעיתי הנך יפה עיניך יונים:

15 *beautiful* (#H3302 יפה) literally; "to be bright, make self fair, beautiful."

Chapter one started off with the unclaimed Shunemite in darkness. Here, Solomon praises this person for her brightness, which is embedded within the definition of "beautiful." This compliment is not directed at the Shunemite, rather, a person who has transformed into a Shulamite.

In Hebrew, a description has more to do with a quality, character trait, or ability. Rarely does holy text describe people by their physical attributes.

Von Dobshutz reminds us that Greeks think, and speak, in spatial terms. Conversely, Hebrews think and speak in temporal terms.[7] The reason for her "illumination" is explained in the commentary for verse, 10. Nowhere is this principle more apparent than in the names of the two sisters, Rachel (רחל) and Leah (לאה). Whereas, Jacob saw dullness in the eyes of Leah, he saw a "spirit of greatness" in Rachel's eyes (רוח = spirit; אל = great one).

Translating without reading the surrounding text produces dull scripture. Most see "Rachel" as coming from the Hebrew word for "lamb." They ignore that the Shulamite came to us through the matriarchs.

It may sound disconnected when Solomon does not respond to the Earthly Shunemite, but ask one of today's Earthly Shunemites if their messiah dialogues with them. He does not. They rely, instead, on ancient holy text.

your eyes are doves (עיניך יונים) literally; "eyes-of-you doves."

Inadequate translators attempt to impose their wrong-headed, Western thinking on this Hebrew verse. Inferior translators throw in extra words ("look like") that are not in the original text. The author is not saying, "Your eyes *look like* doves." The author is saying, "Your eyes *are* doves." That's perfectly obvious when you read the text in Hebrew.

Here is how a proper analogy works: Marriage is not only the beginning of a new life, but the end of an old life. For some, searching for a partner becomes a skill they are unwilling to discard. In other words, they are always on the make.

We may be familiar with the term, "not all that glitters is gold." Few people, however, are familiar with its origin. "Not all that tempts your wandering eyes; And heedless hearts, is lawful prize; Nor all that glitters, gold." *–Thomas Gray*

Loyalty is an important quality of love. Doves are known for their loyalty. Thus, the Shulamite's eyes were focused on her fidelity. Her eyes did not wander. Her "eyes *are* doves." Also, doves nest near a source of water. If water equals truth, then the analogy is complete.

Solomon speaks to his loyal Shulamite, not the Shunemite. His relationship with the Shunemite is distant. She is an undesignated, administrative candidate.

16 [HEAVENLY SHULAMITE:] How handsome you are, my beloved! Oh, how charming! And our bed is verdant.	הנך יפה דודי אף נעים אף־ערשנו רעננה:

16 *handsome* (#H3302 יפה) literally; "to be bright, make self fair, beautiful."

Chapter one starts off with Abishag, the Shunemite, in darkness. The Heavenly Shulamite, by contrast, is bathed in light. Solomon's handsomeness is her light source. When their children display the personality of their parents (the Heavenly Solomon and the Heavenly Shulamite), they too become a source of light. (2Sa 23:3-4)

our bed is verdant (ערשנו רעננה) literally; "bed-of-us verdant."

Hidden beneath the surface translation is proof that the author continues with the "covered" theme. The Hebrew word for this bed is *eh-res* (#H6210 ערש). Unlike regular beds, this bed is defined as "covered bed, canopied." In addition, this bed is described as "verdant."

This is how we know who is speaking. Since the Heavenly Shulamite is our eternal mother, and the Messiah is our eternal father, their children are described as a great crowd that no man can number. (Re 7:9)

As the commentary on verse four makes clear, their bed is within the Heavenly Solomon's chambers—located in Heaven.

The Earthly Shunemite, by contrast, has no children. One day she may—but not until chapter five. "Little children, yet a little while I am with you. Ye shall seek me: And as I said unto the Jews, Whither I go, ye cannot come; so now I say unto you." –*Joh 13:33*

HEAVENLY SHULAMITE: "And there shall be night no more; and they need no light of lamp, neither light of sun; for the Lord God shall give them light: and they shall reign for ever and ever." –*Re 22:5* The Shulamite is not in darkness. The Shunemite is in darkness.

17 [HEAVENLY SHULAMITE:] The beams of our house are cedars; our rafters are firs.	קרות בתינו ארזים רהיטנו ק ברותים:

17 *The beams of our house are cedars* (קרות בתינו ארזים) literally; "beams-of house-of-us cedars."

At this moment, we still have many Earthly Shunemites among us. The Heavenly Shulamites, by contrast, are already assembling and ruling from Heaven. Shulamites no longer live in their Brother's house. They now live in their husband's house—thus the word "our." "And if I go and prepare a place for you, I come again, and will receive you unto myself; that where I am, [there] ye may be also." –*Joh 14:3*

Despite Abishag's pleads "take me away." That's impossible. Just being the most beautiful woman in Israel is not enough. She must continue developing her administrative skills to serve in Solomon's kingdom. Solomon values a woman's kingdom abilities above all else.

Like the Shunemite, queen Esther had to be trained for her future administrative duties. "So it came to pass, when the king's commandment and his decree was heard, and when many maidens were gathered together unto Shushan the palace, to the custody of Hegai, that Esther was taken into the king's house, to the custody of Hegai, keeper of the women. And the maiden pleased him, and she obtained kindness of him; and he speedily gave her her things for purification, with her portions, and the seven maidens who were meet to be given her out of the king's house: And he removed her and her maidens to the best place of the house of the women." –*Es 2:8-9*

Why are the beams of this heavenly abode described as "cedar?" Because the Shulamite's husband is described as a "cedar" tree. "Thus saith the Lord Jehovah: I will also take of the lofty top of the cedar, and will set it; I will crop off from the topmost of its young twigs a tender one, and I will plant it upon a high and lofty mountain: In the mountain of the height of Israel will I plant it; and it shall bring forth boughs, and bear fruit, and be a goodly cedar: and under it shall dwell all birds of every wing; in the shade of the branches thereof shall they dwell.'" –*Ezk 17:22-23* David also claimed to be a "cedar."

The reference to the "fir" tree hints at the Shulamite's heavenly calling. There are balsamiferous trees among the fir family. The fir's balsamic oil is used medicinally (usually containing benzoic or cinnamic acid) and as a perfume.

Balsam plants and trees were always highly prized by Hebrews. The first mention of "balsam oil" occurs at Ex 25:6, with reference to its use as an ingredient in the holy anointing oil, for the tabernacle. In the future, the new tabernacle is relocated to Heaven. "And there was opened the Temple of God that is in Heaven; and there was seen in his Temple the ark of his covenant." –*Re 11:19*

EARTHLY SHUNEMITE: Today, some still struggle with what an Earthly Shunemite is. That remains a matter of interpretation for each faith. The apostle Paul claimed to have a heavenly hope. Yet, while a Shunemite, he never claimed to be equal to a Heavenly Shulamite (while he was on earth). "Not that I have already obtained, or am already made perfect: but I press on, if so be that I may lay hold on that for which also I was laid hold on by Christ Jesus. Brethren, I could not myself yet to have laid hold: but one thing [I do], forgetting the things which are behind, and stretching forward to the things which are before, I press on toward the goal unto the prize of the high calling of God in Christ Jesus." –*Ph 3:12-14*

Let me end this chapter with a story: six injured men shared the same hospital room. Only one had enough mobility to sit up. He was placed nearest the window.

Every afternoon this man would raise himself and encourage the other patients by describing what he saw outside his window. In those sweet moments, his roommates forgot their pain and listened, spellbound.

The other men lived for that special hour, when the patient nearest the window told them about a world they were no longer a part of.

Maybe it was their physical limitations, or maybe it was his reassuring voice. But when he described the park, the pond, the swans, and the children who chased them, the other patients were inspired to regain their health. He described the blossoming love between pedestrians who strolled by. He described, in warm detail, the hope that he could see in young lovers' eyes.

One morning, the man by the window died, unexpectedly. For a time, the men grieved over the roommate who had encouraged them. Soon, their pains and complaints began to return. Their hopelessness crept back into their conversations.

Finally, one man asked the nurse if he could be moved next to the window. The other injured men smiled, waiting for his description of the park, the children, the lovers.

Slowly, painfully, he propped himself up on one elbow, only to discover the window faced an ugly, unpainted wall.

Your partner may have injuries you can't repair. Your partner may be trapped in a dark room, without windows. Your life narrative might bring him more relief than an opiate. Some people make better windows than windows. Your kind words, and enlightened perspective, is a window of wonders to someone living in pain. Your partner needs your hopeful take on the outside world.

Chapter 2:8
Shunemite Intercedes for Brothers

Be extra vigilant in the second year of marriage. For a Hebrew, "two" hints at potential badness. In chapter two, Solomon speaks twice. There are two divisions of the Bride Class (Shunemite and Shulamite). There are two crops of figs. There are two kingdoms. There are two resurrections. "Come" is used twice in the same verse (13). "Face" and "voice" are used twice in the same verse (14). "Foxes" is written twice-in-a-row, which hints at potential badness. In the same verse (15), the word "vineyards" is used twice. And the holy name of God is hidden twice within this chapter. "Two" portends danger.

2 [EARTHLY SHUNEMITE:] I am a rose of Sharon, a lily of the valleys.	ב אני חבצלת השרון שושנת העמקים:

1 *Sharon* (שרון) literally; "Sharon."

This may hurt, but expect to watch other couples be happier, richer, and louder than you. Wait. No obstacle can withstand patience. Wait. As every matriarch discovers, entire seasons will pass without reward. As your mate's peculiarities add up, what can you do? Wait!

The definition of "Sharon" is not certain, but it seems to mean, "perpetual justice, right and fair." Matriarchs long to be acknowledged and treated fair, but justice takes time.

"A rose of Sharon, a lily of the valleys." What a lovely self-image to embrace, while *waiting*. After all, how can you resolve a disagreement unless you first establish what's right and fair?

There's a simple, but often overlooked, marital solution provided by God. In Israel, some sins were committed willfully, others unwittingly. To resolve accumulated transgressions, God instituted a, once-a-year, Day of Atonement (Yom Kippur). The Day of Atonement provided a "scapegoat" to place their petty transgressions on, then forget. F-O-R-G-E-T!

After that, revisiting old sins was not tolerated. A marriage becomes toxic, with old resentments, after only a few years. It's easy to say, "I forgive," but most couples lack the enterprise to do the necessary work that follows. The day after proved who had the wisdom of God, and who didn't. Replace your anniversary with a "Day of Atonement."

Marital problems pre-date your marriage. When God instituted annual forgiving, He left you with no alternative, other than facing your biggest obstacle—the old you. Forgiving removed the camouflage grumblers hid behind.

Annual forgiveness scoured away the residue of anger, the cost of hatred, the waste of broken vows. Forgive to the same degree that you love. The actress, Marlene Dietrich, said it well. "Once a woman has forgiven her man, she must never reheat his sins for breakfast."

lily of (שׁוֹשַׁנַּת) literally; "lily-of."

Throughout this song, Solomon will be harvesting these lilies for a heavenly life—not all at once, however. It stands to reason that this Solomon-like Jesus would not start harvesting these lilies until around 33 A.D. How could he share his kingdom prior to being crowned as king? (Mt 28:18)

How long would it take to marry 144,000 wives? If each wife was given the traditional seven days, Jesus could marry 144,000 wives within 395 years. This gives Jesus plenty of time between the years of 33 A.D. and 2023 (as of the last edition). (Ge 29:27-28)

The Hebrew word *sho-shan* (שׁוֹשָׁן) means "lily." Is queen Esther's city, Shu-shan, related in some way? Yes.

Queen Esther did not reside in Jerusalem. Shushan was in a foreign country where the undisclosed Jew, Esther, distinguished herself among thousands of lily-like women. "And the king loveth Esther above all the women, and she receiveth grace and kindness before him above all the virgins, and he setteth a royal crown on her head, and causeth her to reign instead of Vashti." –*Es 2:17*

2 [HEAVENLY SOLOMON:] Like a lily among thorns is my shepherdess. [She is] among the daughters.	כשושנה בין החוחים כן רעיתי בין הבנות:

2 *thorns* (חוחים) literally; "thorns."

The Solomon-like Messiah is not speaking to the Shunemite. Like queen Esther, the Shunemite is not among the "daughters" at Jerusalem. Solomon is speaking to the Heavenly Shulamite.

Note the contrast in Solomon's compliment: lilies vs thorns. Do not confuse thorns with weeds. Weeds serve no kingdom purpose. Thorns, on the other hand, do active harm. They aggressively impair the "walk" (הלכה). The Heavenly Shulamite has none of these "thorn-like" qualities. "Thorns [and] snares are in the way of the perverse: He that keepeth his soul shall be far from them." –*Pr 22:5*

Too many people neglect to cull out their "thorn-like" qualities. For instance, opting for singleness doesn't count if your thorny personality doesn't attract a mate. If you don't have a mate, you still owe it to society to be considerate. Thorny character flaws could make you a bad representative of God's family. Obnoxious is obnoxious, no matter what liberties you claim for yourself. (Ro 16:17)

If a woman fails to develop character, she not only chisels away her own reputation, but the reputation of everyone in her household.

A wife who obsesses on "fixing" her husband only succeeds in demeaning him. Snide remarks and barbed comments will destroy the peace of her household. Why scatter "thorns" where our children walk? Thorns add pain to their "walk," while lilies are cool and soft to "walk" on.

daughters (בנוֹת) literally; "daughter-class."

There will be many types of "daughters" under discussion in this book. Solomon's "shepherdess" is from the daughters in Heaven. His "shepherdess" became a recent daughter of Jehovah. (So 8:1)

I have departed from traditional translations by inserting, "[She is]." Inserting "[She is]" has two advantages: (1) It avoids the confusion that there may be other "daughters" in Heaven who are like thorns. (2) It also avoids lumping the Shulamite in with the daughters of Zion. She is not among the daughters of Zion! She has a different mother. She has different brothers.

3 [HEAVENLY SHULAMITE:] Like an apple tree among the trees of the forest, is my beloved. [He is] among the sons. I delight to sit in his shade, and his fruit is sweet, to my taste.	כתפוח בעצי היער כן דודי בין הבנים בצלו חמדתי וישבתי ופריו מתוק לחכי:

3 ***Like an apple tree*** (כתפוּח) literally; "like-apple-tree."

The word itself (כתפוּח) does translate as "apple," but it also indicates its *fragrance,* or *scent*. It comes from the root, *naw-fakh* (#H5301 נפח) meaning "blow; pant; struggle for breath." (Ge 2:7; Jer 15:9) Since this apple tree is standing among fruitless trees, this definition gives the impression of an infant being birthed, gasping for its first breath amongst great persons. Maybe you are familiar with the related Hebrew word *ru-akh* (רוּחַ), which means "wind, spirit, or breath."

Regarding this definition, M. C. Fisher wrote: "Relationship [to *naphach*] seems at first semantically strained, but the ideas of 'breathe' and 'exhale an odor' are related. The by-form *puach* (פּוּחַ) means both 'blow' (of wind) and 'exhale a pleasant odor, be fragrant.'"[9]

It's extremely important for the reader connect *spirit* to *apple*. If you fail to make that connection, you will completely miss the surprising connection at So 8:5.

Her beloved, Solomon, serves as a marker, a door to Heaven. If he is "like" an "apple tree," then he is related in some way to the actual "apple tree," described at So 8:5. This "lily of the valley" could follow her nose to locate her beloved (the Shunemite already wears a sachet of his scent So 1:13). Unlike the fortunate Shulamite, chapter two requires our poor Shunemite to command every resource (physical, intellectual, and spiritual) to locate and follow her hard-to-find beloved.

> **NUMERICS:** *apple* (הַתַּפּוּחַ) literally; "apple; blow; breathe; kindle." This is the first of five uses. At the *remez* level, five portends judgment, with a potential for salvation. It means salvation for the righteous, but punishment for the wicked. By the final occurrence (at So 8:5), the faithful Shunemite will receive her judgment—which involves an apple tree.

the forest (הַיָּעַר) literally; "the-forest."

Even as a tree is used to symbolize an individual or a ruler, holy text also uses forests, symbolically, for nations and their rulers. (Ezk 31)

Since the Shulamites are joint rulers with Solomon (Re 5:9-10), they too could be described as forests among men—from which Solomon builds his house. "And his own house hath Solomon built thirteen years, and he finisheth all his house. And he buildeth the house of the forest of Lebanon; a hundred cubits [is] its length, and fifty cubits its breadth, and thirty cubits its height, on four rows of cedar pillars, and cedar-beams on the pillars." –*1Ki 7:1-2*

The metaphorical forest can be dangerous for a Shunemite, because every tree begins to look the same. When we compare all earth's famous leaders, we quickly realize there is no end to the forest of world leaders—and they all cast large shadows over the earth.

In whose shadow do you stand? Who do you follow: Jehovah, Socrates, Buddha, Moses, Bernie Madhoff?

It takes a certain kind of woman to appreciate a certain kind of man. Some unchosen Shunemites love the "famous Solomon." Some unchosen Shunemites love "Solomon the wise." Marriage, however, is different. It's not a popularity contest. In a marriage, partners must administer their partner's ideologies—be a partner in his enterprise.

I have departed from traditional translations by inserting, "[He is]." The sentence could survive without inserting "[He is]" with a simple comma. Inserting "[He is]" has two advantages: (1) It avoids the confusion that her husband is her Father. He is not. (2) It also avoids lumping Solomon in with the sons of the earth. He is no longer among the sons of earth! He has a different Father. He has a different mother. He has different brothers and sisters. (3) It mirrors and balances a similar phrase in verse two.

in his shade (בְּצִלּוֹ)   literally; "in-shade-of-him."

The chosen Shulamite enjoys Solomon's actual shade. The unchosen Shunemite does *not* enjoy the actual person of Solomon. While Solomon is busy choosing foreign, but politically connected women. Abishag waits, hopes, and weeps. The unchosen Shunemite has no one to talk to, no one to watch over her.

How does this sentiment work in real life? Well, consider a song written by George Gershwin that has found an audience in every generation, *Someone to Watch Over Me*. The lyrics are as follows: "There's a somebody I'm longing to see; I hope that he turns out to be; Someone who'll watch over me; I'm a little lamb who's lost in the wood; I know I could always be good; To one who'll watch over me; Although he may not be the man some girls think is handsome; To my heart he carries the key; Won't you tell him please to put on some speed; Follow my lead, oh, how I need; Someone who'll watch over me."

It doesn't take a religious person to crave a messiah. We all need a messiah. It doesn't take a George Gershwin to recognize a core human desire for a redeemer—a desire for "perpetual justice." This basic human desire is nothing to be ashamed of. The promise of a deliverer existed long before the the first page of holy text was ever written.

my taste (לחכי) literally; "to-taste-of-me."

The Hebrew word *khake* (#H2441 חך) means "taste, inside of mouth, organ of speech." It's important to see the connection to a related Hebrew word *khaw-kam* (#H2449 חכם) which means "to be wise, teach wisdom, deal wisely."

When you combine those two concepts you can appreciate what she partakes of. "Oh taste and see that Jehovah is good: Blessed is the man that taketh refuge in him." *–Ps 34:8* "How sweet are thy words unto my taste! [Yea, sweeter] than honey to my mouth!" *–Ps 119:103*

God's fruit makes us wise when we eat it. God's fruit makes us even wiser when we learn to appreciate it. This means, you have the ability to change your "taste" to accommodate your partner—if you want to.

NUMERICS: *fruit* (פרי) literally; "reward; reached for; plucked." This is the first of three uses. At the *remez* level, three is a very significant number. On the third day, God created the seed-within-the-seed; recursive life; life in perpetuity. By the final occurrence (at So 8:12), you will discover how this Shulamite can also bear this fruit that gives eternal life.

4 [HEAVENLY SHULAMITE:] He has taken me to the banquet hall, and his banner over me is divine love.	הביאני אל־בית היין ודגלו עלי אהבה:

4 *He has taken me* (הביאני) literally; "he-took-me".
In verse four of chapter one, the pathetic Shunemite begged to be taken away, but she remains unclaimed—on earth. No banquet hall for her, yet. In verse four of chapter two, however, Solomon took his brides to this prophetic banquet hall (or house of wine). No earth person will have that priviledge. The prophetic banquet hall is in Heaven.

and his banner (ודגלו) literally; "and-banner-of-him."
The tribes of Israel were sectioned into 12 categories—traveling under unique family banners. Like ancient Solomon's wives, the Heavenly Shulamite becomes part of a new tribe, and has a new "banner" (דגל)—divine love (אהבה). God is LOVE. (1Joh 4:8) See commentary, at So 6:4.

It's simple logic. Heavenly Shulamites are granted a "new banner," identifying them as children of Jehovah. "Behold what manner of love the Father hath bestowed upon us, that we should be called children of God; and [such] we are. For this cause the world knoweth us not, because it knew him not." –1Joh 3:1 The Shulamite will have a different Father than the Earthly Shunemite—since the death of Jesus. Jesus is our "eternal father," but the Shulamite travels under Jehovah's banner—her Father.

divine love (אהבה) literally; "divine-love."

The journey to her husband's house is a legal ceremony, binding the Shulamite to her new family. Jehovah, the Father of Jesus, is certainly a tribal patriarch to His heavenly family. So, He becomes the banner over His son (our Messiah) *and* His daughter (the Shulamite). They are unified under His banner of LOVE. Jehovah is LOVE. (1Joh 4:8)

> **HEAVENLY SHULAMITE:** Like David, the Shulamites will challenge giants. They can defeat giants, because they come in the name of Jehovah: "We will triumph in thy salvation, And in the name of our God we will set up our banners: Jehovah fulfil all thy petitions." –Ps 20:5

5 [EARTHLY SHUNEMITE:] Re-constitute me with raisins, revive me with apples, for I am faint without divine love.	סמכוני באשישות רפדוני בתפוחים כי־ חולת אהבה אני:

5 *Re-constitute me* (סמכוני) literally; "support-me."

Life isn't easy for an unclaimed Shunemite. While the Heavenly Shulamites are on their way to the banquet house, Abishag, the Shunemite, pleads for marginal nourishment. The two fruits that will revive her are both identified with the Heavenly Solomon: grapes and apples. (So 2:3; 7:9) What Solomon has, is what she wants. What Solomon has, is what will "re-constitute" her.

With greater responsibilities come greater trials. Abishag was originally selected to be a nurse. She was the faithful and discreet slave of a dying king of a dying kingdom. (Mt 24:45-51) But, who nurses her? After David's death, she is irrelevant.

So, our Shunemite awaits the approval of the new king, Solomon. Christians await the approval of their new king, Jesus; Jews await their Messiah; Muslims await their Messiah.

Abraham had eight sons—not just Isaac. All eight sons bring something to the table. Abraham loved all of his sons. He was a good father who made sure his sons were literate, of good character, and shared their father's ideology. Abraham did good.

Yet, today, all these sons of Abraham treat each other with contempt and cruelty. There is very little cooperation between them. What would Abraham say?

Where did we go wrong?

All Abraham's sons were taught that God would progressively reveal Himself. God's wholeness has yet to be realized. There will always be gaps in our understanding. Why should we fill every unknown gap with suspicion, bigotry, and accusations? Men do it to women; Jews do it to Christians; Christians do it to Muslims. Yet, all these have an implied duty to Abraham. While we wait for our messiah, let us look after one another with "raisins" and "apples." "I do submit, with Solomon, to the Sustainer of the worlds." –*Koran 27:44*

faint without (חוֹלה) literally; "being-faint-of."

The verb *khaw-law* (#H2470 חלה) means "to be weak, sick, afflicted, or in pain." This word (חוֹלה), however, has two additional letters: The *vov* (ו) and the *tav* (ה). The *vov* (ו) is a man's number, six. So, this may refer to the limitations of humanity. This is doubly emphasized by the *tav* (ה), since the *tav* (ת) indicates the end, a limitation, or a boundary. Overall, this compound word hints at the painful limitations of the human speaker. It's acceptable to translate this as "homesick for divine love." Both types of illness relate to family.

A related word *kheel* (#H2427 חיל) means "to be in labor, pain." That too relates to a type of family pain. In the subtext, this connects to So 5:4. Again, the word in this verse inserts a *vov* (ו), which brings mankind into the translation. In any case, the unchosen Shunemite's suffering comes from humanity.

> *Things turn out best for the people who make the best out of the way things turn out.*
> *–Art Linkletter*

The word prior to it (כי) connects to fruits, or lack of them. The particle is the full form of the prepositional prefix, indicating it causes something. כי will flavor the sentence with what Abishag is lacking. Our unchosen Shunemite is lacking Solomon's fruit—*CHILDREN!*

Solomon's fruit will gain her respect in his kingdom. Any way you look at this verse, this Earthly Shunemite longs, hungers for, *FAMILY!*

This verse connects to verse three. This verse, however, is spoken by Abishag—the Shunemite. It's a dangerous life for a Shunemite. "For the enemy hath persecuted my soul; He hath smitten my life down to the ground: He hath made me to dwell in dark places, as those that have been long dead. Therefore is my spirit overwhelmed within me; My heart within me is desolate." *–Ps 143:3-4*

My dear daughter, every friend, every neighbor, and every family member hopes you can retain your golden heart. No one wants to see your love sullied. Yet, they all know some unexpected turn in life will find you, eventually. Know this: you are being hunted—like game. Life will knock you down with some unexpected misfortune. Resolve now, to help your partner get back up. Only a demented family murders its wounded. When everyone else abandons him, come back for your husband.

The unchosen Shunemite cannot allow herself to succumb to her difficult life. Moses allowed himself to succumb, when the Israelites "embittered his spirit." As a result, Moses could not enter the promised land. (Ps 106:32-33) The same dark reality that hunted Moses, hunts you. The same dark reality that hunted the Shunemite, hunts you.

> **EARTHLY SHUNEMITE:** David's wives were taken captive by the Amalekites. His wives' names hint at how to deal with your future "two years of famine." (Ge 45:6) Ahinoam means "brothers are pleasant." Abigail means "my father has made himself joyful."
>
> David was hunted by King Saul for two years. "Then David and the people that were with him lifted up their voice and wept, until they had no more power to weep. And David's two wives were taken captive, Ahinoam the Jezreelitess, and Abigail the wife of Nabal the Carmelite. And David was greatly distressed; for the people spake of stoning him, because the soul of all the people was grieved, every man for his sons and for his daughters: but David strengthened himself in Jehovah his God." –*1Sa 30:4-6*
>
> It's no coincidence that David's name means "beloved." This may have been the *saddest* day of his life, but David was only moments away from the *happiest* event in his life. David resolved to save his family. David fought to retrieve everything he lost in battle. That's when, David was notified that King Saul had died. Suddenly, David became the third king of Israel (first/

Jehovah; second/Saul; third/David). Never underestimate what's around the corner, that is, when you're on the right road.

6 [HEAVENLY SHULAMITE:] His left arm is under my head, and his right arm embraces me.	שמאלו תחת לראשי וימינו תחבקני:

6 *His left arm* (שְׂמֹאלוֹ) literally; "left-arm-of-him."
Most Western readers get headaches trying to figure out how two lovers could get so entangled in such a contortion. Please . . . it's so much more innocent than that. The Shulamite was like a lamb being transported by the fine shepherd. His left arm is under her head and his right arm wraps around her back side.

"He will feed his flock like a shepherd, he will gather the lambs in his arm, and carry them in his bosom, [and] will gently lead those that have their young." –Is 40:11 This verse answers George Gershwin's song mentioned earlier, in chapter one. How else would carry his lamb to Heaven?

"Left" is another way of saying "north." The lamb's head is facing north. Orientation is established by Jerusalem's Temple. Facing the rising sun equals, east. (Job 26:7)

his right arm (וִימִינוֹ) literally; "and-right-arm-of-him."
Again, Hebrews used the Temple to determine direction: east is in front of them, west is behind, north to the left, and south to the right.

This verse seems so tame. On deeper reflection, however, there is profound depth within this innocent comment. Infatuation is about feeling-overload. Love is about protection, shepherding, and character. Brush aside temporal goose-bumps. Instead, tally-up what someone's love will bring to your children's life—and their children's children. Only then can you appreciate real love—which may be more quiet than a loud infatuation. That may not sound thrilling, but God recommends pragmatism in marriage. Solomon was pragmatic when he picked his brides. (Mk 10:40)

This verse will be repeated at So 8:3. If "two" conveys the idea of potential badness, then let this Shunemite be warned: she may not make it. Many don't!

7 [EARTHLY SHUNEMITE:] Daughters at Jerusalem, the pleadings of mine are on the gazelles, and on the does of the field: Do not arouse the watchers, or awaken LOVE, until He wills it so.	השבעתי אתכם בנות ירושלם בצבאות או באילות השדה אם־תעירו ואם־תעוררו את־ האהבה עד שתחפץ: ס

7 ***the pleadings of mine*** (השבעתי) literally; "the-entreaties-of-me."

No shepherd is carrying this poor Shunemite. Yet, despite her hardships, here is where the Earthly Shunemite selflessly intercedes for her Brothers. She is beginning to display a quality that benefits Solomon's government: love.

As our Messiah's chosen are being carried off to Heaven, the remaining Earthly Shunemite asks them to deliver a message. In fact, she appeals to the Daughters of Jerusalem four times. (So 2:7; 3:5; 5:8; 8:4)

The unchosen Shunemite wants the Messiah's associate rulers to give her Brothers more time. An ambassador's main function is the reconciliation of two alienated parties—earth and Heaven. A prophet's main function is the reconciliation of two alienated parties—in this case, earth and Heaven.

Some may argue that the Earthly Shunemite has no enforceable authority. So, under what authority could Abishag intervene for her Brothers? These Earthly Shunemites, in fact, do play an important role in kingdom outworkings. "We are ambassadors therefore on behalf of Christ, as though God were entreating by us: we beseech [you] on behalf of Christ, be ye reconciled to God.'" –*2Cor 5:20*

So, why is this Shunemite ambassador so alarmed? It seems she wants the Daughters of Jerusalem (her mother in Heaven) to stop doing something. (Gal 4:26; 2Cor 5:20)

Everything about this verse conveys the idea of a last chance. This is a declarative oath that seeks a final, divine, reconciliation. "Take heed to yourselves: if thy brother sin, rebuke him; and if he repent, forgive him. And if he sin against thee seven times in the day, and seven times turn again to thee, saying, I repent; thou shalt forgive him." –*Lk 17:3-4*

The parables of Jesus will often incorporate the number, seven (שׁבע) in two ways: pleading, and pleading to desist. So, why would *Song of Songs* repeat something four times (So 2:7; 3:5; 5:8; 8:4), unless it's worthy of re-examination?

Let me give you an intriguing hint: the Shunemite doesn't repeat this prophetic "pleading" four times—she repeats it three-and-a-half times. (Re 11:2-3; 12:6) The last time she says it, she only repeats half of what she asked for previously.

> **NUMERICS:** *pleading* (שׁבע) literally; "to seven; repeated declaration; prophetic cycle brought to a full; prophetic week." This is the first of five uses. At the *remez* level, the number five portends judgment with a potential for salvation. It means salvation for the righteous, but punishment for the wicked. By the final occurrence (at So 8:4), the faithful Shunemite will be judged worthy and will receive immortal life. The Brothers, however, must await a separate judgment.

on the gazelles (בִּצְבָאוֹת) literally; "on-gazelles."

The fastest messenger system, in the days of Solomon, was a horse. To reach a capital city atop a lofty mountain, required something swifter and more sure-of-foot. A gazelle is faster than a horse—on a mountain. (So 2:9; 8:14)

This Shunemite does not live in Heaven. She is earthbound. By invoking the word "gazelles," she is either appealing to Jesus, or a wife of Jesus, persons who can come and go to the heavenly Temple.

The most striking quality of a gazelle is swiftness. It can move fast in both directions, up and down. Judicial LOVE will one day react with all the swiftness of a gazelle. For instance: Babylon's swift fall caused her supporters to flee like gazelles. (Is 13:14)

arouse the watchers (תְּעִירוּ) literally; "charge-city-watchers."

This compound word is very worthwhile to disassemble. The letter *tav* (ת) invokes boundaries, legal limits, or a conclusion. The word *aw-yar* (#H5892 עִיר) means "a city, a place guarded by waking, or watchers, a walled place." The Hebrew word *ee-roo* (#H5900 עִירוּ) means "a citizen, an Israelite."

A prophetic execution was looming far beyond this walled city. On earth, there are four angels (watchers) holding back the four winds of destruction. (Re 7:1) Whereas the Earthly Shunemite wants relief from her difficult life, she never requests luxury at the expense of Solomon's citizens.

Solomon respects her selfless attitude. It has always mattered to Solomon that, great or small, everyone receive justice. He was moved by a prostitute who showed selfless love for the life of her innocent child. (1Ki 3:25-26)

Abraham negotiated with God for the lives of innocents in Sodom. Moses pled with God, to spare the lives of the Israelites. Both prophets had the moral presence of mind to ask God to be merciful to others. This Shunemite's plea for unworthy citizens is noticed.

>**NUMERICS:** *arouse* (#H5894 & H5895 עִיר) literally; "watcher; angel-at-work; guard of city." This is the first of five uses. At the *remez* level, the number five portends judgment, with a potential of salvation. In this context, it means salvation for the righteous, but punishment for the wicked. By the final occurrence (at So 8:4), the faithful Shunemite will be chosen to become a Shulamite bride. As a new bride, and mother, she will fret over her earth-children's judgment.

>*awaken* (תְּעוֹרְרוּ) literally; "you-awaken."

The Hebrew word *oor* (#H5782 עוּר) contains the idea of "stir up." Notice how close it is to the previously cited word *aw-yar* (#H5895 עִיר). This verb appears in the polel stem at So 2:7; 3:5; and 8:4. In this form, it hints at *more* than being awoken. It hints at sparking fury.

This is a perfect example of how translators are forced to exclude information (for the sake of brevity). The additional letter *resh* (ר) hints that this word is meant for an elevated person, a prominent person. By the time you finish examining the word "LOVE," you will know exactly who that prominent person is, and why the Shunemite doesn't want this person awakened—yet.

This "gazelle" delivers prayers to someone who frightens the Shunemite—Jehovah. This unusual word contains ideas that could quickly get out of her control.

>**NUMERICS:** *awaken* (עוּר) literally; "open the eyes, stir up." This is the first of seven uses. At the *remez* level, the number seven is a messianic number. In this instance, it hints at an elevation

of station. By the final occurrence (at So 8:5), the Earthly Shunemite has found and married the Solomon-like messiah—becoming a Shulamite, one of the "Jerusalem Above." (Gal 4:26)

LOVE (אהבה) literally; "DIVINE-LOVE."
God is love. (De 7:13; 1Joh 4:16-17) This is further emphasized by the first letter *aleph* (א). *Aleph* (א) is also the number one (in Hebrew). Jehovah is one (יהוה אחד). (De 4:6)

Unconditional love has recently become a highly touted ideal, among Western-thinking people. But Jehovah's superlative love is conditional. Only those who respond and implement His generous offer of adoption will benefit from it. "For this is the love of God, that we keep his commandments: and his commandments are not grievous." –*1Joh 5:3*

In this instance, this describes a quality of Jehovah. His disobedient angelic sons (demons) found out the hard way that their Father's love *was* conditional.

My dear daughter, hopefully, your marriage will bring added dimensions to God's love. Hopefully, your unique love will bring new meaning to all our lives. Good improves love. Vindictiveness poisons love. Nothing proves this as dramatically as how we treat our loved ones.

Love receives its value based on who it attaches to. A lover of idols will devalue the word "love" (אהב). A lover of trists will devalue the word "love" (אהב). A lover of God, however, will add value to the word "love" (אהב). In this case, the Shunemite loves God. So, the "love" (אהב) that connects them becomes a superlative attachment.

The obligation that comes with principled love (as the Shunemite will learn), is enforcement of kingdom law. "All their wickedness is in Gilgal; for there I hated them: because of the wickedness of their doings I will drive them out of my house; I will love them no more; all their princes are revolters." –*Ho 9:15*

Whether you believe that "son" in Ps 2 is Solomon, Jesus, or Muhammad, those who refuse to conform to His son's kingdom are doomed. The Shunemite fears for Solomon's wayward children. For them, she begs for more time.

The Heavenly Shulamites have already requested reducing the time and requested executing those who have refused to come into the tabernacle (tent of God). (Re 6:10) The Earthly Shunemite is at odds with the Shulamites' request.

He wills it so (שתחפץ) literally; "time-of-lawful-will."

The Hebrew word *khaw-fates* (#H2654 חפץ) contains the formal intent of "inclined, predisposed, willed." The ultimate authority she wants to influence is Jehovah. He has already set an end date for this secular system. Abishag is only quibbling over a miniscule extension.

She doesn't want the Heavenly Shulamites to launch Armageddon. But, the Shulamites are having an entirely different conversation in Heaven. (Re 6:10)

"If so be that it is a righteous thing with God to recompense affliction to them that afflict you, and to you that are afflicted rest with us, at the revelation of the Lord Jesus from Heaven with the angels of his power in flaming fire, rendering vengeance to them that know not God, and to them that obey not the gospel of our Lord Jesus:" –*2Th 1:6-8* Jehovah's love has conditions—always has, always will.

8 [HEAVENLY SHULAMITE:] Proclaim my beloved: *Look! There he comes, leaping across the mountains, bounding over the hills.*	קוֹל דּוֹדִי הִנֵּה־זֶה בָּא מְדַלֵּג עַל־הֶהָרִים מְקַפֵּץ עַל־הַגְּבָעוֹת׃

8 *Proclaim* (קוֹל) literally; "voice."

You cannot understand the word *kole* (#H6963 קוֹל), unless you see how it's used elsewhere. "A voice of tumult from the city, a voice from the Temple, a voice of Jehovah, ["voice of Jehovah" קוֹל יהוה] that rendereth recompense to his enemies." –*Is 66:6* Who is the "voice" of Jehovah? Who is the "spokesman" of Jehovah? According to John, the Shulamite's husband. (Joh 1:1; 18:37)

So, when the Heavenly Shulamite asks the "voice of Jehovah" to speak up, she is responding directly to the Earthly Shunemite's pleading in verse seven.

Look (הנה) literally; "behold."

When Joshua was appointed as the overseer (not king) of the nation of Israel, he was instructed to make a copy of God's law, and to "meditate" thereon day and night. (Jos 1:8 *KJV*) In Jos 1:8, God used the Hebrew word *hag-hah* (הגה). It basically means "meditate." (Ps 35:28)

Our word, *ha-nah* (הנה), is slightly different than "meditate," but is still related. Rather than journeying for an answer, *ha-nah* (הנה) advocates insight. It beckons for awareness. We already know that in the last days, the Messiah will walk among us in what's described as his invisible "presence." (Mt 24:3)

Shulamites set the example by being quick to hear this "Voice of Jehovah."

he comes (בא) literally; "he-comes."

The Messiah "comes" to us at the command of his Father, who is the personification of "LOVE." "The voice of Jehovah [קוֹל יהוה] is upon the waters: The God of glory thundereth, Even Jehovah upon many waters. The voice of Jehovah [קוֹל יהוה] is powerful; The voice of Jehovah [קוֹל יהוה] breaketh the cedars; Yea, Jehovah breaketh in pieces the cedars of Lebanon." –*Ps 29:3-5*

There was a time when Jesus neither knew the day nor the hour. (Mk 13:32) That never meant Armageddon wouldn't come. When the Father calls His son, ("voice of Jehovah"), Jesus will charge, headlong, against the evil ones on earth.

> **NUMERICS:** *comes* (בֹּא) literally; "enter; depart." This is the first of six uses. At the *remez* level, six is a man's number, or describes a person from earth. By the final occurrence (at So 5:1) you will discover how the Heavenly Solomon will "come" and retrieve the Shunemite from earth.

the hills (הגבעות) literally; "the-hills."
The Hebrew term *gheh-bah* (#H1387 גבע) can refer to a natural elevation, but a hill is lower than a mountain (הר).

It's no accident that an earthly king is addressed as, "his eminence." The English word *"eminence,"* has a secondary definition of "A rise of ground; hill." Its first definition is more familiar: "A position of great distinction or superiority." Symbolically, "hills" represent the under-kingdoms of a larger kingdom.

Both Isaiah and Micah foretold that "the mountain of the house of Jehovah" would become firmly established above the top of other mountains and would be lifted up above these *hills*. (Is 2:2; Mic 4:1)

While highlighting the greatness of the Father, Isaiah shows that God will quantify the nations and their prefects: "weigh the hills in the scales." (Is 40:12) In this same line of thinking these foreign hills were leveled, so His children could return home—unhindered. "Return, ye backsliding children, I will heal your backslidings. Behold, we are come unto thee; for thou art Jehovah our God. Truly in vain is [the help that is looked for] from the hills, the tumult on the mountains: truly in Jehovah our God is the salvation of Israel." –*Jer 3:22-23*

9 [HEAVENLY SHULAMITE:] My beloved is like a gazelle, or a young stag. Meditation: *There he stands, behind our wall, gazing through the windows, peering through the lattice.*	דומה דודי לצבי או לעפר האילים הנה־זה עומד אחר כתלנו משגיח מן־החלנות מציץ מן־ החרכים:

9 *Meditation:* (הגה) literally; "Meditate."

Verse eight included a call to "proclaim." Verse nine includes a call to "meditation." And, it's the only call to meditation in the book of *Song of Songs*.

In this meditation the operative word is "stands." When a king sits, he does so to perform an act of judging. (Is 28:6) When a king stands, he does so to execute the judgment he previously made. (Is 2:19)

our wall (כתלנו) literally; "walling-of-us."

The Father chose 144,000 wives for the greater Solomon, Jesus, but one facet of his heavenly city is its "wall." This verse shows the Heavenly Solomon stands within its walls, peering down at earthly Zion. "Wall" is such a general metaphor that it's correct to say that there are walls around Heavenly Jerusalem.

Religion and marriage may not appear connected, but your Bible shows they are. Joseph Epstein claims, adhering to the tenants of a religion keeps families together. When that religious boundary is breached, a community's integrity loses its glue. Minus community support, couples are more vulnerable to self-destructive philosophies.[10]

Maybe Israel's self-rule destroyed her long before the Romans set foot on her soil. Maybe Western independt thinking is a similar cancer that destroys marraiges long before divorce proceedings.

At the destruction of ancient Jerusalem, in 70 A.D., Josephus described how the Romans broke through several walls, before destroying the Temple. This will not happen with the Jerusalem Above.

One day, God's people, will dwell in a city without literal walls, yet enjoy peace and security. (Ezk 38:11) "The holy city, New Jerusalem," which comes down out of Heaven, is said to have "a great and lofty wall" of jasper, the height of which is 144 cubits. (Re 21:2, 12, 14, 17-19) Since the Hebrew word for "cubit" (*amah* #H520 אמה) is spelled exactly the same as "handmaid" (*amah* #H519 אמה), it's somewhat easy to calculate the length of this wall: 1,000 cubits. (see So 8:9)

> **HEAVENLY SHULAMITE:** Like all future Shulamites, there will be times when you too will face crude assaults on your virtue, or solicitations that are nothing more than naked attempts to cheapen your marriage. Being polite and refined is one thing . . . but there comes a time. Even the peace-loving Jesus took a rope to those who disregarded the boundaries of his Father's house. Your house has boundaries too. Do what you must.

the windows (החלנות) literally; "the-windows."

Windows are not for entering or exiting. Windows are for spying out of—not into. In other words, the Earthly Shunemites were being watched (examined). (Jos 2:15; 1Sa 19:12; Ac 20:9)

In Jerusalem, windows facing the street were usually covered by lattices. (Jg 5:28; Pr 7:6) Today's Earthly Shunemites can't see who watches them from Heaven. But Solomon's eyes are roving about the earth, looking for the righteous. (2Ch 16:9) That "watching" includes an event soon to take place "on the streets," at So 3:2.

The Hebrew word for "lattice" is *kheh-rek* (#H2762 חרכ) which means "a woven net, or a woven wooden lattice (covering a window)." There are multiple definitions of this word (חרכ) as found in the book of *Habakuk*, "And makest men as the fishes of the sea, as the creeping things, that have no ruler over them? He taketh up all of them with the angle, he catcheth them in his *net*, and gathereth them in his *drag*." –*Hab 1:14-15*

Heavenly Solomon spies through the lattice to "net" good humans with his discernment. After all, this messiah is a fisher of men. (Mt 4:19)

It would be a costly mistake to think the Solomon-like messiah is neither interested, nor watching. "Say unto wisdom, Thou art my sister; And call understanding [thy] kinswoman: That they may keep thee from the strange woman, From the foreigner that flattereth with her words. For at the window of my house I looked forth through my lattice [אשׁנבי] And I beheld among the simple ones, I discerned among the youths, A young man void of understanding." –*Pr 7:4-7*

This too is the Shulamite's direct response to the Earthly Shunemite's pleading in verse seven. The Heavenly Shulamites are carefully selected, but the Earthly Brothers don't seem to fare well in this examination. "For all this I laid to my heart, even to explore all this: that the righteous, and the wise, and their works, are in the hand of God; whether it be love or hatred, man knoweth it not; all is before them." –*Ec 9:1*

10 [HEAVENLY SHULAMITE:] My beloved commanded me. [HEAVENLY SOLOMON:] "Arise, my darling, my beautiful one, and come with me.	ענה דודי ואמר לי קומי לך רעיתי יפתי ולכי־לך:

10 *commanded* (ואמר) literally; "and-commanded."

Her "beloved" is the Solomon-like Messiah. The person he is speaking to is a new Shulamite (one of the 144,000). His "voice" is her call to Heaven. First, he says: "Arise." Second, he says: "come with me."

There are two callings for mankind, one to a heavenly resurrection, another to an earthly resurrection. The Shulamite has been watched, quantified, and found worthy.

It appears she was dead, but transformed, "in the twinkling of an eye." (1Cor 15:52) Since this verse incorporates, "commanded," we know this is past-tense. This shows the speaker has recently become a Shulamite.

> **NUMERICS:** *arise* (רעי) literally; "raise up (resurrect)." This is the first of four uses. At the *remez* level, four is a very significant number. We view our three-dimensional world with limited eyesight. The fourth dimension is inside us. Only God can see the heart. By the final occurrence (at So 7:8), Jehovah is the ultimate evaluator of His son's brides. He will evaluate what's within the Earthly Shunemite and—if found worthy—cause her to be reborn as a Heavenly Shulamite.

11 [HEAVENLY SOLOMON:] For here, the winter is past; the rains are over and gone.	כי־הנה הסתיו ק עבר הגשם חלף הלך לו:

11 *the winter* (הסתו) literally; "the-winter."

In Heaven, there is no winter, no rain, no suffering. The uncommon word for "winter" is *seth-awv* (#H5638 סתו). This word is rarely used, but the Heavenly Solomon employs it for some important reasons. Not only does this word mean, "winter," but more importantly, it also carries the idea of being the final, in a chain of seasons—the most severe, in a chain of seasons.

The first letter in this word (סתו) is *samech* (ס). It's the only round letter in the Hebrew alphabet. It hints at a cycle, or season. It seems that this prophetic group of Shulamites were hidden away for a season, but now they are being awakened. Without the connection of "rain" in the same sentence, it would likely have been translated as, "the dark part of the day," or just "hidden away."

What had passed was an extended dark and gloomy "winter season." For all remaining Shunemites, their burdens will be great, but temporary.

Their "winter" may be uncomfortable, but in Hebrew, there is something happening beneath the soil, and deep within the trees. The sap is beginning to rise, and the seeds are standing at the door of a break-through. Spring. Can nature know all this? Of course. Nature knows when spring is near. If man is like the "tree," described earlier, then Jehovah is causing mankinds' symbolic sap to rise.

Even outside of holy text, trees, sap, and humans are often equated. Jack Benny and Fred Allen were rivals in the early days of radio. They were constantly sniping at one another. After Jack Benny's hometown planted a tree in his honor, the tree withered and died. Allen quipped "How can a tree survive in Waukeegan when the sap lives in Hollywood?"

The Jewish calendar starts its day with darkness. Holy text repeats: "And God called the light Day, and the darkness he called Night. And there was evening and there was morning, one day." *–Ge 1:5* This verse shows how day progresses from darkness, to light.

For a Jew, winter symbolizes a final sleep. So, that may explain why the seed in the earth and the sap in the tree considers their darkness as their beginning—with Spring just around the corner. At the beginning of *Song of Songs*, the Shunemite's day started in darkness, but Solomon's announcement suggests brighter things to come—the light of spring.

the rains (הגשם) literally; "the-rain."

After decades (seven) of exile, God called Israel back from Babylon. When they arrived home, however, their behaviors and teachings were still out of sync. Many thought showing up was good enough. They were wrong. "And they made proclamation throughout Judah and Jerusalem unto all the children of the captivity, that they should gather themselves together unto Jerusalem; and that whosoever came not within three days, according to the counsel of the princes and the elders, all his substance should be forfeited, and himself separated from the assembly of the captivity. Then all the men of Judah and Benjamin gathered themselves together unto Jerusalem within the three days; it was the ninth month, on the twentieth [day] of the month: and all the people sat in the broad place before the house of God, trembling because of this matter, and for the great rain." *–Ezr 10:7-9*

Many husbands and wives arrive at marriage with the mistaken idea that "showing up" is good enough. Jehovah made it clear there would be a favorable season for growth and self-improvement. This should see us through the bad times.

12 [HEAVENLY SOLOMON:] Flowers appear on the earth; the seasonal rhythm for me has come. The cooing of doves is heard in our land.	הנצנים נראו בארץ עת הזמיר הגיע וקול התור נשמע בארצנו:

12 *rhythm* (הזמיר) literally; "the-rhythm-for-me."

Like the previous word, "winter," the word "rhythm" (#H2158 זמיר) is quite rare. Oddly enough, the Bible's 300 songs rarely use this word. This word has more to do with a, thumping, time keeping, or the rhythm of a season. This verse hints at a prophetic season.

Psalm 96 teaches us that a prophetic song is more than just a melody. In Psalm 96 we learn a song is also an action, or a behavior that God considers melodious. "Oh *sing unto Jehovah* a new song: Sing unto Jehovah, all the earth. Sing unto Jehovah, *bless his name*; Show forth his salvation from day to day. *Declare his glory among the nations*, His marvellous works among all the peoples. For great is Jehovah, and greatly to be praised: He is to be feared above all gods. For all the gods of the peoples are idols; But Jehovah made the Heavens. Honor and majesty are before him: Strength and beauty are in his sanctuary. Ascribe unto Jehovah, ye kindreds of the peoples, *Ascribe unto Jehovah glory and strength*. Ascribe unto Jehovah the glory due unto his name: *Bring an offering*, and *come into his courts*. Oh *worship Jehovah* in holy array: Tremble before him, all the earth. *Say among the nations*, Jehovah reigneth: The world also is established that it cannot be moved: He will judge the peoples with equity.'" –*Ps 96:1-10* Each of the italicized words are behaviors—life patterns, rhythmic events.

When these worship behaviors are observed three times a year, they are like a circulatory system, pumping life's blood to, and from, the heart. The next verse (13) informs us that she is coming to life.

This word (הזמיר) is only used once in *Song of Songs*. This behavioral "rhythm" harmonizes the Shulamite to a season—a harvest of wives by the greater Solomon. "And they sing as it were a new song before the throne, and before the four living creatures and the elders: and no man could learn the song save the hundred and forty and four thousand, [even] they that had been purchased out of the earth." –*Re 14:3*

> **NUMERICS:** *rhythm* (זמר) literally; "rhythm; strum." There is only one use in *Song of Songs*. At the *remez* level, one is a very significant number. Jehovah is, one. (De 6:4) Everything emanates from one source, Jehovah. So, this "song" has something to do with Jehovah.

13 [HEAVENLY SOLOMON:] The fig tree forms its early fruit. The blossoming vines spread their fragrance. Arise. Come my darling, my beautiful one. Come with me.	התאנה חנטה פגיה והגפנים ׀ סמדר נתנו ריח קומי לך ק רעיתי יפתי ולכי־לך: ס

13 *fig tree* (תאנה) literally; "fig-tree."

Along with the olive and the vine, the fig tree (*Ficus carica*) is one of the most prominent plants of the Bible. The fig tree is noted for its remarkable longevity. While the tree can produce fruitage in the wild, superior fruitage requires cultivation. Yet, it's quite adaptable to various kinds of soil, even rocky soil. The fig tree may reach a height of about 30 feet, with a trunk diameter of about two feet.

While appreciated for its fruit, the fig tree is also valued for its shade. The leaves are large, measuring as much as eight inches, in width. The first mention of the fig was when Adam tried to sew its leaves to cover himself and Eve. (Ge 3:7) In some parts of the Middle East, fig leaves are still sewn together and used for wrapping fruit.

There are two crops of figs produced each year. Early figs mature in June or early July. This "early" crop grows from the old branches, and they produce the best fruit. Early figs are comparable to the first resurrection.

The later figs mature in August, or early September. This "late" crop grows from the new branches, and make up the main crop. The "late crop" produces greater quantities, but lower-quality fruit. This crop is comparable to the second resurrection.

Ask yourself: "Who embodies the 'early fruit'?" The answer is obvious: Shulamites.

These under-Messiahs (Shulamites) are called to administrate under Jesus. "Blessed and holy is he that hath part in the first resurrection: over these the second death hath no power; but they shall be priests of God and of Christ, and shall reign with him for a thousand years." –*Re 20:6*

This first resurrection doesn't happen all at once. The first resurrection begins in the first chapter of *Song of Songs* and will complete its full number (144,000) by the last chapter. Then, the "season of the song" will be over.

blossoming (סמדר) literally; "blossoming."

Around February, the first-fruit buds appear. The fig's leaves will come two months later (April). This corresponds with the flowering of grapevines, which will begin about April. This explains why the fig and grape vine are mentioned jointly in many texts. Fig trees were often planted in vineyards—their botanical schedules are eternally synchronized.

This helps to understand the double image conjured to describe peace in Israel. The expression "sitting under one's own vine and fig tree" symbolized peace (the Hebrew root of Shulamite is: *sha-lom* / שׁלוֹם) for those who were synchronized with this symbolic "fig tree." (Zec 3:10)

This provides us with further insight as to why it's so desirable to be a Shulamite. She is the fruit that Jesus longed to find, but was disappointed. (Mk 11:19-23; Pr 7:4-7)

arise (קוּמִי) literally; "arise-my."

This entire song is about the first resurrection. There is nothing comparable to this superlative resurrection. To frame this divine book in any other way misses the fundamental premise.

Many commentaries (Fox, Ben Isaac, Pope, Adeney, Gill, Littledale, or whoever), each fails to distinguish between the two types of resurrections. Since these sages missed the boat on such a major point, why should we give their work any further significance?

come with me (וּלְכִי־לָךְ) literally; "and-coming to-you."

Come where? From where? Refer back to the first sentence of verse 12. Solomon is asking the Shulamites to travel to Heaven with him. Solomon is harvesting wives from the gardens of earth.

Earthly wives would be wise to synchronize their marital rituals to the seasons of the Jewish calendar. When your personal stories are combined with God's, His cycles lend a spiritual foundation to your relationship story.

Your anniversaries may find you in happy times, or at a relationship low. In those low periods, a ritual can revive you. Personal rituals remind you, who you are, why you are, and why you must continue.

Start a family ritual. Tell your story and don't stop. The best rituals have three phases: (1) Setting a day to vacate the secular world's rhythm. (2) The celebration, itself. (3) A sober discussion on how to re-enter the rhythm of the secular world, while keeping your sacred relationship intact.

Each year will bring its own challenges, but every challenge gives birth to new versions of marital wisdom.

> **NUMERICS:** *vine* (גֶפֶן) literally; "bending; twining." This is the first of four uses. At the *remez* level, the number four is a very significant number. We view our three-dimensional world with limited eyesight. The fourth dimensional vine is inside us. By the final occurrence (at So 7:12), God will cause the vine in the Shulamite's heart to blossom with LOVE.
>
> **PUZZLE:** The God you worship enjoys weaving additional messages beneath the surface message. That mathematical complexity is what separates holy text from Jewish newspapers. The Hebrew language doesn't weave these messages, naturally. That takes the mind (and deft hands) of

God. In this verse, the sacred name of God is hidden between the third and the fourth Hebrew words.

14 [HEAVENLY SOLOMON:] My dove in the clefts of the rock, in the hiding places on the mountainside, show me YOUR FACES. Let me hear YOUR VOICES, for your voices are sweet, and your faces are lovely.	יונתי בחגוי הסלע בסתר המדרגה הראיני את־מראיך השמיעיני את־קולך כי־קולך ערב ומראיך נאוה׃ ס

14 *in the clefts* (בחגוי) literally; "in-clefts-of."

The rock dove builds its nest high, in rocky places. Noah discovered a new world, with the help of the third third bird—a dove. Our Messiah will also take her to high places.

the mountainside (המדרגה) literally; "the-mountainside."

If a mountain represents a kingdom, then these doves have nested within the shadowy crags of his kingdom, crying out for, God-rule. (Mt 6:10) Today, some of earth's Shunemites can be heard, cooing the same song as the Shulamites.

show me YOUR FACES (הראיני את־מראיך) literally; "show-me FACES-OF-YOU."

Consider a similar situation, where a king called his queen, to view her pretty face, with the opposite result. "On the seventh day, when the heart of the king was merry with wine, he commanded Mehuman, Biztha, Harbona, Bigtha, and Abagtha, Zethar, and Carkas, the seven chamberlains that ministered in the presence of Ahasuerus the king, to bring

Vashti the queen before the king with the crown royal, to show the peoples and the princes her beauty; for she was fair to look on. But the queen Vashti refused to come at the king's commandment by the chamberlains: therefore was the king very wroth, and his anger burned in him." –*Es 1:10-12* Unlike the antagonistic Vashti, our Messiah's royal brides will heed their king's call. It has been foretold. (Da 2:45)

15 [HEAVENLY SOLOMON:] Catch for us the foxes, the little foxes that ruin vineyards, our vineyards, that are in bloom.	אחזו־לנו שועלים שועלים קטנים מחבלים כרמים וכרמינו סמדר:

15 *catch* (אחזו־) literally; "catch."

The Hebrew word *aw-khaz* (#H270 אחז) means "to seize (often includes, holding in possession)." It's the next letter (*vov* ו) is also the sixth letter in the Hebrew alphabet and has a number value of six. "Six is a man's number." Solomon will do more than harvest his human lilies, he will also round up the conniving human foxes. "For the mountain of Zion, which is desolate: The foxes walk upon it. Thou, O Jehovah, abidest for ever; Thy throne is from generation to generation. Wherefore dost thou forget us for ever, [And] forsake us so long time?" – *Lam 5:18-20* Man, Zion, and foxes, are all negatively connected in this verse from *Lamentations*.

Who is the "us" in verse 15? The answer becomes clear in the next chapter, at So 3:7-8. The angelic Brothers are being called, by Solomon, for a fox hunt. "Why do the nations rage, And the peoples meditate a vain thing? The kings of the earth set themselves, And the rulers take counsel together, Against Jehovah, and against his anointed, [saying], Let us break their bonds asunder, And cast away their cords from us. He that sitteth in the Heavens will laugh: The Lord will have them in derision. Then will he speak unto them in his wrath, And vex them in his sore displeasure: Yet I have set my king Upon my holy hill of Zion. I will tell of the decree: Jehovah said unto me, Thou art my son; This day have I begotten thee. Ask of me, and I will give [thee] the nations for thine inheritance, And the uttermost parts of the earth for thy possession. Thou shalt break them with a rod of iron; Thou shalt dash them in pieces like a potter's vessel. Now therefore be wise, O ye kings: Be instructed, ye judges of the earth. Serve Jehovah with fear, And rejoice with trembling. Kiss the son, lest he be angry, and ye perish in the way, For his wrath will soon be kindled. Blessed are all they that take refuge in him!" –Ps 2:1-12

Where did our matriarchs get their courage to do the right thing? While Abraham hesitated, Sarah boldly threw Ishmael's butt out. "And the child grew, and was weaned. And Abraham made a great feast on the day that Isaac was weaned. And Sarah saw the son of Hagar the Egyptian, whom she had borne unto Abraham, mocking. Wherefore she said unto Abraham, Cast out this handmaid and her son. For the son of this handmaid shall not be heir with my son, even with Isaac.'" –Ge 21:8-10

Isaac intended to bless Esau, but Rebekah courageously inserted Jacob. "And Jehovah said unto her, Two nations are in thy womb, And two peoples shall be separated from thy bowels. And the one people shall be stronger than the other people. And the elder shall serve the younger.'" –Ge 25:23

Both these matriarchs were safeguarding God's kingdom arrangement. They protected the messianic root stock, from "foxes," by putting God's kingdom interests above all else. They made a proactive decision to play a role, no matter how small. There was nothing selfish about their harsh actions.

foxes (שועלים) literally; "foxes, or burrowers."

Look at the original Hebrew. Foxes (שועלים) appears twice—a quick repeat. Two indicates potential badness, to a Hebrew. The fox is well known for its craftiness. It was this destructive characteristic that Jesus inferred when describing political rulers, like king Herod. He called Herod "that fox." (Lk 13:32) Herod had burrowed himself into God's vineyard—the nation of Israel—with the assistance of Rome.

In the world-to-come, the "craftiness" of the fox will no longer be cultivated. As Paul reminds couples: "But we have renounced the hidden things of shame, not walking in craftiness, nor handling the word of God deceitfully; but by the manifestation of the truth commending ourselves to every man's conscience in the sight of God." –*2Cor 4:2*

When we consider that *Song of Songs* ends with the Shulamite proclaiming that she is a "wall," the following verse may be of further interest. "Now Tobiah the Ammonite was by him, and he said, Even that which they are building, if a fox go up, he shall break down their stone wall." –*Neh 4:3*

Can a mere fox destroy your marriage? Be a wall!

the vineyards (כרמים) literally; "vineyards."

Check the original Hebrew, vineyards (כרמים) is used twice—a quick repeat. Two indicates potential badness, to a Hebrew.

As Jude 1:3-5 reminds us, there are two kinds of brothers. Not everyone who claims to be a spiritual Jew, is. Be forewarned: the Messiah will round up these "foxes," from among our very own earthly "vineyards." So, you already know them.

These foxes might be related to you. "Thy mother was like a vine, in thy blood, planted by the waters: it was fruitful and full of branches by reason of many waters. And it had strong rods for the sceptres of them that bare rule, and their stature was exalted among the thick boughs, and they were seen in their height with the multitude of their branches. But it was plucked up in fury, it was cast down to the ground, and the east wind dried up its fruit: its strong rods were broken off and withered; the fire consumed them." –*Ezk 19:10-12*

There are frauds among us. There are wolves among us. There are foxes among us.

16 [HEAVENLY SHULAMITE:] My beloved is mine, and I am his. He nourishes us among the lilies.	דודי לי ואני לו הרעה בשושנים:

16 *My beloved is mine* (דוֹדִי לִי) literally; "lover-of-me to-me."

I'm always startled at the common person's belief that the women of the Bible were oppressed and without rights. Nothing could be further from the truth. In this verse, the Shulamite claims her legal property rights. The Heavenly Solomon belongs to her. He is her property.

A recently married teen-aged bride could stop the King of Israel from drafting her husband into a war. Since her husband was her legal property (according to Hebrew Law) she could legally demand that he stay home for a year—until he could provide her with a child. (De 24:5)

The early apostles understood Hebrew women's rights, and advocated for them. "The wife hath not power over her own body, but the husband: and likewise also the husband hath not power over his own body, but the wife. Defraud ye not one the other, except it be by consent for a season, that ye may give yourselves unto prayer, and may be together again, that Satan tempt you not because of your incontinency." –*1Cor 7:4-5*

If you think these Hebrew Christian women were feisty, consider how bold pre-Christian Hebrew women were. When their husband died, they would march into the house of their husband's brother and demand (legally) that his brother impregnate her. If he refused, she would take his sandal off his foot and slap him with it. (De 25:5) Does that sound like an oppressed woman?

To this day, Jewish couples sign a contract of marriage (*ketubah*). When the husband fails to live up to that contract, the wife will pull him over to the living-room wall (where it's generally posted) and make him re-read his duties.

It's non-religious women who are adrift in a world that doesn't value, or respect women. All holy text advocates for a woman's God-given rights—from *Genesis* to *Revelation*.

he nourishes (הרעה) literally; "the-one-feeding."

The Hebrew word *raw-aw* (#H7462 רעה) means "tend a flock, i.e. pasture it; feed it." "Then shalt thou delight thyself in Jehovah; and I will make thee to ride upon the high places of the earth; and I will *feed thee with the heritage* (והאכלתיכ) of Jacob thy father: for the mouth of Jehovah hath spoken it." –*Is 58:14*

A good man shouldn't feel burdened by his biblical obligations. A good king behaves like a steward, always looking after God's valuables. You are God's valuables. Today's earthly sisters are God's valuables and were promised that they would be nurtured by Jacob's heritage.

In the commentary text, at So 2:5, the Shunemite was described as, "the faithful and discreet slave." That role should not be confused with king David's 288,000 [144,000 x 2], humans looking after the king's valuables.

David devided these "faithful and discreet slaves" into 12 divisions. He assigned specific individuals, within those 12 divisions, to better serve his citizens. "And over the herds that fed in Sharon [meaning: perpetual justice]. Shitrai [meaning: officer] was the Sharonite: and over the herds that were in the valleys was Shaphat [meaning: shining deliverance] the son of Adlai [meaning: smoky tent of me]." –*1Ch 27:29*

For Christians, king Jesus maintained that same structure within his earthly church. "Tend the flock of God which is among you, exercising the oversight, not of constraint, but willingly, according to [the will of] God; nor yet for filthy lucre, but of a ready mind; neither as lording it over the charge allotted to you, but making yourselves examples to the flock. And when the chief Shepherd shall be manifested, ye shall receive the crown of glory that fadeth not away." *–1Pe 5:2-4*

Thanks to those obedient under-shepherds, Solomon's citizens grazed in "perpetual justice." They're not tempted by nutritionless philosophies. "There is more hunger for love in this world than for bread." *–Mother Theresa* Why invest your time and emotions in people who will never appreciate you?

17 [EARTHLY SHUNEMITE:] Until the day breaks and the shadows flee, turn my beloved, and be like a gazelle, or like a young stag on my mountain section.	עד שיפוח היום ונסו הצללים סב דמה־לך דודי לצבי או לעפר האילים על־הרי בתר: ס

17 ***day breaks and the shadows flee*** (שיפוח היום ונסו הצללים) literally; "when-he-breaks the-day and-they-flee the-shadows."

This merism shows the contrast, or extent, of the Heavenly Solomon's activity: From dawn to darkness. To that extent, he shepherds her, in Sharon. From Pentecost to Armageddon, the Heavenly Solomon has nurtured the Shunemites in Sharon [perpetual justice].

PUZZLE: Here is where our forsaken Shunemite begins to decode the holy language. For the first time, she begins to speak in such a manner that praises the holy name of God. Starting in the second word and the second letter, you will find letter skips of four that will spell out the holy name of God--YHWH. I have used a 20% shading screen to bring them to your attention throughout the Hebrew text.

For what purpose did Jehovah add these equidistant letters skip (ELS) markers? Beneath the playful puzzles of holy text, lies a unique signature of God: *His holy name!*

This ingenious method does not interfere with the surface text, but it will disappear if a bad scribe adds or subtracts one letter from the scroll. Like the watermark on your government's money, this divine tracking system acts like a watermark for holy text.

The watermark on money and postage stamps, and other government documents are employed by government agencies to discourage counterfeiting. Watermarks, you're your Bible's ELS system, can vary in their visibility; while some are obvious on casual inspection, others require an expert's eye to notice.

This method goes beyond identifying scribal errors, however, it also seperates holy text from an extra-biblical text, protecting God's people from frauds who try to pass off so-called inspired writings, hoping to include them in the Bible canon.

my mountain section (הרי בתר) literally; "mountain-me section."

Go back and review the first word in this verse, "Until." This hints that there is a time limit. This thought is connected to "my mountain section." Previous translators have translated these words (my mountain section) different than mine.

The Hebrew word *har* (#H2022 הר) is quite common. It's within the common phrase, "Har-Mageddon" (or, Mountain of Magiddo). The suffix, *yod* (י) is commonly translated as "me or mine." The Hebrew word *beh-ther* (#H1335 בתר) means "a section, part, piece." In the past, (without explanation) it has been erroneously translated as "ruggedness."

"My mountain section" implies that the Shunemite, has already fled to the mountain of God. (Lk 21:21) She is on a specific section (1 of 144,000) of God's mountain, desperately beseeching her beloved to come to her. The king of the North (a fox) is nipping at her feet.

"My mountain section" invokes the famous parable, "How think ye? if any man have a hundred sheep, and one of them be gone astray, doth he not leave the ninety and nine, and go unto the mountains, and seek that which goeth astray?" –*Mt 18:12*

The Shunemite speaks, specifically, of her "section." If the entire mountain represents Solomon's entire earthly government, why would she speak of a section? Remember, the Shunemites have kingdom duties. They don't serve as under-kings, or under-priests, but they do serve. The Shunemites serve as nurse-like ambassadors. (2Cor 5:20) Until they secure their royal crown they must accept, and execute, their limited assignments, in their very limited territories.

Nations are commonly referred to as women. In the case of Moab: "Kerioth is taken, and the strongholds are seized, and the heart of the mighty men of Moab at that day shall be as the heart of a woman in her pangs." –*Jer 48:41* Egypt was also referred to as a "woman." (Jer 46:11) The Shunemite's arch-enemy, Babylon, was also referred to as a "woman." (Re 17:4-6) This poor Earthly Shunemite plays a fractional role in kingdom service. So, like the 288,000, it's reasonable to describe her limited earthly assignment as her "mountain section."

EARTHLY SHUNEMITE: Every earthly ambassador has a personal responsibility to announce: "Flee to the mountains." (Lk 21:21) "Get thee up on a high mountain; O thou that tellest good tidings to Jerusalem, lift up thy voice with strength; lift it up, be not afraid; say unto the cities of Judah, 'Behold, your God!'" –*Is 40:9*

PUZZLE: The God you worship enjoys weaving additional messages beneath the surface message. In this verse, the sacred name of God appears every four letters, starting with the second letter in the second Hebrew word.

Notice the young Shunemite is prone to giving Solomon orders. Her elder Shulamite, on the other hand, watches her husband to know how to react. She owns her husband, but she studies him carefully before offering her counsel.

Let me end the chapter with one of Aesop's stories: During the Grecian wars, a soldier diligently tended to his faithful horse, and in return, the horse served him well.

After the decorated soldier retired, he treated this same horse with little regard. The former soldier forced his war horse to labor long hours in community transport, and sweat under the hot sun as a plow horse. Yet, he provided no shelter against the cold nights. Adding insult to injury, he underfed the horse.

One day, the soldier's homeland came under Roman attack. So, the brave soldier saddled his faithful charger.

The startled war horse cautioned her dear master: "Do I look fleet? Do I look like the horse that brought you home? Years of domestic disrespect has turned me into nothing more than an ass. It will take years of rehabilitation to restore me to the war horse I once was."

Chapter 3:[11]
Solomon's Presence

In this chapter, Abishag the Shunemite comes close to Solomon. (1Ki 1:3) Yet, Solomon never dialogues with her. Instead, he calls out "commands," regarding her. Some girls can live for years on a scant memory of a fleeting brush with romance. This is no substitute for children of her own.

3 [EARTHLY SHUNEMITE:] In the nights on my bed, I looked for THE ONE MY SOUL LOVES. I looked for him, but did not find him.	ג עַל־מִשְׁכָּבִי בַּלֵּילוֹת בִּקַּשְׁתִּי אֵת שֶׁאָהֲבָה נַפְשִׁי בִּקַּשְׁתִּיו וְלֹא מְצָאתִיו:

1 *In the nights* (בַּלֵּילוֹת) literally; "in-the-nights."

My dear daughter, I know a secret about my daughter. She smiles a lot, and I know where she finds those smiles. She builds bridges, bridges that delight others.

Too many people live isolated existences. Such people discover, it's not easy to be happy. While others succumb to their darkness, my daughter thinks past the darkness—and she can't hide her delight.

There was an odd, but related, example given by Rabboni Jesus, prior to resurrecting Lazarus . . . and I bet, like my daughter, Jesus hid a wry smile. "Jesus answered, 'Are there not twelve hours in the day? If a man walk[s] in the day, he stumbleth not, because he seeth the light of this world. But if a man walk[s] in the night, he stumbleth, because the light is not in him.' These things spake he: and after this he saith unto them, 'Our friend Lazarus is fallen asleep; but I go, that I may awake him out of sleep.'" –*Joh 11:9-11*

The key to understanding his puzzle is found at the word "in." Jesus was connecting the resurrection of Shulamites to the resurrection of Lazarus. The Jewish day starts with darkness.

Chapter one, of *Song of Songs*, also began with the Earthly Shunemite in troubling darkness. The last half of a Jewish day contains the light. Chapter eight, of *Song of Songs*, ends with light "in" the Shulamite—like a burning flame. (So 8:6) Like my happy daughter, when the Shulamite travels in darkness, she brings light with her.

What a fantastic lesson for marriage. Too many marriages are discarded before they've made it through the darkness. Sunlight begins at the latter half of the day. Some short-sighted mates reason: If marriage is a bond, then marriage must be a form of bondage. If divorce dissolves this bondage, then divorce must be a form of liberation.

Divorce has been the Western culture's solution to every marital setback. Western ideology rewards those who opt out, rather than seeing their problems through, to the light of day. But, we didn't learn "quitting" from our matriarchs.

my bed (מִשְׁכָּבִי) literally; "bed-of-me."

What happened to the "verdant bed," at So 1:16? This empty bed helps us to identify the speaker. Solomon hasn't come for Abishag, the Shunemite, "she has not known a man." (1Ki 1:4) The Shunemite's empty bed taunts her, but there is no place for her—in Heaven—yet.

Abishag, the Shunemite, has a disturbing night, much like the king of Babylon. "I saw a dream which made me afraid; and the thoughts upon my bed and the visions of my head troubled me." –*Da 4:5* This king's vision was a mental image, not reality. Both saw something they couldn't explain, but their visions came from the same source.

my soul (נַפְשִׁי) literally; "soul-of-me."

Some translators have rendered this as "heart." The Hebrew word for heart is *labe* (#H3820 לב). But, we see the Hebrew word for soul, *neh-fesh* (#H5315 נפש), which generally means "a breathing creature, beast, creature or man." The Shunemite is a human, with all the frailties of a human. She still bumps into things of the night.

We have all been there. The musical classic, *Somewhere* encapsulates her strong, but undefined hopes. "There's a place for us; somewhere a place for us; peace and quiet and open air wait for us; somewhere; there's a time for us; some day a time for us; time together with time to spare; time to look, time to care; someday; somewhere; we'll find a new way of living; we'll find a way of forgiving; somewhere." *–Leonard Bernstein and Stephen Sondheim*

The "discreet maidens" waited with their oiled lamps for the groom to arrive. (Mt 22:35-38) This Shunemite is like a "discreet maiden." She is not the bride. So, like the "discreet maidens," she too waits in darkness.

The word "soul" will appear in the next four verses in the same phrase. This word (soul) creates some problems when translating to English. In the past, English translators have removed the word (soul). I have capitalized it (because of location—the Hebrew object identifier points to the bundled thought).

Unfortunately, there doesn't seem to be any alternative way to translate, without destroying the structure—in the English. The Hebrew is just fine. The problem takes place when you translate Hebrew into English.

> **NUMERICS:** *searched* (בקש) literally; "striving, enquiring, seeking." This is the first of five uses. At the *remez* level, five hints at judgment, with a view to salvation. By the final occurrence (at So 6:1) we will see that she has help. Her new Brothers will escort her to the Messianic Solomon.

NUMERICS: *find* (מצא) literally; "appear, attain, acquire, meet, presence." This is the first of eight uses. At the *remez* level, eight describes starting over. If seven completes the week, then the eighth day is the beginning of a new week.

This potential bride of the Messiah is following all her matriarchs counsel of wisdom. When we reach the final occurrence, at So 8:1, we will see she "finds" her Messiah.

PUZZLE: The God you worship enjoys weaving additional messages beneath the surface message. That's what separates holy text from Jewish newspapers. The Hebrew language doesn't weave these messages naturally. It takes the mind (and deft hands) of God. In this verse, the sacred name of God appears every 13 letters, starting at the third letter in the third Hebrew word. It took the Israeli Solomon 13 years to construct his personal house. (1Ki 7:1)

2 [EARTHLY SHUNEMITE:] I will get up now, and go about the city, through its streets and through its squares. I will search for THE ONE MY SOUL LOVES. So, I searched for him, but did not find him.	אקומה נא ואסובבה בעיר בשוקים וברחבות אבקשה את שאהבה נפשי בקשתיו ולא מצאתיו:

2 *I will get up* (אקומה) literally; "I-will-get-up."

What city does the Shunemite "go about" in? Verse 11 gives us the answer. The Shunemite's habitat is earthly Zion, not "The Jerusalem Above." This Zion has an ugly history of rejecting God's messiahs. God only blesses Zion when its citizens embrace a duly-anointed king. (Ho 8:4)

We have to admire the initiative of this Earthly Shunemite. She lacks kingdom skills, but she keeps an oiled lamp for the bride and groom. She makes a good bride's maid, but she has a big problem. She loves the groom.

We have already witnessed her grim life. The life of the Shunemite is one many modern women would quickly abandon. Every day, alcoholics tell themselves, "I can't do it." Every day, drug addicts tell themselves, "I can't do it." Every day, business failures tell themselves, "I can't do it."

So, why does this relentless Shunemite continue on?

Love.

Even when you fall short of your love goal, never forget which star you chart your life by. The Shunemite uses the same star as Solomon: the God of love. (1Joh 1:7-8)

and go about (ואסובבה) literally; "and-I-will-go-about."

If we pay attention, we discover a lot of people "going about" in this Zion. The Shunemite, watchers, and other spirit persons are "going about" in this earthly city. "And the angel answered and said unto me, 'These are the four winds of Heaven, which go forth from standing before the Lord of all the earth.' [The chariot] wherein are the black horses goeth forth toward the north country; and the white went forth after them; and the grizzled went forth toward the south country. And the strong went forth, and sought to go that they might walk to and fro through the earth: and he said, 'Get you hence, walk to and fro through the earth. So they walked to and fro through the earth.'" –*Zec 6:5-7*

Why would she go about in these "streets?" The answer is hidden in So 2:9. If you recall, Solomon is watching the street from behind his lattice. This Earthly Shunemite isn't stupid. She knows where to go to get into her beloved's line of sight. He's paying attention to the "going's about" in the earthly streets of Zion.

The Earthly Shunemite is in earthly Zion. Again, verse 11 supports that this city is Zion. (2Sa 5:7-10)

but did not find him (ולא מצאתיו) literally; "but-not I-found-him."

He's in Earthly Zion, but hidden behind a lattice. She can't see him, but he can see her. (So 2:9) A similar event is described in *Matthew:* "And as [were] the days of Noah, so shall be the coming of the Son of man. For as in those days which were before the flood they were eating and drinking, marrying and giving in marriage, until the day that Noah entered into the ark, and they knew not until the flood came, and took them all away; so shall be the coming of the Son of man." –*Mt 24:37-39* The Shunemite will lead a group that recognizes, and embraces, Solomon as their rightful king. Many won't. (1Ki 1:5-8; 1Ki 3:1)

The Shunemite's "beloved" is often present, but not seen. "Therefore speak I to them in parables; because seeing they see not, and hearing they hear not, neither do they understand . . . Lest haply they should perceive with their eyes, And hear with their ears, And understand with their heart, And should turn again, And I should heal them. But blessed are your eyes, for they see; and your ears, for they hear." –*Mt 13:13-16*

EARTHLY SHUNEMITE: So 3:2 connects to So 2:2. Should you be wondering if queen Esther's city of Shushan is related to "lily" (*sho-shan*)? King Ahausurus chose Esther from Shushan. Esther's story, is Abishag's story.

David's death left many wives. Under Hebrew law, Solomon became Abishag's kinsman redeemer. (De 25:5) If you have drawn a different conclusion, as Judah did, then re-read 1Ki 2:22-25.

3 [EARTHLY SHUNEMITE:] The watchers found me, as they made their rounds in the city. "THE ONE MY SOUL LOVES, you saw!"	מצאוני השמרים הסבבים בעיר את שאהבה נפשי ראיתם:

3 *made their rounds* (הסבבים) literally; "the-going-round-ones."

The Hebrew word *doom-maw* (#H1820 דמה) means "desolate, to bleed out, a ceremonial death." It comes from the Hebrew word *dawm* (#H1818 דם) which means "blood." This word (דמה) was used in *Hosea* to describe the ceremonial execution of the unfaithful wife of Jehovah, Israel. (Ho 4:5)

A second chance is hidden within the book of *Isaiah*—not for God's executed wife, but for their remaining children. "The burden of Dumah. One calleth unto me out of Seir, 'Watchman, what of the night? Watchman, what of the night?' The watchman said, 'The morning cometh, and also the night: if ye will inquire, inquire ye: turn ye, come.'" –*Is 21:11-12*

Ancient Jerusalem was ceremonially executed (*doom-maw* דמה) in 70 A.D. The components for a new Zion, however, awaits his second return, or his coming presence.

Given these facts, the Shunemite has every reason to believe that the inhabitants of earthly Zion would know her beloved. The above quote from *Isaiah* shows she studied Isaiah's prophecy. Note that she inquired again.

The watchman operates in the same frame of mind, and instructs the listener to "inquire again." The Shunemite does "inquire again." The Shunemite returns again, and has a different experience with the same watchers. (So 5:7)

So, why would the watchers, politely, ask her to come back again? Yet, when she does come back, they violently strike her. What could justify this seeming contradiction? So 5:7 awaits you, anxious to explain.

you saw (ראיתם) literally; "you-saw."

This is not a question. She knows what they saw. They witnessed the untimely death of her Messiah. Followers of Jesus know the angels (or watchers) were dispatched to comfort Jesus, the night before he died. Jesus, the Heavenly Solomon, told his disciples he would return. This Shunemite is holding him to that promise.

She also knows, they know, where her beloved is. "Then he cried in mine ears with a loud voice, saying, Cause ye them that have charge over the city to draw near, every man with his destroying weapon in his hand. And behold, six men came from the way of the upper gate, which lieth toward the north, every man with his slaughter weapon in his hand; and one man in the midst of them clothed in linen, with a writer's inkhorn by his side. And they went in, and stood beside the brazen altar." –*Ezk 9:1-2*

Modern disciples are familiar with the angelic watchmen and their "marking" work.

4 [EARTHLY SHUNEMITE:] Scarcely had I passed them when I found THE ONE MY SOUL LOVES. I held him and would not let go until I had brought him to my mother's house, to the room of the one who conceived me.	כמעט שעברתי מהם עד שמצאתי את שאהבה נפשי אחזתיו ולא ארפנו עד־שהביאתיו אל־בית אמי ואל־חדר הורתי:

4 ***had I passed them*** (שעברתי מהם) literally; "that-I-passed from-them."

These watchers are aligned with Solomon's interests, not her's. To her, these watchers are related, but distant relatives, uncles. These uncles have a gruesome place in Solomon's timetable. *Step aside!* the watchers seem to say.

Throughout history Jehovah has demonstrated his own set of boundaries. "So we passed by from our brethren the children of Esau, that dwell in Seir, from the way of the Arabah from Elath and from Ezion-geber. And we turned and passed by the way of the wilderness of Moab. And Jehovah said unto me, 'Vex not Moab, neither contend with them in battle; for I will not give thee of his land for a possession; because I have given Ar unto the children of Lot for a possession.'" –De 2:8-9

The Israelites didn't like it, but Jehovah had outside relationships with other nations, including Moab. God expected Israel to honor His previous promise to Lot. Good or bad, Jehovah has a larger family than Israel.

when I found (שמצאתי) literally; "that-I-found."

The Hebrew word *maw-tsaw* (#H4672 מצא) means "to attain, find, acquire, meet, present." Consider one possible application: Andrew told Simon Peter, "We have found the Messiah." (Joh 1:41) The woman at the well returned to tell the men in her village, "I have found the Messiah." (Joh 4:29) Mary Magdalene returned to report the resurrection of Jesus to the apostles, "We found him." (Lk 24:9)

A more accurate rendering, however, would be "inner discovery." This word (found) has appeared four times, consecutively. (So 3:1; 3:2; 3:3; 3:4) "Four" can apply to the inner (fourth) dimension. There seems to be some emphasis on her inner discovery—by means of the numeric count.

He's invisible. How could the Shunemite "find" this invisible Messiah? At this very moment, you are less than a mile from hundreds of people who have "found" God. They can't see Him, and don't claim to see Him. Yet, they still claim to have "found" Him—and—have been converted by the experience. He doesn't talk to them, but the word "found" has such a wide range of definition that each of us could say, we have "found" God, in one sense or another.

There have been many temporary messiahs. Every Israelite king went through a ceremonial anointing process—including Solomon. The same is true for priests who served in the Temple. They are all gone now. They were merely prophetic place holders for the final Messiah, Jesus.

THE ONE MY SOUL LOVES (שאהבה נפשי) literally; "THE-ONE-SHE-LOVES soul-of-me."
Why would the divine author repeat this same phrase in each of the last four verses, and why place the definite direct object marker (את) before each use? Could this be further proof that these four expressions apply to the inner dimension? This inner song animates the Shunemite and is an ongoing theme throughout these eight chapters.

and would not let go (ולא ארפנו) literally; "and-not I-would-let-go-him."
Like Jacob, the Earthly Shunemite makes no apologies for godly ambitions. Jacob man-handled an angel and never expressed an iota of regret. "And he said, 'Let me go, for the day breaketh.' And he said, 'I will not let thee go, except thou bless me.' And he said unto him, 'What is thy name?' And he said, 'Jacob.' And he said, 'Thy name shall be called no more Jacob, but Israel: for thou hast striven with God and with men, and hast prevailed.'" –*Ge 32:26-28*
Since her intentions are honorable, there is nothing left to do, except go get what she wants. (Pr 3:1; 4:4; 6:21)

the one who conceived me (הורתי) literally; "one-conceiving-me."
There are a number of ways to interpret this Hebrew word (הורתי). Keep in mind, however, that she is an *Earthly* Shunemite. Since man's body was made "out of dust from the ground," the earth is occasionally likened to mankind's "mother." (Ge 2:7)

"Then Job arose, and rent his robe, and shaved his head, and fell down upon the ground, and worshipped; and he said, 'Naked came I out of my mother's womb, and naked shall I return thither:'" *–Job 1:20-21*

When we combine the birth of Adam (at Ge 2:7) with the death of Job (at Job 1:21), notice that Adam came from mother "Earth" and Job went back to mother "Earth." Both described their mother as the "earth."

So, fleshly humans could legitimately describe their mother as the "earth." The Shunemite wants to show the whole "earth" her beloved. But, they don't see what she sees.

When this verse is compared to So 8:2, the reader is left wondering, "Why is the Shunemite's mother described as "conceiving" her, but the Shulamite's mother is described as "teaching" her? Because these are two different daughters, with two different mothers, with two different purposes. "Earth" embodies the Shunemite's origins, and that's where she sends the following message from.

5 [EARTHLY SHUNEMITE:] Daughters at Jerusalem, the pleadings of mine are on the gazelles, and on the does of the field: Do not arouse the watchers, or awaken LOVE, until He wills it so.	השבעתי אתכם בנות ירושלם בצבאות או באילות השדה אם־תעירו ׀ ואם־תעוררו את־ האהבה עד שתחפץ: ס

5 *the pleadings of mine* (השבעתי) literally; "the-entreaties-of-me."

The Shunemite has persistently attempted to be among the intimates in Solomon's household. Like Jacob, she has relentlessly chased, grabbed, and wrestled, for her family position. Yet, the exhausted Shunemite still finds time to intercede for her Earthly Brothers.

The Shunemite pleads three times, but appeals to the Shulamites with this 15-word refrain only twice. (So 2:7; 3:5) The Shunemite wants Solomon's associate rulers (Shulamites) to give her Earthly Brothers more time. The seeds of division (10-tribe vs two-tribe kingdoms) have already been sown. Abishag's Brothers will be among the symbolic 10-tribe.

The Shunemite is more than a citizen—maybe a prophet. A prophet's main function is to reconcile two alienated parties—earth and Heaven—Ephraim and Manasseh. Thus begins the "dance of two camps." (So 6:13)

Why is this Shunemite prophetess so alarmed? It seems she wants the daughters at Jerusalem to stop doing something. The proof is hidden within the word, "pleadings." Notice the similarity between, pleading (שׁבע) and *Shabbat* (#H7673 שׁבעת). *Shaw-bath* (שׁבעת) means "cease," or "desist."

So, why would the divine author repeat variations of this verse four times (So 2:7; 3:5; 5:8; 8:4), unless it's worthy of re-examination? God is challenging us to ask, "Cease doing what?"

on the gazelles (בצבאות) literally; "on-gazelles."
The fastest way to deliver a message, in the days of Solomon, was on a horse. To reach a capital city atop a lofty mountain required something swifter and more sure-of-foot than a horse. A gazelle is faster than a horse—on a mountain.

By mentioning gazelles and does, the Shunemite is invoking the swift delivery of her "prayer" to delay the Father's judicial love—which won't be favorable for her brothers.

She must be asking the fleet-footed Solomon to quickly deliver her prayer, since she later identifies Solomon as this "gazelle." (So 8:14)

arouse the watchers (תעירו) literally; "charge-city-watchers."
This compound word is very worthwhile to disassemble. The word *aw-yar* (#H5892 עיר) means "a city, a place guarded

by waking, or watchers, a walled place." The Hebrew word *ee-roo* (#H5900 עִירוּ) means "a citizen, an Israelite." The *tav* (ת) invokes boundaries, legal limits, or conclusion. Most Earthly Shunemites are dead. They wait, in death, for the call of their "swift" Messiah. (Re 3:20)

When a person dies, they were described as entering "the gates of death." (Ps 9:13; 107:18) Old age delivered them to the gates of *sheol*. (Is 38:10; Mt 16:18) This song will use the word "gates" repeatedly. Death is a metaphor that means they will wait with Job, deep in their earth "mother," waiting to be re-born into a new world—whether her "new world" be earth or Heaven.

In the mean time, a prophetic execution was looming over the earth. In fact, there were four angels (watchers) holding back the four winds of destruction. (Re 7:1) Whereas the Shunemite longed for relief from her difficult life, she did not want romance at the expense of her Earthly Brothers.

Like the Shunemite, Abraham negotiated with God for the lives of the innocents in Sodom. Moses pled in behalf of the guilty Israelites. All three of these prophets had the moral presence of mind to ask God for mercy.

The bedraggled remnant of Shunemites remain vigilant, against impossible odds, pleading for the symbolic Ephraimites (also known as, the Earthly Brothers).

awaken (תְּעוֹרְרוּ) literally; "you-awaken."

The Hebrew word *oor* (#H5782 עוּר) contains the idea of, "stir up." This verb appears in the polel stem at So 2:7; 3:5; and 8:4. In this form, it hints at more than being awakened. It hints at, fury. The Shunemite believes when God does respond, He will be furious . . . and He will.

This is a perfect example of how translators are forced to exclude some information (for the sake of brevity). The additional *resh* (ר) hints that this word is meant for an elevated person, a prominent person. It is. By the time you finish examining the word "LOVE," you will know exactly who that prominent person is: the God of Solomon.

LOVE (אהבה) literally; "DIVINE-LOVE."

God is love. (1Joh 4:16-19) This is further emphasized by the first letter, *aleph* (א). *Aleph* (א) is also the number one (in Hebrew). Jehovah is, one (יהוה אחד). (De 6:4)

That love is conditional, however. Love costs. True lovers pay without complaint, however. Only those true lovers will benefit from it. "For this is the love of God, that we keep his commandments: and his commandments are not grievous." *–1Joh 5:3*

The flip-side to this superlative love is that Jehovah's attribute of justice requires strict conformity to His son's kingdom. (Ps 2) Those who refuse to conform, are doomed. And God's patience is wearing thin. Don't forget: Unlike the Earthly Shunemite who asks for more time, the Heavenly Shulamites are requesting the opposite—revenge. (Re 6:10)

The Shunemite and Shulamites are making opposite requests to the same person.

He wills it so (שתחפץ) literally; "time-of-lawful-will."

The Hebrew word *khaw-fates* (#H2654 חפץ) contains the formal intent of "inclined, predisposed, willed." The person the Shunemite wants to influence is Jehovah, Himself. Solomon's God has already announced a conclusion of this system of things. The Shunemite is only quibbling over a miniscule difference in time. "And Jesus said unto him, 'To-day is salvation come to this house, forasmuch as he also is a son of Abraham. For the Son of man came to seek and to save that which was lost.'" *–Lk 19:9-10*

6 [EARTHLY SHUNEMITE:] Who is this, coming out from the wilderness, like a column of smoke, perfumed like myrrh and incense, made from all the spices of the merchant?	מִי זֹאת עֹלָה מִן־הַמִּדְבָּר כְּתִימֲרוֹת עָשָׁן מְקֻטֶּרֶת מוֹר וּלְבוֹנָה מִכֹּל אַבְקַת רוֹכֵל:

6 *Who is this* (מִי זֹאת) literally; "who this?"

Who is this? Notice that all these descriptions are not concretely physical. The wording is similar, but not equal, to So 8:5. Hebrew poetry loves progressive imagary. A clue to the identity of this person can be found in the description, "columns of smoke." "And Jehovah will create over the whole habitation of mount Zion, and over her assemblies, a cloud and smoke by day, and the shining of a flaming fire by night; for over all the glory [shall be spread] a covering." –Is 4:5

This same person proved to be darkness to the ancient Egyptians, but a pillar of light to the Israelites. Smoke signals were used to communicate messages between cities. (Jg 20:38-40) In the third chapter of *Song of Songs*, this person is the "signal" between the Jerusalem Above and the Zion below. (Heb 12:22) The next verse names the "column of smoke."

Another clue that explains who is coming from the wilderness, can be found in the words, *la-bon-ah mik-al* (מִכֹּל לְבוֹנָה). The first word (לְבוֹנָה) means, "white-stuff." The second word (מִכֹּל) phonetically, sounds like "Michael." "And at that time shall Michael stand up, the great prince who standeth for the children of thy people; and there shall be a time of trouble, such as never was since there was a nation even to that same time: and at that time thy people shall be delivered, every one that shall be found written in the book. And many of them that sleep in the dust of the earth shall awake, some to everlasting life, and some to shame and everlasting contempt." –Da 12:1-2 Jehovah is not Michael. Verse six is describing Solomon.

wilderness (מדבר) literally; "wilderness."

A commonly mistranslated Hebrew word is *mid-bawr* (#H4057 מדבר) which should be translated as "wilderness." Often, it's mistranslated as "desert," as though "*mid-bawr*" was a wasteland—baron of life. Wilderness is teaming with life, but absent of human engineering.

Starting with the first letter, *mem* (מ), we get the concept of birth. Birth is not random, or haphazard. It's majestically precise. For example: A woman's contractions can be predicted, timed, and helps physicians to gauge her nearness to delivery. The next three letters are *daw-bar* (#H1696 דבר) which means "word, arrange, answer, speak, command, teach, etc." The primary thought being, an orderly method of arranging, describing, or orderly communication.

Fully understanding *mid-bawr* (מדבר) helps to understand why Jesus went into the "wilderness" for 40 days to meditate. God's creation helps us to straighten out our crooked thoughts, or align our thoughts with the mind of God. (Ro 1:20)

NUMERICS: *incense* (קטר) literally; "turn into fragrance by fire, incense, kindle." There is only one use in *Song of Songs*. At the *remez* level, one. (De 6:4) Everything emanates from one source, the Father. She was chosen by Jehovah for His first-born son. Like her future husband, she too must die to enter Heaven. In this context, her death will be a sweet fragrance to Jehovah.

7 [EARTHLY BROTHERS:] Here, maybe, on this side! It's Solomon's litter, escorted by 60 warriors, valiant warriors of Israel,	הנה מטתו שלשלמה ששים גברים סביב לה מגברי ישראל:

7 ***Here, maybe, on this side*** (הנה) literally; "on-this-side."

This is the Earthly Brothers speaking. The Hebrew word *hane-naw* (#H2008 הנה) means "hither or thither (used both of place and time): here, hither, now, on this (that) side." The Earthly Brothers recognize the presence of this messiah, but with uncertaintly. Nonetheless, they stand ready to administer his kingdom decisions.

This verse mirrors So 2:17, where the Shunemite refers, specifically, to her "mountain section." The Earthly Brothers version, "Maybe, on this side," is spoken with less certitude.

litter (מטתו) literally; "litter-of-him."

This describes a portable couch or bed, usually covered with a canopy and hidden with curtains, designed to obscure a person of importance can be carried around. The significance of this word demonstrates that Solomon is no longer in Jerusalem. He is mobile. The 60 are aware of his presence and they soldier at his earthly base of Zion.

It's also important to note that this messianic king remains veiled, behind the curtains of the litter (behind the veil of death).

Predictably, the word *mit-ta* (מטה) is also used to describe a "litter," for the transport of the dead. This messiah seems to be coming to transport the dead back to the Heavenly Jerusalem. (Ps 45:9) This is just logical, since it was already predicted, at Da 12:1-2.

Notice the way *mit-ta* (מטה) is translated as "bier" (or litter) in the following quote: "And David said to Joab, and to all the people that were with him, Rend your clothes, and gird you with sackcloth, and mourn before Abner. And king David followed the bier [מטה]. And they buried Abner in Hebron: and the king lifted up his voice, and wept at the grave of Abner; and all the people wept." –*2Sa 3:31-32*

While trees burst into their seasonal colors, lovers vow their vows. While the blossoms on fruit trees sprout, couples pledge their lives to one another. The sun returns each year to see who has kept their promises. The Messiah never forgets. He keeps his promises. Despite death and centuries . . . he comes back. The world is full of frauds, but the Messiah defrauds no one. Solomon returns for a reason. He made a vow to return for his Shulamites. (Joh 14:3)

60 warriors (ששים גברים) literally; "60 warriors."
Do these 60 warriors have something to do with the 60 queens mentioned at So 6:8? Of course. Warriors are a different facet of the same government. Holy text uses the number 60 to indicate a circle, a season, or completed "cycle" of family time.

Although 60 could symbolize a season of the human family, 60 usually means much more than that. Generally, it indicates a new crop of a family-type. How fitting that this eternal father would return to earthly Zion. (Is 9:5-6) This crop, however, includes sons ready for war. Consider our family's history of war:

"This charge I commit unto thee, my child Timothy, according to the prophecies which led the way to thee, that by them thou mayest war the good warfare." *–1Ti 1:18* "For though we walk in the flesh, we do not war according to the flesh (for the weapons of our warfare are not of the flesh, but mighty before God to the casting down of strongholds), casting down imaginations, and every high thing that's exalted against the knowledge of God, and bringing every thought into captivity to the obedience of Christ; and being in readiness to avenge all disobedience, when your obedience shall be made full." *–2Cor 10:3-6*

valiant warriors of Israel (מגברי ישראל) literally; "from-valiant-warriors-of Israel."

The Hebrew word for warrior is *gheh-ber* (#H1397 גבר). Notice the double-repeat of "warriors." David's mighty warriors let nothing encroach on their anointed king. These 60 warriors will do no less for Solomon when he returns to Zion. The number 12 hints at relocation. The number 60 [5 x 12 = 60] hints at an earthly family. What are these 60 getting ready for? Which "Jerusalem" are they from?

"And in the days of those kings shall the God of Heaven set up a kingdom which shall never be destroyed, nor shall the sovereignty thereof be left to another people; but it shall break in pieces and consume all these kingdoms, and it shall stand for ever." –*Da 2:44* They (the Messiah and his entourage) arrive at earthly Zion—the earthly outpost for those coming and going from the Jerusalem Above.

8 [EARTHLY BROTHERS:] all of them wearing the sword, all experienced in battle, each one with his sword at his side, prepared for the terrors of the night.	כלם אחזי חרב מלמדי מלחמה איש חרבו על־ירכו מפחד בלילות: ס

8 *experienced in battle* (מלמדי מלחמה) literally; "ones-being-experienced-of battle."

These angelic warriors escort the Heavenly Solomon and guarantee the safety of Solomon's household.

". . . the king granted the Jews that were in every city to gather themselves together, and to stand for their life, to destroy, to slay, and to cause to perish, all the power of the people and province that would assault them, [their] little ones and women, and to take the spoil of them for a prey." –*Es 8:11*

Angels are always on call, but Earthly Brothers can also play a vital role in safeguarding the household of the greater Solomon. Even our Israeli women fight beside us. "I commend unto you Phoebe our sister, who is a servant of the church that is at Cenchreae: that ye receive her in the Lord, worthily of the saints, and that ye assist her in whatsoever matter she may have need of you: for she herself also hath been a helper of many, and of mine own self." –*Ro 16:1-2*

From the beginning, Israel chafes at injustice. "But when he was well-nigh forty years old, it came into his heart to visit his brethren the children of Israel. And seeing one [of them] suffer wrong, he defended him, and avenged him that was oppressed, smiting the Egyptian: and he supposed that his brethren understood that God by his hand was giving them deliverance; but they understood not." –*Ac 7:23-25*

terrors of the night (מפחד בלילוֹת) literally; "for-terror of-the-nights."

Our family's warriors have always faced the most horrible adversaries—and will continue to battle all the terrors our enemies hurl at Zion. "So that with good courage we say, The Lord is my helper; I will not fear: What shall man do unto me?'" –*Heb 13:6* The king of these 60 warriors is, of course, the Heavenly Solomon.

9 [EARTHLY BROTHERS:] King Solomon made for himself a carriage. He made it from the trees of Lebanon.	אפריון עשה לו המלך שלמה מעצי הלבנון:

9 ***carriage*** (אפריון) literally; "carriage."

Notice also, this is a different word than, litter (מטתוֹ). This word *a-peree-on* (אפריון) appears nowhere else in the Bible, and there is no consensus on its definition. There is a biblical passage that sounds close, and even resembles the definition used here. "They have over them as king the angel of the abyss: his name in Hebrew is Abaddon, and in the Greek [tongue] he hath the name Apollyon." –*Re 9:11*

A word related to messiah, and even contains the definition used here, is *mesheekhaw* (#H7882 מְשִׁיחָה), which means "from the chasm." This second word pushes deeper into the meaning of "messiah." This "carriage" is coming from that "chasm."

Returning to the earlier symbolic definition for "tree" we get a composite view of the great people being assembled for this carriage. Lebanon is north of Zion. The word "wreaths" (at verse 11) hints at what kind of trees compose this carriage.

from the trees of Lebanon (מעצי הלבנון) literally: "from-trees-of the-Lebanon."

Do you recall the "six men" (So 3:3) who entered at the north gate? These 60 warriors work in harmony with those "six men." These related numbers (6/60) was your first hint.

Also, cedar had been used extensively in the construction of the various royal edifices. (1Ki 7:2-12) King Jehoiakim, who heard the words recorded, at Jer 22:6, used cedar paneling for his luxurious palace. (Jer 22:13-15) Therefore, the royal home included cedar. Many facets of royal life included cedar—including Solomon's transport.

So, this heavenly transport could appropriately be compared to the finest people, the finest timber, taken from earth. Somewhere there is a place for them. Peace and quiet, and open air, wait for them. Somewhere. The Jerusalem Above is that place.

10 [EARTHLY BROTHERS:] Its posts he made of silver, its base of gold. Its seat was upholstered with purple. Its interior lovingly inlaid by the daughters at Jerusalem.	עמודיו עשה כסף רפידתו זהב מרכבו ארגמן תוכו רצוף אהבה מבנות ירושלם:

10 Its posts (עמודיו) literally; "posts-of-him."

Posts always hold something up. The marital covenant is an outward sign of the Shulamite.

So, earthly Zion's invitation to come out and see this new Solomon is supremely important. The proper support of a wife doesn't depend on knowing that her husband will prevail, rather, trusting that good will prevail—whether her husband survives or not. If her husband has enemies, she should defend him with her life. Be your husband's post-like support.

seat (מרכבו) literally; "seat-of-him."

Generally, "seat" and "stand" have very predictable meanings. To a Hebrew, "seat" means consider, as in a trial deliberation. "Stand" means to pronounce judgment.

In this case, the Father has committed all judging to His son. On the Day of Atonement (day of the covering), the high priest entered the Most Holy and splattered half of the bull's blood before the "mercy seat" and then did the same with the blood of the goat. (Le 16:14-15)

Thus, the "mercy seat" did more than cover the stone tablets, jar of manna, and Aaron's rod, it played a thematic role in the covering of sins. The inspired writer of the book of *Hebrews* points out what the greater Solomon already knew: these items were symbolic. (Heb 9:11-14, 24-28)

its interior lovingly inlaid (תוכו רצוף אהבה) literally; "interior-of-him being-inlaid from-divine-love."

This was additional public testimony of the Shulamite's love for Solomon. It proved her concern for his comfort and how he is viewed by others. So great was her love that she was willing to work hard on his presentation.

Counterfeit love doesn't look after the best interests of their partner. A fraud sneaks, makes excuses, and is always in the market for a better husband. The Bride of our Messiah is not like that.

If you don't make daily opportunities for kindness, then don't get married. Such people should never inflict themselves on others.

The Hebrew word *raw-tsaf* (#H7528 רצף) means "joining of objects together." This shows the reader the Shulamite's special skill. As her name suggests, she weaves peace, and artfully joins alienated groups. The Shulamite knits everything together—in love. This phrase explains So 7:5 (royal weaving).

It doesn't take long for a wife to discover the ugly details of her man. There is a moment in every relationship when you will want to turn and run. Don't.

When a woman understands the art of *raw-tsaf* (רצף), she takes the broken pieces of her life, and the broken pieces of his life, and constructs something for the clouds. Remember: a carriage is how we present ourselves to the public. She is so concerned for his public appearance that she is willing to invest her time and skills for his public persona.

> **NUMERICS:** *seat* (מרכב) literally; "seat (as in chariot)." There is only one use in *Song of Songs*. At the *remez* level, one is a very significant number. Jehovah is, one. (De 6:4) Everything emanates from one source, Jehovah. So, as chapter eight will prove, this litter has one destination—their Father.

11 [HEAVENLY SHULAMITE:] Come out you daughters at Zion, and look at king Solomon wearing the wreath, the crown with which his mother crowned him on a day of his wedding, a day his heart rejoiced.	צאינה ׀ וראינה בנות ציון במלך שלמה בעטרה שעטרה־לו אמו ביום חתנתו וביום שמחת לבו: ס

11 ***daughters at Zion*** (בנות ציון) literally; "daughters-of Zion."

Most are surprised there is no consensus on the definition of Zion. A closely related word *tsee-yoon* (#H6725 ציון) means "a monumental, or guiding pillar, sign, waymark." (Pr 8:34) Blend that thought with the mysterious incident at Ge 28:18-22 commonly referred to as "Jacob's ladder."

At Ge 28:18, Jacob set up a "pillar" for the house of God. "Zion" was where God anointed humans to rule over Israel. Zion was on a different hill than the Temple. Jehovah lived on one hill (Moriah) and Israel's king lived on the other (Zion).

Most Bible readers never distinguish Zion from Jerusalem, but *Song of Songs* forces the distinction. We have the "daughters at Jerusalem" speaking to "the daughters at Zion." These "daughters at Zion" are Earthly Shunemites. (2Sa 5:7-10) The "daughters at Jerusalem" are Shulamites. (1Ki 3:1)

These are two different groups. "But you have approached a Mount Zion <u>and</u> a city of the living God, Heavenly Jerusalem, and myriads of angels, in general assembly, and the congregation of the firstborn who have been enrolled in the Heavens, and God the Judge of all, and the spiritual lives of righteous ones who have been made perfect, and Jesus the mediator of a new covenant." –Heb 12:22-24 *Revelation* claims that Jesus <u>descends</u> atop Mt. Zion.

The Heavenly Jerusalem is high above earthly Zion. Jehovah's rule emanates through Jesus; Jesus' rule emanates through Heavenly Jerusalem; Heavenly Jerusalem's rule emanates through earthly Zion. (Re 14:1-3; Da 2:44)[12]

wearing the crown (בעטרה) literally; "with-the-crown."

The Heavenly Solomon wears this crown, to display his mother's approval of these ongoing weddings. A capable wife is considered "a crown to her owner," because her good conduct brings honor to her husband, raising him in the estimation of others. (Pr 12:4)

The Shulamites are like a "crown of beauty" denoting they were the product of God's workmanship. (See So 8:1) This verse teaches us that the "mother" participated in their creation too. This was prefigured in her crown of 12 stars. So, his crown must carry special significance too.

There is a big surprise waiting for earthly Zion. It was prophesied, then promptly ignored for centuries. "And the nations shall see thy righteousness, and all kings thy glory, and thou shalt be called by a new name, which the mouth of Jehovah shall name." –Is 62:2

which his mother crowned him (שׁעטרה־לּוֹ אמּוֹ) literally; "which-she-crowned upon-him mother-of-him."

The Hebrew word *gheb-ee-raw* (#H1377 גבירה) means "mistress, or foreign queen." But, that's not our word. Where that title is used, it generally applies to the mother or grandmother of a Hebrew king, or a foreign queen. (2Ki 10:13) Our word simply tells us this woman is his "mother." The woman who crowns Solomon will be identified later, in the eighth chapter.

If the Jerusalem Above is our mother, who is her mother? And who is the mother of Heavenly Solomon? Which "woman" placed a crown on Solomon's head? Again, the answer is waiting for you, in the eigth chapter.

on a day (ביום) literally; "on-day."

It's important for translators *not* to insert "the" or "on a day of his wedding." There is no such thing as an indefinite article in Hebrew. Yet, this sentence has an definite article—in the English translation. Given the context, an English indefinite article was necessary.

Translating by way of context, gives us better insight. Here's why: there was no such thing as "the" day of Solomon's wedding. Instead (with 1,000 wives), Solomon married continuously, over a period of time. The same with Jesus.

The Heavenly Solomon harvests lilies continuously, over a period of 40 years. So, those who expected one big wedding—are wrong. Holy text teaches otherwise.

"And after the three days and a half the breath of life from God entered into them, and they stood upon their feet; and great fear fell upon them that beheld them. And they heard a great voice from Heaven saying unto them, 'Come up hither.' And they went up into Heaven in the cloud; and their enemies beheld them. And in that hour there was a great earthquake, and the tenth part of the city fell; and there were killed in the earthquake seven thousand persons: and the rest were affrighted, and gave glory to the God of Heaven." –*Re 11:11-13*

Let me end this chapter with a story: There was once a blind girl who despised her life, because she was blind. She began to hate everything, and everyone. Well, almost everyone, with the exception of one young man who did favors for her. She sensed he cared for her. And, over time, she learned to care for him.

When the young man finally professed his love, and asked her if she would marry him, she refused. She explained that she would, if only she could see. If she had eyes that could see, that would change everything.

A short time later, a donor bank notified her that some kind person had donated a pair of eyes. That same day, her parents scheduled a surgery.

Just as she suspected, her operation changed everything. Now, she hated no one. She kissed her parents, cheerfully, greeted her neighbors, strolled through beautiful parks, and for the first time, read great literature.

When a knock came at her door she no longer needed to ask who was there. She opened her own door, to see with her own eyes. The young man who did favors for her, stood on her porch.

The girl was shocked. He was blind.

"Now, will you marry me?" he asked.

It saddened her, but she explained, she had a new life in front of her. She couldn't throw that away—not for a blind man. She sent him away with these final words: "I wish you the best, but I could never marry a blind man."

Her parents rushed him off and comforted her. After the boy left, she read the note he left behind. "Please take care of my eyes, my dear one."

Chapter 4:[13]
This is the Gate of the Heavens

"This is the gate of the Heavens." –*Ge 28:17* In Jacob's vision there is a small fact that's often overlooked. The spirit creatures were going up, then down. (So 7:11-12) If this describes angels, shouldn't they be coming down, then going up? (Ge 28:12) Jacob was describing creatures from earth.

4 [HEAVENLY SOLOMON:] See how beautiful you are, my beloved. See how beautiful. Your eyes, behind your veil, are doves. Your hair is like a flock of goats, descending from Mount Gilead.	ד הנך יפה רעיתי הנך יפה עיניך יונים מבעד לצמתך שערך כעדר העזים שגלשו מהר גלעד:

1 *See* (הנך) literally; "see-you."

A funny thing about marriage: no matter who does it, it always seems to disrupt the life they imagined. It only takes a few years of marriage before you are unexpectedly pulled in the "wrong" direction. That, my wise daughter, does not have to be a problem.

Just when Beethoven was beginning to see success, he went deaf. Just when Sir Walter Raleigh realized how the world worked, he was thrown in prison for 13 years. Just when Martin Luther grasped the true meaning of the Bible, he was sentenced to death. All were taken in the wrong direction.

Yet, during Martin Luther's exile he translated the Bible, which helped millions see the Bible in their own language. Sir Walter Raleigh used his time to write *The History of the World*. After Beethoven went deaf, he wrote some of his greatest work, including *Midnight Sonata*.

Adversity can be food for the human spirit. Humans never stay on plan. They can't. Your most rewarding destinations may come from unexpected obstacles.

Jacob is a good example of an outcast, driven away from home. The Shulamite was also an outcast. Like Jacob, she had trouble sleeping. (Ge 28:11; So 3:1) Like Jacob, her wanderings took her to Jacob's heavenly steps. They were both comforted when shown their descendants would inherit that ground—from where the stairs rose. Jacob reiterated this inheritance with a cryptic blessing to Joseph's two sons, Ephraim and Manasseh. (Ge 48:17-20)

how beautiful you are (יפה רעיתי הנך) literally; "you-are-beautiful my-love see you-are-beautiful".

The Heavenly Shulamite has something in common with her new husband. When the Messiah was on earth, he was a rather unremarkable man—in appearance. Holy text had compliments for Rachel. (Ge 29:17) Holy text had compliments for Joseph. (Ge 39:6) Holy text showered compliments on Absalom. (2Sa 14:25) Yet, nothing was said about Solomon's good looks, nor Jesus. In all due respect, you probably won't find an attractive husband.

Whatever Solomon's bride once looked like, now she became a creature of great beauty . . . at least to this appreciative husband.

Don't kid yourself, real love takes skill. For example: even if a wife works outside the home, she still waits for her husband to come home. She is still like a girl on tip-toes, waiting for a kiss. It's sad if her husband never notices.

Develop those skills now! Not only will you benefit, but the ripple effect pays dividends for generations. Acquire the habit of complimenting. Develop charm. In a good marriage both partners feel appreciated, like the Shulamite and Solomon.

Solomon and his Shulamites may not have started as people with stunning looks, yet that doesn't stop Solomon from greeting his Shulamite with enthusiastic compliments. Her true beauty is a combination of character and loyal ambition.

Shulamites are new creations, recreated directly from the deft hands of Solomon's God. (So 7:1) Finally, the eager Solomon can say: "Alas, bone of my bone and flesh of my flesh." As spirit creatures, they don't have bone and flesh, but both resemble their heavenly family. In Solomon's house, the Shulamites don't need to stand on their "tip-toes," for long.

> **NUMERICS:** *see* (הנה) literally; "see, behold, lo." This is the last of nine uses. At the *remez* level, nine implies approaching community responsibility. We are barely half-way through *Song of Songs* and, already, the Shunemite will "see" no more. This newly-minted Shulamite has become part of Jacob's vision. Not far behind, the remaining Shunemite is one chapter away from her transition.

2 [HEAVENLY SOLOMON:] Your teeth are like a drove, freshly shorn, coming up from the wash. Each has its twin, and not one of them is alone.	שניך כעדר הקצובות שעלו מן־הרחצה שכלם מתאימות ושכלה אין בהם:

2   *Your teeth* (שניך) literally; "teeth-of-you."

This phrase is a bridge to So 6:6. Solomon is speaking to the new Shulamite—not the old Shunemite. The Heavenly Solomon never dialogues with the Earthly Shunemite. There are pronouncements and commands directed at this final Shunemite, but no dialogue.

This verse would be difficult to understand if you weren't familiar with the significance of "teeth." (Ps 3:7) If "teeth" are used to symbolize devouring opposition, then the enemies of the messianic kingdom should be terrified that this co-ruler has all her teeth. The following words, "not one of them is alone" means, the 144,000 will reign from Heaven, but spill out of Zion when their children are threatened.

Residing in Heaven and administrating from Zion will chew up Solomon's earthly adversaries. Just as Sarah had a hand maiden, Rachel had a hand maiden, Leah had a hand maiden, the Shulamites will have earthly hand maidens, exactly 288,000—two for each Shulamite.

The ongoing reference to two's and twins, is also conveyed in many of the Bible's parables. "All of which are bearing twins" reminds us of the double features within the messianic kingdom. There are two aspects to Solomon; two aspects to the Bride Class; two crops of figs; two resurrections; etc. I could go on and on.

3 [HEAVENLY SOLOMON:] Your language is just like the scarlet rope, and your advanced speech is agreeable. Like the half of a pomegranate is your temples, behind your veil.	כחוט השני שפתתיך ומדבריך נאוה כפלח הרמון רקתך מבעד לצמתך:

3 *Your language* (שפתתיך) literally; "lip-of-you."

This Hebrew word for lip is *saw-faw* (#H8193 שׂפה). Being a part of the mouth and having much to do with the formation of words, "lip" is figuratively used for language. (Pr 14:3; 1Cor 14:21) Like any container, the inner contents will pass over the container's "lip." Your "lip" is also where your heart pours out its contents.

Before the confusion of language, at Babel, all humans spoke one language (literally, "one lip"). (Ge 11:1-9) After

Babel, only Shem's descendants continued speaking the original, pure, language. (Ge 9:26; 1Ch 1:24-27) The reason being—Shem's pure heart. God promised, in the future, He would give everyone the pure language (lip). In the future, we will all speak Hebrew. (Zep 3:9; Pr 12:19)

Nimrod caused confusion within the original language, because of his evil heart. Is your manner of speech closer to Shem's, or Nimrod's? Nimrod's "gate to the Heavens" (a.k.a., Tower of Babel) came from an evil motive. That concerned the Father. (compare Ge 11:5-6 with Ge 28:11-15)

Jehovah expressed no comparable alarm when Jacob discovered a stairway to Heaven (a.k.a., Jacob's Ladder). Because Jacob was descended from Shem and spoke the pure language, with a pure heart. Jacob's descendants will be approved to ascend these royal steps.

like the scarlet rope (כחוט השני) literally; "like-rope-of-the-scarlet."

The Hebrew word for scarlet is *shaw-nee* (#H8144 שני). The word's origin is uncertain, but it could either mean, the worm, from which they make the scarlet dye, or the actual color—scarlet. This is the same "worm" (שני) from the story of Jonah. (Jon 4:7) That worm disturbed the *improper* peace of Jonah—by eating his *improper* shade plant. This Shulamite's scarlet lips are not afraid to challenge *improper* teachings.

When law has lost touch with justice, and religion no longer resembles truth, then they do *improper* harm. Only the courageous will challenge *improper* religious policy.

The "rope" is juxtaposed with "lips" and "scarlet." The Hebrew word for rope is *khoot* (#H2339 חוט). This is the same rope (חוט) that Rahab displayed from the lip of her window. Displaying that rope resulted in her family's salvation. (Jos 2:18) So, if "lips" are where your language pours from, then this "rope" symbolizes salvation for a family adrift. (So 2:7; 3:5; 8:4)

The Shulamite was not afraid to chastise *improper* advances. You cannot be naïve and righteous. If you do not oppose evil—with intelligence—you will endanger your children, the way Eve endangered her children. Naïve.

  and your advanced speech (ומדבריך) literally; "and-developed-mouthings-of-you."
  The Hebrew word translated as "speech" is *mid-bawr* (#H4057 מדבר). It has a number of definitions. It's related to the words, "wilderness" and "bee." All its variations contain the idea of something well arranged—by way of process. The letter *mem* (מ) hints at something nurtured into existence.
  The Earthly Shunemite is perceiving—from afar—the qualities that this Messiah values. Being classy is *not* about superiority. Having class is about under-stated style, accompanied by good manners. Having class means exuding a genuine interest in the success of others. Having class is about being confident in the matriarchy you came from, and respecting the core values of your family.
  Classy women move through life unaffected by the criticisms of detractors. They always seem to know where the center of the earth is. After all, the laws that govern class come from the same "well arranged" laws that govern the universe—and we know where those laws come from.
  No wonder class means: exuding selflessness, generosity, compassion, and communal hospitality. The Shulamite has tapped into the source of all knowldege—her husband's Father.
  The Heavenly Solomon doesn't speak directly to the Earthly Shunemite, but that doesn't prevent her from watching, and learning, from the Heavenly Shulamite's elegant examples.

  Like the half of a pomegranate (כפלח הרמון) literally; "like-segment-of the-pomegranate."

The explanation has less to do with a "pomegranate," but more to do with "half." In Hebrew, *khaw-tsoth* (#H2677 חֲצוֹת) means "half." "Half" (חֲצוֹה) first occurs at, Ex 24:6.

Ex 24:6 is where Moses sprinkled blood on the two "halves" of the covenant: Moses sprinkled "half" the blood on the implements of the Tabernacle (If Jesus is like the Tabernacle, then the Shulamites are like the implements in the Tabernacle) and sprinkled the other "half" on the Israelites. That is, half on the ruling class and half on the citizens.

Blood makes a covenant legitimate.

When blood was sprinkled on the head of an Israelite, the flecks of blood resembled pomegranate seeds. That's why the prefix "like" (כְ) is used.

your temples (רְקָתֵךְ) literally; "temples-of-you."
This word, "temples" (#H7541 רַקָּה), is rarely used unless relating to death. (Jg 4:21-22; 5:26; So 4:3; 6:7) So, "temples" is a very clever tie-in to the nature of the Shulamite.

She was dead. She had to die.

This recently resurrected person, ascending Jacob's ladder, resembles ancient Israel going through her covenant marriage ceremony, when she was raised from Egypt.

This translation is a variation from So 6:7. Here, the speaker goes from teeth, to lips, to tongue, to temples. These descriptions maintain a horizontal pattern. The literal translation of "temple" (רַקָּה) doesn't specify one body part, or location. It's a flexible term that means, "emaciated, flattened out." In that horizontal path, "temple" fits best.

behind your veil (מִבַּעַד לְצַמָּתֵךְ) literally; "at-behind to-veil-of-you."

Where did the high priest sprinkle blood on the tabernacle's implements? Behind the curtain of the most holy. That curtain was "like" the veil described in this verse.

This clever reference helps to recall the annual ceremony in Jerusalem. This annual anointing ceremony was a renewal of Israel's marital vows with Jehovah. (Ex 24:3) That ceremony included the release of the iconic scapegoat, which symbolized forgetting the previous year's transgressions.

"And she said unto the servant, 'What man is this that walketh in the field to meet us?' And the servant said, 'It is my master.' And she took her veil [צמתך] and covered herself." –*Ge 24:64-65* Rebekah veiled herself to her new husband for the same reason the Shulamite veils herself.

| 4 [HEAVENLY SOLOMON:] Your neck is like the tower of David, built with ascending courseways of 1,000 elegant shields, all of them, shields of warriors. | כמגדל דויד צוארך בנוי לתלפיות אלף המגן תלוי עליו כל שלטי הגבורים: |

    4 *neck* (צוארכ) literally; "neck-of-you."

Now, Solomon's descriptions begin to descend. In Hebrew culture, fleeing was described as turning the "neck" to the enemy—the back of his neck. (Jos 7:8) Therefore, a hand on the back of an enemy's neck was equivalent to conquering him. (Ge 49:8; 2Sa 22:41; Ps 18:40)

The "neck" of the Shulamite was beyond the reach of her enemies. Her neck was like a "tower" beyond the hand of her enemies.

In Egypt, victorious pharaohs are depicted as treading on the necks of their enemies. Likewise, Joshua ordered his army commanders: "'Come near, put your feet upon the necks of these kings.' And they came near, and put their feet upon the necks of them." –*Jos 10:24* Those defeated kings were described in the same position that the Satan was, "cast down to the earth."

tower of David (כמגדל דויד) literally; "like-tower-of David."

Along the east wall, south of the Temple, was what's referred to as "the protruding tower." Still further south, in the vicinity of David's palace, was a tower associated with the king's house, near the Courtyard of the Guard. (Ne 3:25-27) Some think this tower is the one referred to in this verse.

WARNING: This tower should not be confused with the more modern, so-called, "Tower of David." That tower was built much later by Herod the Great—not Solomon.

ascending courseways (לתלפיות) literally; "ascending-courses."

David was barred from building God's Temple because his hands shed blood. (2Sa 7:13) Yet, David's battles brought Solomon closer to a "kingdom of peace."

You will never find this word (לתלפיות) anywhere else in holy text, or extra-biblical sources. So, there is no lexicon to help us with the definition. It must be deduced the way Daniel deduced the four words scratched on the wall in Babylon—at the *sod* level. (Da 5:5-30)

Back to our verse at hand: the translators from the *New English Bible* assume the root comes from *lap-ee* (לפי), and they assume it means "layered, arranged in courses." There simply is no way to verify their conclusion. Using the *Meaning of Hebrew Letters*[14] will allow us to breakdown this word, letter-by-letter, for a constructed definition, the same way Daniel broke down the "four words."

Our composite word breaks down to mean, "to-the-outer-limits, arranged-steps-for-man-to-the-outer-limits." Sound familiar? "And he was afraid, and said, 'How dreadful is this place! This is none other than the house of God, and this is the gate of Heaven.'" –*Ge 28:17* (*And note that Jacob did not say "door" of Heaven, but instead, said "gate." Gate always references death.*)

There may be no equivalent Hebrew word, but there is an equivalent Hebrew experience—Jacob's ladder!

the warriors (הגבורים) literally; "the-warriors."

We have already learned that an exposed neck portends defeat, or death. This Heavenly Shulamite has 1,000 shields from David's mighty men surrounding her neck. That number (1,000 אלף) will be discussed in greater detail, at So 8:11.

One of these warriors who contributed a "shield" was Benaiah. "Benaiah the son of Jehoiada, the son of a valiant man of Kabzeel, who had done mighty deeds, he slew the two [sons of] Ariel of Moab: he went down also and slew a lion in the midst of a pit in time of snow. And he slew an Egyptian, a man of great stature, five cubits high; and in the Egyptian's hand was a spear like a weaver's beam; and he went down to him with a staff, and plucked the spear out of the Egyptian's hand, and slew him with his own spear." –1Ch 11:22-23

Benaiah only contributed one shield. The Shulamite has 1,000 shields, symbolizing 1,000 mighty warriors protecting her neck.

5 [HEAVENLY SOLOMON:] Your two breasts are like two young ones, the twins of a female gazelle that are feeding among the lilies.	שני שדיך כשני עפרים תאומי צביה הרועים בשושנים:

5 *breasts are like* (שדיך) literally; "breasts-of-you-like."

Within this compliment, Solomon makes a sobering point that resolves some upcoming dangers. Notice how quickly three references are made to "two." Two is a potentially bad number, to a Hebrew. That means, unless her children make proper use of her breasts, it could go bad for them.

This word (breasts) can mean more than, a source of milk. It's also used to describe the forepart of the human body (male or female) between the neck and the abdomen. Two Hebrew words denoting the human breast are *shad* (שַׁד) and *shod* (שֹׁד). Both words denote closeness, intimacy, or adoption. (Joh 13:25; 21:20) So, her children must maintain this intimate relationship, or it could go bad for them.

The bosom (שַׁד) adds volumes to a story. For instance: When Naomi placed Obed in her "bosom," she demonstrated Obed was the legal heir of her dead husband, Elimelech. (Ru 4:16) Jesus employed this same symbolism with Lazarus being in "the bosom position of Abraham," signifying "adoption" by God. (Lk 16:22, 23) John described Jesus as being "in the bosom position with the Father." (Joh 1:18)

gazelle (צְבִיָּה) literally; "gazelle."

Later, Solomon will be described as a "gazelle." (So 8:14) Here, the Shulamite is described as a "gazelle." Fawns (עֳפָרִים) and a female gazelle (צְבִיָּה) are mentioned in quick succession. Fawns are rarely mentioned in holy text. The gazelle that most Israelites were familiar with was, the fawn-colored, Gazelle Arabica.

If her breasts are "the twins of a female gazelle," that means those young "twins" are getting their milk from elsewhere—their mother. The milk in the breasts of this Shulamite comes from the elementary teachings of her *mother* ("the woman"). (Heb 5:12-14)

The Bride of Christ provides fundamental truths for disciples, and basic orientation into the messianic family. Those who take milk from this mountain-dwelling mother will quickly ascend to the attention of her Father, Jehovah.

It would be sacrilege for the Shulamite to claim she's the exclusive source of food for her children. Moses made the same mistake when he said, "Hear now, ye rebels; shall we bring you forth water out of this rock?" –*Nu 20:10*

Moses didn't give Israel water. Jehovah did.

Like Moses, if our religious leaders made the same arrogant claim, it too could prevent us from entering the Promised Land. (Nu 20:12) Did Moses sin when he over-stated his role in giving Israel water? If so, the Earthly Shunemite class could sin by claiming to be the only source of milk.

Moses corrected his rash statement, but by that time, it was too late for Moses. (De 8:15-18) Idolatry means, giving something, or someone, a prominence that they don't deserve. Let us honor the Shunemite class, but without idolatry.

among the lilies (בשושנים) literally; "at-the-lilies."

We have already discussed the "gate of the Heavens," and "to the outer limits, arranged steps for man to the outer limits." Now let us see where these lilies (*Shulamites/the Jerusalem Above*) were presented, in the Temple area.

Before Solomon's Temple was built, Jacob erected two pillars: One, when he departed, and another when he returned. (Ge 28:18 and Ge 35:14-15)

Was Jacob's example the narrative model for David, when David provided the instructions, to erect two pillars at the front of the Temple? Why would he top both pillars with lilies? "And he set up the pillars at the porch of the Temple: and he set up the right pillar, and called the name thereof Jachin; and he set up the left pillar, and called the name thereof Boaz. And upon the top of the pillars was lily-work: so was the work of the pillars finished." *–1Ki 7:21-22*

Shulamites may have once been a "lily of the valley," but, Jehovah, prophetically elevated the "lily" atop both Temple pillars. Jehovah made the Israelites look up (in prophetic expectation) to these anointed lilies.

Another symbolism for a "pillar," in Israel, was for marking the location of the dead. (Ge 35:20; 2Sa 18:18) That may shed additional light on Jacob's intent when he erected pillars. He may have understood the price required to ascend this stairway (or ladder, as it's commonly rendered in substandard translations). Why else would Jacob anoint his pillars? Because, this location marked the stairway for those on their way to be anointed.

The wise husband conforms his speech to the occasion. A wise husband steers clear of lectures. The best thing a wise man can do for his family is love them, through actions. Caring people find ways to convey that message in their daily routine.

Husbands: Can you go one week without lecturing?

If you consider Solomon a worthy example, note his kind words. Researcher Paul Persall has discovered some very important reasons for married couples to be kind. We are hardwired for it. We need it. When we open our hearts and reach out to others, our brains release endorphins—the morphine-like chemical that produces feelings of exhilaration, also known as "runner's high."

Acts of kindness will cause your brain to release "Substance P," a neurotransmitter chemical. This natural reaction has a healthy effect on the body.

This Shulamite could run another 100 miles on a compliment like that. For instance: a steady flow of endorphins and Substance P strengthens our immune system, keeps us feeling happy, and energized. These natural chemicals heighten our sense of well-being.

Kindness increases our capacity to become calmer, more centered, and better able to focus, despite stressful circumstances. Physiologically, these brain chemicals improve circulation, reduce blood pressure, increase body warmth, and improve weight control.

The true index of character is not how much we know, but how we behave when we don't know. Holy text was right. Our opinion of the world is a confession of our character. (1Sa 25:25) People grow from experience . . . when they meet life with kindness and integrity. When we change our behaviors, we change our chemistry, and in turn, our future.

6 [EARTHLY SHUNEMITE:] When the day he breaks, and the shadows flee, I shall go my way to the mountain of myrrh, and to the hill of frankincense.	עד שיפוח היום ונסו הצללים אלך לי אל־הר המור ואל־גבעת הלבונה:

6 ***day he breaks and the shadows flee*** (היום ונסו הצללים אלך) literally; "when-he-breaks the-day and-they-flee the-shadows."

Now, the Earthly Shunemite speaks. This sentence is a merism, showing the contrast, or extent of her activity, from the darkness of night, to the brightness of day. To that extent, she will duplicate the noble work of her role-model, the Shulamite. From Pentecost to Armageddon, the Earthly Shunemite helps deliver food to her sheep-like Brothers.

The world is replete with God's knowledge. It's the duty of religion to convert that raw information. "For the invisible things of him since the creation of the world are clearly seen, being perceived through the things that are made, [even] his everlasting power and divinity; that they may be without excuse: because that, knowing God, they glorified him not as God, neither gave thanks; but became vain in their reasonings, and their senseless heart was darkened." –*Ro 1:20-21*

I shall go my way (אלך לי) literally; "I-will-go to-my."

It's odd that this Earthly Shunemite would speak of going to the "mountain of myrrh" and the "hill of frankincense." Neither myrrh, nor frankincense comes from Israel. Both are imported from distant lands.

Her choice of words shows where she expects to be when her beloved returns. He will arrive like the sun, but her beloved will find her, far away, in a kingdom of darkness, where death rules—*sheol*.

Abishag, the rejected Shunemite, can no longer hold on. She's only human. Humans have very short life spans. The musical classic, *God Help the Outcasts* encapsulates her strong, but dark hopes. "They tell me I'm just an outcast; I shouldn't speak to you; still I see your face and wonder; were you once an outcast too? God help the outcasts; hungry from birth; show them the mercy; they don't find on earth; the lost and forgotten; they look to you still; God help the outcasts; or nobody will." *–Stephen Schwartz and Alan Menken*

My dear daughter, you have a great deal in common with this Earthly Shunemite. People who expect the same old you are bound to be disappointed. From birth, you were indomitable. Not disrespectful, but indomitable. You grew with every obstacle you overcame. You have already learned that fear is just another bad habit to discard.

Once again, the Earthly Shunemite is passed over. Yet, she does not quit. If you despair, work on in despair. Like the Shunemite, you too must remain a lady. If you must retreat, retreat within your community of faith.

In conclusion, the Earthly Shunemite discovers what most of the world has missed: there is a protocol to enter the gate of Heaven. Others have built their own gates to Heaven, which they call ziggurats, pyramids, or cathedrals.

Generations of religious leaders have offended God by their comical attempts at pure worship. Their hymns are sung in the key of contempt. Too many wives are pickling in their bile, and are constantly on war footing. Love is *not* like that.

> **NUMERICS:** *comes* (בוֹא) literally; "comes; abide; depart; enter." This is the first of six uses. At the *remez* level, six is a man's number. By the final occurrence (at So 5:1), you will discover where Heavenly Solomon will "come" on earth.

PUZZLE: The God you worship enjoys weaving additional messages beneath the surface message. That's what separates holy text from Jewish newspapers. The Hebrew language doesn't weave these messages, naturally. That takes the mind of God.

The Shunemite continues to decode the holy language. She continues to speak in such a manner that praises the holy name of God. Starting in the second word and the second letter, you will find letter skips of four that will spell out the holy name of God. She gets it.

7 [HEAVENLY SOLOMON:] Altogether you are beautiful, my shepherdess, and there is no flaw in you.	כלך יפה רעיתי ומום אין בך: ס

7 *my shepherdess* (רעיתי) literally; "shepherdess-of-mine."

Since the Shulamite has been tested and found worthy, only the Shulamite can claim to be this shepherd's "shepherdess." Conversely, the Shunemite can only dispense food. "He saith unto him the third time, Simon, son of John, lovest thou me? Peter was grieved because he said unto him the third time, Lovest thou me? And he said unto him, Lord, thou knowest all things; thou knowest that I love thee. Jesus saith unto him, Feed my sheep." *–Joh 21:17*

There is an old saying: "If you cannot build a road, start with the curb. God will provide the road." Do your part, God will lend you the rest. Your "insurmountable problems" cannot withstand persistence. If you will contribute a behavior, God will provide a supporting chemical—which makes the next behavior easier, and so on, and so on.

Although couples place much importance on their wedding day, it isn't the biggest day of their life. The biggest day of their life is every day thereafter. Because it's not the pledge to love someone that matters, but the fulfillment of that pledge. In other words, the real work has just begun.

One of the easiest ways a wife can elevate her mood and completely change her chemistry, is to ask for a promotion. Your family is your business, and Proverbs 31 teaches us that a dedicated woman can make a big difference in the success of her man's household. When we look beyond ourselves, we discover a peace-of-mind impossible without family.

Dr. Robert M. Rose conducted an experiment with rhesus monkeys, proving when monkeys acquire leadership roles—they produced more testosterone.[15] But this chemical (testosterone) is not just for males. When females are injected with this chemical, they express more interest in their mates. If you want to acquire more testosterone, give yourself a promotion. Become the "shepherdess" in your family.

flaw (ומום) literally; "and-flaw."

As the Messiah and his Shulamite ascend these symbolic steps, the immature Shunemite can only look on, in bewilderment. The still immature Apostle Paul explained: "Not that I have already obtained, or am already made perfect: but I press on, if so be that I may lay hold on that for which also I was laid hold on by Christ Jesus. Brethren, I could not myself yet to have laid hold: but one thing [I do], forgetting the things which are behind, and stretching forward to the things which are before, I press on toward the goal unto the prize of the high calling of God in Christ Jesus." –*Ph 3:12-14*

Paul, as a Shunemite, felt a vast chasm between himself and the Heavenly Shulamite. The Shunemites were in man's camp, while the Shulamites had crossed over to a heavenly camp. (So 6:13)

8 [HEAVENLY SOLOMON:] With me from Lebanon, my bride, with me from Lebanon may you come. Descend from the top of Amana, from the top of Senir, the summit of Hermon, from the lairs of lions, from the mountains of leopards.	אתי מלבנון כלה אתי מלבנון תבואי תשורי ן מראש אמנה מראש שניר וחרמון ממענות אריות מהררי נמרים:

    8 *Descend* (תשׁורי) literally; "you-descend."

    The Shulamites (the heavenly Bride Class) are Christ's joint rulers. These would ascend Jacob's steps to receive their anointing, then come down to administer God's laws. "For the Lord himself shall descend from Heaven, with a shout, with the voice of the archangel, and with the trump of God: and the dead in Christ shall rise first." –*1Th 4:16*

    But, Jacob erected two pillars. (Ge 28:18; Ge 35:20) The first, no doubt, symbolized the 144,000 with a heavenly hope. The second, however, symbolized a different elevated group—the 288,000 maidservants of the 144,000. These 288,000 maidservants had an earthly hope. Sarah, Leah, and Rachel had a maidservant. It would not be unusual for the 144,000 to have maidservants, too. (Ge 25:12; 35:25-26) Our Messiah, Jesus, will preside over two mountains. 1) Jerusalem Above. (Gal 4:25) 2) Zion below. (Ro 16:20)

    Jesus was a "pillar of death" for his disciples. Atop the two pillars in Solomon's Temple were carvings of lilies. Our pillar, Jesus, was crowned with lilies, a metaphor of his brides. "A worthy woman is the crown of her husband; But she that maketh ashamed is as rottenness in his bones." –*Pr 12:4*

    Amana (אמנה) literally; "supporting, a column, a pillar."

Amana (#H548 אמנה), a mountain in Lebanon (elevation 3,566 feet), also means "something fixed, a covenant, an allowance." Amana is not Senir. Senir has an elevation of 9,232 feet.

Both Amana and Senir are below Heaven. This name (*Amana*) is also a direct connection to the vision of Jacob, in the sense that they both go out to meet Solomon and his Shulamites. The significance of his two "pillars" (in addition to the "steps to Heaven") gains prophetic momentum when Jacob mentions the incident, yet again, on his deathbed. (Ge 48:3) No wonder *Song of Songs* incorporates "pillars" am-mood (#H5982 עמד) throughout, such as So 3:10 and So 5:15.

Senir (שניר) literally; "eighty."

Since Senir means "80," what does Senir have to do with the 80 concubines, at So 6:8? This verse describes "Senir" (or 80 concubines) as a call to Israelites, who died long before Jesus shed his blood, to serve among these 288,000 (*80 x 3,600 = 288,000*). (1Ch 5:23) A Hebrew husband must pay for a wife—not a concubine (a.k.a. half-wife). The blood of Jesus has yet to pay for some—288,000. (compare 1Th 4:16 to Heb 11:13)

The above paragraph defines the number 80, but what defines the number 3,600? Not too surprising, 3,600 only shows up twice in your Bible. First, at 2Ch 2:2 and next, at 2Ch 2:18. Both these scriptures provide more than a definition, they also provide a job description. "And Solomon counted out threescore and ten thousand men to bear burdens, and fourscore thousand men that were hewers in the mountains, and three thousand and six hundred to oversee them." *–2Ch 2:2* "And he set threescore and ten thousand of them to bear burdens, and fourscore thousand that were hewers in the mountains, and three thousand and six hundred overseers to set the people at work." *–2Ch 2:18*

These 3,600 are not from the ruling class, they are from the working class. These lowly workers are given additional authority, to keep fellow workers busy. So, these 288,000 (*80 x 3,600 = 288,000*) work on earth—not Heaven.

An Assyrian inscription describes Senir as "a mountain, facing the Lebanon."[16] This is a description of a lesser (half) kingdom facing a greater (full) kingdom. In other words, a half-wife facing a full-wife.[17]

These 288,000, will not be resurrected as citizens. They must, first, become disciples of Jesus—whom they have never met. After meeting their new Messiah, however, they will convert. Then, they can be used as "princes."

The six founding matriarchs (Sarah, Rebekah, Leah, Rachel, Bilhah, and Zilpah) were all from Haran. These white mountains of Lebanon stood between Jerusalem and Haran.

The greater Solomon, and our heavenly mother, will help these 288,000 to traverse and outwit all Satanic opposition. Together, this duo (144,000 & 288,000) will help us survive the Satan's release from the pit. (Re 5:10)

lairs of lions (ממענות אריות) literally; "from-dens-of lions."

Jehovah likens himself to a lion when executing judgment. (Ho 5:14; 11:10; 13:7-9) And God's foremost judicial officer, Jesus, is "a Lion, of the tribe of Judah." (Re 5:5)

So, what do "lions" have to do with Jacob's steps to Heaven? Solomon's throne holds a clue: "There were six steps to the throne, and the top of the throne was round behind; and there were stays on either side by the place of the seat, and two lions standing beside the stays. And twelve lions stood there on the one side and on the other upon the six steps: there was not the like made in any kingdom." *–1Ki 10:19-20*

The millennial reign brings Earthly Brothers back to Adamic perfection.[18]

mountains of leopards (מהררי נמרים) literally; "from-mountains-of leopards."

The subject in this sentence is "mountains." But what lives on these mountains are leopard-like people who cull the unworthy from kingdom citizenship.

Holy text speaks of the swiftness of the leopard (Hab 1:8) and its manner of lying patiently near towns, ready to pounce upon its victim. (Jer 5:6; Ho 13:7) Where are the friends you had 10 years ago? If they are like some of my fox-like friends, they were removed from the mountain by these symbolic leopards.

Let us not blame the lack of religious leadership, bad association, or parents. "Blame" is just a lazy person's way of criticizing God's separation work. They may have been culled out by these metaphorical leopards, and lions, because they don't belong with us.

When a concubine displays leopard-like skills, or a full-wife displays lion-like skills, they are both effectively removing the foxes from their husband's vineyard. Yet, when that separation work is completed, the leopard and the kid are depicted as lying down together, in peace, during the Messiah's rule. (Is 11:6) Justice is the way of our family.

Patience is not to be confused with weakness. The term, "lady" has been hijacked by British nobility, who warehouse girls the way some warehouse fragile tea cups. A real lady has helpful hands, but not necessarily manicured hands. A real lady can drive a stake through the Temple of God's enemy, and with the same hands, nurse her children back to good health. (Ge 24:17-20)

The Western understanding of "lady" is not the same as the Hebrew understanding of "lady."

9 [HEAVENLY SOLOMON:] You have stolen my heart, my bride of the sisterhood, you stole my heart with one [glance] from your eye, with one jewel of your necklace.	לבבתני אחתי כלה לבבתיני באחת ק מעיניך באחד ענק מצורניך:

9 *from your eye* (מעיניך) literally: "from-eye-of-you."

The Hebrew word for "eye" is *ah-yin* (#H5869 עין) which means "eye, a fountain, outward appearance, or countenance." The way this word is translated depends on context. Verse 15 is proof. There, *ah-yin* is translated as "fountain." Like a "fountain," the eye exudes what's beneath the surface.

Eyes often reveal more than you want. They may show pity, or the lack of it (De 19:13); they may wink to flirt, or blink in fear, or narrow in disbelief. (Ps 35:19; Pr 6:13; 16:30) One who does not want to assume responsibility will close their eyes. (Mt 13:15; Pr 28:27) Even a person's health, vigor, or state of happiness, is manifested by their eyes. (1Sa 14:27-29; Ps 6:7; 88:9) The stupid person's eyes are "at the extremity of the earth," wandering without any fixed point. Their thoughts are scattered. (Pr 17:24)

"One glance" at her eyes tells this messianic Solomon all he needs to know. Jacob saw the same thing in Rachel's eyes, whereas, Leah had dull eyes. (Ge 29:17) Experiments at the Institute of Heart Math revealed DNA changed its shape, depending on the emotions it was exposed to. When your DNA switches off, it closes down your body's growth program, and activates your body's defense software. When the feelings of love, gratitude, and appreciation were exposed to a switched-off DNA, it relaxed, resuming its healthy growth cycle.

The quantum biologist, Bruce Lipton summed up the experiment this way: "Our body's computer can only be in growth mode, or protection mode. It cannot be in both at the same time."[19]

No relationship, however, can be in constant reassurance mode. Confront, but quickly get your confrontations out of the way. According to Lipton, when confrontations linger, they physically weaken your entire family. Get your questions answered, then get on with happiness. Notice how much time the Heavenly Solomon spends doting over, and reassuring, his wife.

jewel (עֲנָק) literally; "jewel-of."

Ancient Jerusalem, and the Jerusalem Above, are both described as jewels. (Ezk 20:6; Da 11:16) The holy city, New Jerusalem, has a radiance "like a most precious stone, as a jasper stone shining crystal-clear." The 12 foundations of its wall "were adorned with every sort of precious stone," a different stone for each foundation: jasper, sapphire, chalcedony, emerald, sardonyx, sardius, chrysolite, beryl, topaz, chrysoprase, hyacinth and amethyst.

The city's 12 gates were the only jewel made by a living thing—pearls. Clams build their pearl around years of pain—a single grain of sand. (Re 21:2, 9-21) Like the pearl, the Shunemite's life doesn't start pleasant, but her sufferings gain her entrance into Heavenly Jerusalem. (Joh 10:9)

The greater Solomon's compliments are the by-product of divine love. Kindness isn't just a fluffy, feel-good, warm-fuzzy concept. Only a powerful force can transform both the giver and the receiver at this profound level.

Kindness works miracles that can be validated with verifiable through quantum sciences of biology, physiology, psychoneuroimmuniology, and physics. The power of cheerfulness fuels endurance. The cheerful person can accomplish more than a soldier, yet still remain pleasant.

necklace (מִצַוְּרֹנָיִךְ) literally; "necklace-of-you."

Necklace-style chains were also used for architectural ornamentation, the two Temple pillars (Jachin and Boaz), for example. "Also he made before the house two pillars of thirty and five cubits high, and the capital that was on the top of each of them was five cubits. And he made chains in the oracle, and put [them] on the tops of the pillars; and he made a hundred pomegranates, and put them on the chains. And he set up the pillars before the Temple, one on the right hand, and the other on the left; and called the name of that on the right hand Jachin, and the name of that on the left Boaz." –*2Ch 3:15-17* Symbolic adornment. You would think Bible readers would have picked up these clues centuries ago.

NUMERICS: *sisterhood* (אחות) literally; "sisterhood." This is the first of seven uses. At the *remez* level, seven is a messianic number. It hints at an elevation of station. By the final occurrence (at So 8:8), the Shunemite has found, and married the Messiah. Since they are both children of Jehovah, they are brother and sister. There is a proper and dignified way to find, and marry, the right man. The number seven provides additional clues for a good woman seeking a good husband.[20]

10 [HEAVENLY SOLOMON:] How beautiful your expressions of endearment are, my sister bride. How much better your expressions of endearment are than wine, and the fragrance of your perfumes—more than spices.	מה־יפו דדיך אחתי כלה מה־טבו דדיך מיין וריח שמניך מכל־בשמים:

10 *expressions of endearment* (יפו דדיך) literally; "they-are-delightful loves-of-you."

Have you ever heard of someone who fell out of love? Have you ever been someone who fell out of love? All holy text is written with the bold expectation that humans have command over their feelings. Those who have lost the glow of love are expected to fall back in love . . . if God requires it. That isn't a very popular thought, in Western culture, but it's an immutable, biblical, truth.

Can you imagine that? A God who holds us accountable for our behaviors—despite our feelings!

"Thou shalt not hate thy brother in thy heart: thou shalt surely rebuke thy neighbor, and not bear sin because of him. Thou shalt not take vengeance, nor bear any grudge against the children of thy people; but thou shalt love thy neighbor as thyself: I am Jehovah." –Le 19:17-18

Expressions of endearment are supposed to mean something. The Shulamite's expressions of endearment may not be the most outrageous promises you have ever heard, but she intends to live up to them.

Behaviors *instill* feelings. According to previously cited research, happiness isn't just a state of mind. Happiness effects your heart rate, your body chemistry, and it contributes to better health.[21] Happiness lowers levels of cortisol, which is related to abdominal obesity, type II diabetes, hypertension, and immune disorders. This proves there is a unique biology for happiness. We have an obligation to our family to be happy.

bride (כלה) literally; "bride."

The Hebrew word *kal-law* (#H3618 כלה) means "bride, son's wife, spouse." In keeping with the previous paragraph, a "bride" is someone who has made vows. Our Grandfather, Jehovah, set the bold example when He told His wife (Israel), "and thou shalt love Jehovah thy God with all thy heart, and with all thy soul, and with all thy might." –De 6:5 That takes a lot of gall, to *demand* that someone love you. Our Grandfather is a gutsy husband. I've always admired His boldness.

What if Jehovah's bride said "But I'm not feeling it." Well, she did. (Ps 2:2-3) His answer was revolutionary: Make yourself feel it. Brides who complain that they no longer "feel it" are ignoring the Godly injunction: Do loving <u>behaviors</u>, then you will create loving <u>feelings</u>. According to God (and science), <u>behaviors</u> come first, the <u>feelings</u> will follow.

perfumes (שמניך) literally; "perfumes-of-you."

Ointments, perfumes, and incense were not limited to the holy formula used in the sanctuary. By Solomon's day there were all sorts of perfumes available. They were used for scenting houses, garments, beds, royalty, and others who could afford them. (Es 2:12; Ps 45:8; Pr 7:17)

In Nehemiah's day, there was an exclusive trade group of ointment mixers. (1Sa 8:13; Ne 3:8) In the ancient world the market for perfumed products was lively and profitable. This included the raw materials to make perfume. These raw materials did not originate in Israel. Items such as myrrh, frankincense, spikenard, saffron, cane, cinnamon, aloes, cassia, as well as various spices, gums, and aromatic plants were transported long distances to reach Israel's ointment makers. (Re 18:11-13)

What has that got to do with the Shulamite's "expressions of endearment?" Like these exotic perfumes, she mixes her words with the same craftsmanship as these ointment makers—and her words ascend great distances, as a beautiful fragrance. (Re 5:8)

11 [HEAVENLY SOLOMON:] Your lips drip sweetness, as comb honey, my bride. Milk and honey are under your tongue. The fragrances in your garments are like the fragrances of Lebanon.	נפת תטפנה שפתותיך כלה דבש וחלב תחת לשונך וריח שלמתיך כריח לבנון: ס

11 *comb honey* (נפה) literally; "comb-honey."

Holy text uses two kinds of honey to describe abundance. In the Old Testament, comb honey (from bees) is referred to as *no-feth* (#H5317 נפה). It's not to be confused with the sweet syrup that oozes from fruit, which the Old Testament refers to by a separate word, *deb-ash* (#H1706 דבש).

"The fear of Jehovah is clean, enduring for ever: The ordinances of Jehovah are true, [and] righteous altogether. More to be desired are they than gold, yea, than much fine gold; Sweeter also than honey [דבש] and the droppings of the honeycomb [נפה]." –*Ps 19:9-10*

Your family can still achieve great things, without manipulating, or strong-arming, those who disagree with you. Disagreement is inevitable in every marriage. That's okay. Just remember not to get grid-locked in opposing positions. The shortest route to a lovely day is to set your disagreements aside and re-focus on that day's family goals. Don't kid yourself, love is a highly developed skill.

honey and milk (דבש וחלב) literally; "honey and-milk."

Often, milk is used symbolically. (Ge 49:12; Lam 4:7) Resources of a nation is sometimes called "milk." (Is 60:16) The Promised Land is repeatedly described as "a land flowing with milk and honey." This term was a description of the abundance that was theirs for the taking. There is a world-to-come that holds the same promise. It guarantees prosperity for Jehovah's household. (Ex 3:8; De 6:3; Jos 5:6; Jer 11:5; Ezk 20:6; Joe 3:18)

In this verse, the Heavenly Solomon compliments his partner as having honey and milk under her tongue. This is a Hebrew idiom. It means, her tongue gave lovely expressions to kingdom-building.

It's a sad day, when a person becomes content with the thoughts they have already thought, and the deeds they have already done. We all have a duty to beat at the doors of something larger than yesterday. Our God loves growth.

garments (שלמתיך) literally; "garments-of-you."
The first time this Hebrew word *salma* (שלמה #H8008) is used, it shows up in a verse discussing Solomon. "And it came to pass at that time, when Jeroboam went out of Jerusalem, that the prophet Ahijah the Shilonite found him in the way; now [Ahijah] had clad himself with a new garment [שלמה]; and they two were alone in the field. And Ahijah laid hold of the new garment [שלמה] that was on him, and rent it in twelve pieces. And he said to Jeroboam, Take thee ten pieces; for thus saith Jehovah, the God of Israel, Behold, I will rend the kingdom out of the hand of Solomon, and will give ten tribes to thee (but he shall have one tribe, for my servant David's sake and for Jerusalem's sake, the city which I have chosen out of all the tribes of Israel)." –1Ki 11:29-32

Since this word (שלמה) is very close to Solomon (שלמה), it's also curious that the subject prophesies dividing up Solomon's portion. (So 8:12)

| 12 [HEAVENLY SOLOMON:] A garden barred in, is my sister bride, a garden barred in, a spring sealed up. | גן ׀ נעול אחתי כלה גל נעול מעין חתום: |

12 *barred in* (נעול) literally; "being-locked."
The Hebrew word *naw-al* (#H5274 נעל) means "to fasten up, with bar or cord, bolt, inclose, shut up." Since the divine author adds the letter *vov* (ו), we further understand that this word pertains to a "human."

The Shulamite has already been released from this "garden." What's the "garden?" The "garden" is, *sheol*. This is confirmed again in verse 16.

This Shulamite has departed this great "garden," but the Shunemite has yet to enter the "garden" of kingdom seeds. And, when she enters the "garden," will her Messiah come for her, too. The waiting Shunemite still feels like an outcast.

But, her Messiah had to wait for the proper season to harvest these human seeds.

We are all going through stages. In only five minutes you can make a radical change in the way your family life feels. Solomon sets the family tone by how he speaks. You too have an amazing amount of choice in setting the emotional environment of your household.

Look for ways to extend your love in small ways. Start with your children, but use them as envoys to reach out, and extend your husband's realm, but not before making that realm worthy of extending.

When Christians are baptized, Jesus becomes their eternal father. The Shulamite isn't the only one he teaches. The eternal father teaches people of all kinds—but first, those within his household.

my sister bride (אחתי כלה) literally; "sister-of-me bride."

This is the last of five consecutive verses where the word, "bride" appears. For those who dispute this translation (sister bride) let them reconcile So 8:1. Some translators have gone so far as to remove the word "sister." Is that any way to convey God's thoughts—removing God's words from His holy text?

She is a sister, and in the following chapters, we will prove they share the same Father and Mother. We will learn where and how she was born.

The Shulamite is the sister of this groom. Deal with it. If a Bible reader struggles with this image, they will really struggle with the image of the "Bride Class" being composed of men. (Re 14:4) Deal with it.

Adam was all alone, without a human family. God did not like that. Humans require more than God. God, Himself, designed humans to need more than God. God is not enough.

It's not good for man to dwell alone. Socrates startled his students when he introduced the possibility that humans could not be intelligent, on their own. Socrates suggested that if two unenlightened humans were put together, by questioning one another, they could achieve an intelligence, unachievable in solitude.

By his theory, single people do not grow as fast, or as much, as married couples. In the Hebrew culture, it's considered a sin to remain single—for the same reason.

sealed up (חתום) literally; "being-sealed."

The Hebrew word *khaw-tham* (#H2856 חתם) means "to seal, make an end, mark, stop." Since the divine author adds the letter *vov* (ו), this word pertains to "a human." This is connected to the Hebrew word *ah-yin* (עין) which means, eye. When a spring erupts, it resembles an eye, crying. A spring releases what hides beneath the surface. To seal it up, is to stop it from crying or revealing what's beneath the surface.

"And I saw another angel ascend from the sunrising, having the seal of the living God: and he cried with a great voice to the four angels to whom it was given to hurt the earth and the sea, saying, Hurt not the earth, neither the sea, nor the trees, till we shall have sealed the servants of our God on their foreheads. And I heard the number of them that were sealed, a hundred-and-forty-and-four thousand, sealed out of every tribe of the children of Israel." –*Re 7:2-4*

13 [HEAVENLY SOLOMON:] Your plants are a paradise of pomegranates, with choice fruits, with henna and nard;	שלחיך פרדס רמונים עם פרי מגדים כפרים עם־נרדים:

13 *Your plants* (שלחיך) literally; "plants-of-you."

We have already established that the Hebrew word for daughter (*beth* בת) has a companion idiom. Hebrews affectionately refer to daughters as an, "apple branch." You are probably familiar with a number of scriptures that refer to the Messiah as "the twig of Jesse." (Is 11:1) You may even be familiar with texts that describe the sons of Israel as a "vine." (Ps 80:8) Their attention to their vineyard's health means it will grow stronger and more bountiful over the course of time.

pomegranates (רמונים) literally; "pomegranates."

Eating a pomegranate reminds us of the effort required to peel through the tough outer skin. Yet, when we expend the effort, we are rewarded with its symmetry and sweetness—like God's word.

There are only so many Shulamite mothers (144,000), but there are countless children. During the millennial reign, many will be resurrected. They will not, however, be resurrected as acceptable worshipers. That will take time.

Like the Israelites returning from exile, they were brought back with a goal. They must conform to God. Resurrected Brothers must be instructed in God's teachings. Then, they will be given an opportunity for adoption (improperly known as, grace). It was also prophesied that many of those children will not make it. (Re 20:8)

14 [HEAVENLY SOLOMON:] nard and saffron, cane and cinnamon, with every kind of incense tree: myrrh, aloes, and all the finest spices;	נרד ׀ וכרכם קנה וקנמון עם כל־עצי לבונה מר ואהלות עם כל־ראשי בשמים:

14 *cane* (קנה) literally; "calamus."

The Hebrew word *kaw-neh* (#H7070 קָנֶה) means "by resemblance a rod (for measuring), reed, stem, branch, cane." At Ge 41:5, 22 it's used as "reed" and at 1Ki 14:15. In certain texts, such as this verse, it doubles as an aromatic plant by which she (the Bride) is measured. (Ex 30:23; Is 43:24) This is the same word (קָנֶה measured) used in Ezekiel's vision. Solomon provides many ways to show how his Shulamite is measured—successfully.

The Messiah's children are created from a prescribed recipe. The distinctive aroma of God's ingredient is discussed in some detail here. Why? Simply having the ingredients does not make it so. *Doing* is required.

Holy text provides the precise recipe to make our personality pleasing. Ancient Israel was given gifts in men, but many did not listen to those men. So, they were rejected by the Father. (Jer 3:8) It's our individual responsibility to submit to God's teachings and blend those teachings into your family—for God. (Eph 4:7-8)

Nard, saffron, cane, cinnamon, myrrh, aloes and other spices are with us as humans, waiting to exceed their individual component. Truly, in the case of the Shulamites, the whole is better than the parts—so is your family.

15 [HEAVENLY SOLOMON:] You are a garden fountain, a well of flowing water, streaming down from Lebanon.	מַעְיָן גַּנִּים בְּאֵר מַיִם חַיִּים וְנֹזְלִים מִן־לְבָנוֹן:

15 *fountain* (מַעְיָן) literally; "fountain-of."

The Hebrew word for "fountain" is *mah-yawn* (מַעְיָן #H4599) which means "a spring, fountain, source of satisfaction." The way this word is translated depends heavily on context. Verse nine is proof of how context works. There, a related word is translated as "eye." What's the connection?

In a land without refrigerators, restaurants, and drinking fountains, nothing is more beautiful than a "fountain." Digging a well involves work. A "fountain" bubbles forth without work, an unexpected surprise. Unlike a well, a "fountain" is an effortless gift from God.

Moses described the Promised Land as a land of "springs and watery deeps issuing forth in the valley plain and in the mountainous region." (De 8:7) He was right. Springs are plentiful in Israel, with an average of six for every 40-square miles. (see commentary at So 4:8)

Because the mountains of Ephraim are mainly porous rock, the winter rains easily filter down to great depths. The waters run along solid rock and then resurface as springs on the west side of the Jordan Valley.

It's interesting to note that this verse adds yet another water source. It mentions water streaming down from Lebanon. If "Lebanon" represents Heaven (and it does), then the water of truth becomes abundant when the Shulamite gathers her children and teaches them heavenly values. "And he showed me a river of water of life, bright as crystal, proceeding out of the throne of God and of the Lamb, in the midst of the street thereof. And on this side of the river and on that was the tree of life, bearing twelve [manner of] fruits, yielding its fruit every month: and the leaves of the tree were for the healing of the nations." –Re 22:1-2

well (באר) literally; "well-of."

The Hebrew word *be-ayr* (#H875 באר) means "well, or pit." It usually describes a pit dug out to access a natural (but difficult to reach) supply of water. The word, *be-ayr* appears in place-names such as *Beer-lahai-roi* (Ge 16:14), *Beer-sheba* (Ge 21:14), *Beer* (Nu 21:16-18) and *Beer-elim* (Is 15:8). Digging a well was worth the effort. But, having one was often a matter of life and death.

If the palm was a metaphor for finding water where other trees could not, then what did Abraham represent when he dug wells? He represents a tree that found life.

Abraham established his ownership of a well, at *Beersheba* by naming it. (Ge 21:25-31; 26:20-21) After Abraham's death, the Philistines showed their contempt for God's people by stopping up Abraham's wells. (Ge 26:15-18) These are just a few examples of how multi-faceted the word "well" is.

You too must provide "wells" for your family. It could be a matter of life or death. The work / family balance is critical for every family's happiness. The impossible problem of "balance" is solved when we see every problem as nothing more than a lingering lack of decision.

Like Abraham, Sarah worked until her death. All Israelite women worked. The Shulamite worked. The 288,000 earthly concubines worked, and made sure the earth's children worked. (2Ch 2:2; 2Ch 2:18) Seeing to family business is a great protection for fathers, mothers, and children. Everyone's head was in the game. The Shunemite must learn, she too has a family business! (Pr 31)

To place unreasonable burdens on just one partner is not loving. Western women have traditionally expected husbands to be the breadwinner, but that's not the Israelite way. (Pr 31) Business is just something we do, while we get to know each other. All Israelites were fully engaged in the family business—and each other's lives. Love is bigger than romance. Yet, we must find a way to bring romance into every facet of our life—*every facet of our life!*

> **PUZZLE:** The God you worship enjoys weaving additional messages beneath the surface message. That's what separates holy text from Jewish newspapers. The Hebrew language doesn't weave these messages, naturally. It takes the mind (and deft hands) of God.

The Hebrew sages observed a meaningful structure within *Song of Songs*. So 4:15 marks the center of *Song of Songs*. *Song of Songs* has 222 lines. This forms the exact middle of this Hebrew book, with 111 lines from So 1:2 to 4:15 (note that I excluded the superscript). This is followed by 111 lines from So 5:2 to 8:14. This is very Solomon-like. It parallels the same methodology, of 222 verses (not "lines"), used in the book of *Ecclesiastes*.

16 [HEAVENLY SOLOMON:] Awake, north wind and come in south wind. Breathe upon my garden. Let its spices spread abroad. [HEAVENLY SHULAMITE:] Let my dear one come into his garden and taste its choice fruits.	עורי צפון ובואי תימן הפיחי גני יזלו בשמיו יבא דודי לגנו ויאכל פרי מגדיו:

16 *Breathe upon my garden* (הפיחי גני) literally; "breathe-on garden-of-me."

As discussed earlier, "garden" equates to the common grave of mankind (*sheol*). These words are a call to resurrection. The Shunemite is witnessing the messiah, Solomon, resurrecting his brides to ascend Jacob's steps, to Heaven.

The hint comes from the word, "breathe on" (הפיחי). Not only does it resemble the word "spirit" (רוח), it's also closely related to the word "apple" (#H8598 תפוח) This earthly garden (*sheol*) is where she is born into heavenly life. (So 8:5)

The Egyptian pyramids were constructed for the same purpose as Jacob's ladder. Egyptian royalty intended to ascend to their gods. Their "gate," however, was not Jehovah approved. As we will learn from the commentary at So 6:1, the

Egyptian resurrection is not Jehovah's resurrection. Egyptians can still receive an earthly resurrection. No doubt, they too can live full rich lives in the world-to-come.

Whether we are discussing a Babylonian ziggurat, Egyptian pyramid, the Greek Mt. Olympus, or a modern cult called "Heaven's Gate," there is only one method for reaching the Father's Heaven. Yet, none of these pagan methods incorporated the "apple tree." (So 8:5)

Math is hard at work in the biology of the apple. Morphogenesis, means the origin of the shape. A team from Harvard University decided to tackle the algebraic equation that defines the geometric description.

Biological shapes are often organized by structures that serve as focal points. These focal points can take the form of singularities where deformations are localized in the cusp of an apple, the inward dimple where the stalk meets the fruit. This expands the definitions found at So 5:5.

The mathematics of the "apple tree" is just another version of, Jacob's Ladder. God grants no access to outsiders. All those with a heavenly calling must submit to the terms of the Messiah, and come to Him via "Jacob's ladder," and via the "apple tree."

"Verily, verily, I say unto you, He that entereth not by the door into the fold of the sheep, but climbeth up some other way, the same is a thief and a robber." –*Joh 10:1*

and taste (ויאכל) literally; "and-let-him-taste."

Why was the cupbearer so close to the king? The cupbearer would "taste" the king's wine, prior to it reaching the king's lips. This protected the king from wine of poor quality, or poisoning. The king was eternally in the cupbearer's debt. There is a road to our God, from our heart, that does not go through the intellect.

The Shulamite makes it clear to her new husband, their children are like good wine, and safe to drink.

As the Shunemite watched, she finally puts it all together: "[it is] he that buildeth his chambers [מעלותו] in the Heavens, and hath founded his vault upon the earth; he that calleth for the waters of the sea, and poureth them out upon the face of the earth; Jehovah is his name." –*Am 9:6*

For eons, wise men have been unearthing the foundation stones of God's wisdom—but naming their discoveries after themselves. Socrates, for example, was onto something when he discovered, "individuals could not be intelligent on their own."

Jehovah provided the facts eons earlier. The first badness God commented on was, solitude. "And Jehovah God said, 'It is not good that the man should be alone; I will make him a help meet for him.'" –*Ge 2:18* Our futures are full of magical things patiently waiting to sharpen our wits.

Your husband's growth depends on your participation—and vice versa. Press him into the service of your growth. Few other requests will bring him such indelible joy. You are his family business. Ask him, thank him, and appreciate him.

Let me end the chapter with this story: A bitter salesman met a wise farmer on his way to town. "What are the people like in this town?"

The farmer asked the bitter salesman. "What were they like in the last town?"

"Awful!" snapped back the bitter salesman.

"They will be awful in this town too." replied the wise farmer.

The next day a gracious salesman came along. "What are the people like in this town?" asked the gracious salesman.

"What were they like in the last town?"

"Great!" replied the gracious salesman.

"They will be great here too." said the wise farmer.

This describes the difference between a Shunemite and a Shulamite.

Chapter 5:22
She Awakens as a Shulamite

The drama of this transhuman (Shulamite) turns on the 111th line (of 222). Solomon retrieves those who mastered real love. The deceased Shunemite awakens as a Shulamite. (Da 12:2)

5 [HEAVENLY SOLOMON:] I've come into my garden, my sister bride. I've gathered my myrrh with my spice. I've eaten my honeycomb and my honey. I've drunk my wine, and my milk. Eat friends and drink your fill, my beloveds.	ה באתי לגני אחתי כלה אריתי מורי עם־בשמי אכלתי יערי עם־דבשי שתיתי ייני עם־חלבי אכלו רעים שתו ושכרו דודים: ס

1 *I've come* (באתי) literally; "I've-come."

You may have suspected this, but from infancy I've planted ideas, hopes, and dreams that may sleep dormant for decades, but they await their opportunity to spring to life. I promise, that opportunity will knock, and you will be ready.

Solomon keeps returning to this "garden." (So 2:10) His special ones are waiting there. Those Shunemites wait like seeds, waithing to stretch beyond their wetware.

There were prior references to this locked-up, or barred-in garden. (So 4:12) When holy text mentions "bars," this is an oblique reference to death—even when it doesn't seem so. (Ge 34:20-21, 25) Simon states, "In the Bible we do not find the image of a gate [bars] with reference to the land of living, but only with reference to the land of the dead."[23] But the context tells us, Solomon is entering a garden of death and restores her to life.

and milk (וחלב) literally; "and-milk."

The Hebrew word *khaw-lawb* (#H2461 חלב) means "milk, or richness." If "milk" is what brings life to an infant, then "milk" symbolizes life to the dead Shunemite. As a new lifeform, she too must feed.

This verse also connects to So 4:11 and So 8:10. God warns the spiritually dead to buy life-promoting spiritual "milk." "Ho, every thirsty one, come ye to the waters, And he who hath no money, Come ye, buy and eat, yea, come, buy Without money and without price, wine and milk." –*Is 55:1* The Messiah will use milk to transform his Shulamite.

"Who so does that which is right, and believes, whether male or female, him or her will We quicken to a happy life." –Koran 16:97

Eat friends (אכלו רעים) literally; "eat friends."

The Hebrew word *aw-kal* (#H398 אכל) means "eat, devour, dine." If you recall, at the end of the Prodigal-Son parable, there was a feast. That father celebrated because he gained a *son*. Here, Jehovah gains a *daughter*.

The Hebrew word *ray-ah* (#H7453 רע) means "associate, friend, companion, fellow." Friend (רע) is related to Pharaoh (פרע). A Pharaoh's title means "they look after the friends, or looked to by friends."

"These things have I spoken unto you, that my joy may be in you, and [that] your joy may be made full. This is my commandment, that ye love one another, even as I have loved you. Greater love hath no man than this, that a man lay down his life for his friends. Ye are my friends, if ye do the things which I command you. No longer do I call you servants; for the servant knoweth not what his lord doeth: but I have called you friends; for all things that I heard from my Father, I have made known unto you." –*Joh 15:11-15* This word (friends) is also used by the Shulamite, at So 8:13.

NUMERICS: *come* (בוֹא) literally; "come, abide, enter." This is the final of six uses. At the *remez* level, six is a man's number, and expresses six Cartesian coordinate positions for a precise location. A call by this messianic Pharaoh comes from a very specific place on earth: Zion.

2 [EARTHLY SHUNEMITE:] My [eyes are] shut, but my heart is awakening. Listen! My beloved is knocking. [SOLOMON:] Open to me, my darling sister, my dove, my flawless one. My head signals the finale with dew, my hair with the dampness of the night.	אני ישנה ולבי ער קול ׀ דודי דופק פתחי־לי אחתי רעיתי יונתי תמתי שראשי נמלא־טל קוצותי רסיסי לילה:

2 ***but my heart is awakening*** (ולבי ער) literally; "but-heart-of-me causing-awake."

Interesting that her first sensory perception is not sight. Her first awareness comes from her heart. Let us compare the word "heart" (לב) to the word "womb" (מעה) used later, in verse four. They are completely different words, but located near one another—deep inside. To translate verse four with "heart" is to ignore the context, and the original Hebrew.

The point is: while others are content, sleeping soundly, something disturbs this dead Shunemite. In a dark corner of her soul's cellar, an ancient hope is fighting its way out, refusing to remain filed away in some forgotten grave.

knocking (דופק) literally; "knocking."

Let us examine what triggers her heart. The Hebrew word *daw-fak* (#H1849 דפק) means "to knock, press severely, beat." This same verb (דפק) is used at Ge 33:13, where Jacob cautions against "driving" [דפק] the cattle too hard.

If you drive a living cow too hard, it's heart could fail. Yet, if a defibulator shocks the same heart, that could re-start its failing heart.

Heavenly Solomon has never dialogued with the Shunemite. But now, she has been resurrected as a Shulamite. Still, their new relationship remains buffered, and distant. This becomes clear when we read So 5:6, "I called, but he did not answer." She is awakening as someone (something) she has never been. At last, he can answer her—if she can find him.

open to me (פתחי) literally; "open-me."

The Hebrew word *paw-thakh* (#H6605 פתח) means "to open wide, loosen, appear, draw out, let go free, ungird." The new Shulamite had been expecting this "knock" for centuries. Had she not rehearsed for this moment, then she might have slept past this opportunity, forfeiting a spectacular entrance onto this prophetic stage. "Behold, I stand at the door and knock: if any man hear my voice and open the door, I will come in to him, and will sup with him, and he with me." –Re 3:20

It's important to identify the two separate groups that Jesus continually refers to. In this case, the Messiah speaks of a small group, his musical Bride Class, who can master the song. In the book of *Luke*, he also identifies a separate group who attend the wedding. "And be ye yourselves like unto men looking for their lord, when he shall return from the marriage feast; that, when he cometh and knocketh, they may straightway open unto him." –Lk 12:36 What's this other group supposed to do? Wait at the gates of Zion. Zion is on earth.

Although, "waiting at the gates of Zion" is a separate event than being called to Jerusalem. "Waiting at the gates of Zion" may be what this Shulamite is referring to, at So 7:13.

signals the finale with dew (נמלא־טל) literally; "being-full dew."

The Hebrew word *maw-law* (#H4390 מלא) means "full, accomplish, confirm, consecrate, be at an end, be expired, fulfil." The "dew" symbolizes the completion of his work. (Re 18:4) If she looked, she would see the evidence in his hair.

The Hebrew word *tal* (#H2919 טל) means "dew." "And the remnant of Jacob shall be in the midst of many peoples as dew from Jehovah, as showers upon the grass, that tarry not for man, nor wait for the sons of men." –*Mic 5:7* These symbolic dew drops crown him.

Joseph's sons (Ephraim and Manasseh) are finally in place. Jacob's blessing on Joseph's two sons is displayed in Solomon's hair. (Re 17:17) It's time.

dampness of night (רסיסי לילה) literally; "dampness-of night."

The dampness is "the remnant of Jacob." Since the word "dampness" (רסיסי) has two *samek's* (ס), we learn this "dampness" is part of an ongoing cycle of irrigation. The Hebrew word *lah-yil* (#H3915 ליל) means "twist away light, night, adversity." The word "night" is connected to verses So 1:6; 3:1; 3:8; 5:2. This marks an end to adversity.

"The burden of Dumah. One calleth unto me out of Seir, Watchman, what of the night? Watchman, what of the night?" –*Is 21:11* "Behold, I will put a fleece of wool on the threshing-floor; if there be dew on the fleece only, and it be dry upon all the ground, then shall I know that thou wilt save Israel by my hand, as thou hast spoken." –*Jg 6:37* It's time.

3 [HEAVENLY SOLOMON:] I've taken off MY CLOAK. Must I put it on [again]? I've washed MY FEET. Must I soil them [again]?	פשטתי את־כתנתי איככה אלבשנה רחצתי את־רגלי איככה אטנפם:

3 *taken off MY CLOAK* (פָּשַׁטְתִּי אֶת־כֻּתָּנְתִּי) literally; "I-took-off CLOAK-OF-ME."

The Hebrew word *koot-to-neth* (#H3801 כֻּתֹנֶת) means "cover, cloak, coat, garment, robe." This term is rarely used to describe women's clothing. This word usually describes mens' clothing. (Ge 37:3; Is 22:21; etc.) Notice his garment has a different Hebrew word than her garment, in verse seven (כֻּתָּנְתִּי = cloak-of-me vs. רְדִידִי = wrap-of-me). But which kind?

"And when they had mocked him, they took off from him the robe, and put on him his garments, and led him away to crucify him." –Mt 27:31 The Father removed his fleshly "cloak" when he was resurrected. When he knocked at the Shunemite's door, for some reason, she expected to see him in his original flesh ("cloak"). Her hesitation is not appropriate.

Must I put it on [again]? (אֵלְבָּשֶׁנָּה) literally; "must-I-put-her-on."

The cloak that Solomon does not want to put on again is his flesh. This Heavenly Solomon has, and will continue to have, the ability to materialize. His son-of-man flesh, however, has been sacrificed, once and for all time.

For instance: Jesus materialized for the benefit of his apostles. Like this Shulamite, Thomas also demanded too much from Jesus. Thomas made Jesus show him his wounds. "Unless I see in his hands the print of the nails and stick my finger into the print of the nails and stick my hand into his side, I will certainly not believe."

Extraordinarily, eight days later, Thomas had his chance. Jesus again appeared to the disciples, and finally, Thomas was convinced. In the middle of all this, the Messiah imparted some sage advice for Thomas that this new Shulamite failed to heed: "Happy are those who do not see and yet believe." (Joh 20:24-29)

So, what was Jesus saying to Thomas? The same thing Solomon is saying to the new Shulamite: *don't look for flesh!*

MY FEET (אֶת־רַגְלַי) literally; "feet-of-me."

The Hebrew word *reh-gel* (#H7272 רֶגֶל) means "a foot, as in walking, or journey." A young Jewish Rabbi (Jesus) awakened the dreams of a conquered nation. The Romans attempted to stop the walk of this Jesus by nailing his feet to a stake. (Joh 20:25-27; Lk 24:39; Ps 22:16) When he was removed from the stake, his body (and feet) were cleaned and wrapped for burial. Does the Shulamite need to see the feet of this messiah again? (This word "feet" connects to So 7:1)

Must I soil them (אֲטַנְּפֵם) literally; "must-I-soil-them."

The Hebrew word *taw-naf* (#H2936 טָנַף) means "to soil, defile." The Pharisees demanded miracles, and the crowds demanded the overthrow of Roman oppressors. That's why they were rejected. (Jer 3:8) Contrast their self-serving demands to that of the repentant prostitute: "And turning to the woman, he said unto Simon, Seest thou this woman? I entered into thy house, thou gavest me no water for my feet: but she hath wetted my feet with her tears, and wiped them with her hair.'" –Lk 7:44

There are Shulamites willing to wash the feet of Jesus. Too many women can only embrace a relationship that matches (in their mind's eye) a romanticized plot from some Hollywood movie.

Do you burden your man with expectations that kill the spirit of romance?

Ask yourself: Which has more strength? A famous movie scene; a famous pop song; or longings rooted in principle? These are questions the Shulamite must decide immediately.

4 [EARTHLY SHUNEMITE:] My beloved thrust out his hand, granting elevation in rank [sealed]. My womb groans with mankind.	דּוֹדִי שָׁלַח יָדוֹ מִן־הַחֹר וּמֵעַי הָמוּ עָלָיו:

4 ***thrust out his hand*** (שלח ידו) literally; "he-thrust hand-of-him through."

This is one of the more difficult verses in *Song of Songs*. Most students are surprised that there is no consensus for rendering this verse. There is no evidence for translating this as "latch opening," as many do. That rendering is a scholar's bluff. Call their bluff. They have no proofs.

The Hebrew word *shaw-lakh* (#H7971 שלח) means "to send for, send out, appoint." So, with a wave of the Messiah's hand, the Shunemite has been dispatched for duty—as a Shulamite. With a wave of his hand, the Messiah does something that "sealed" explains in increasing detail. She has been "authorized."

granting elevation in rank [sealed] (מנ־החר) literally; "granting the-appointing."

The Hebrew word *mane* (#H4482 מנ) means "to apportion, a part, hence a mere musical bar." As part of the 144,000, she not only masters the song, she is a part of the song. That means, with one wave of his hand, her beloved has anointed her as one note in this divine musical.

This new Shulamite must respond immediately, or she will miss her "que" in the ongoing song of the universe. If she is off time, the greatest of all songs will finish without her.

The Hebrew word *khore* (#H2715 חר) means "white or pure (from cleansing of fire), noble in rank." Whatever bad ideologies she once had, has been burned away. The Messiah is both the husband (*eesh* / איש), and fire (*aysh* / אש). For this honor, however, she must relinquish her human life. That will come in only a few verses.

and my womb (ומעי) literally; "and-womb-of-me."

The Hebrew word *may-aw* (#H4578 מעה) means "intestines, abdomen, uterus, womb." It's a flexible word that doesn't always translate the same way. The best example of this word (womb) is used by Naomi, "Turn again, my daughters: why will ye go with me? have I yet sons in my womb (מעה), that they may be your husbands?'" –*Ru 1:11*

Naomi's quote captures the true context of this word (*may-aw* / מעה). Naomi's "womb" cannot deliver another son for Ruth to marry (through brother-in-law marriage). Likewise, this "seal" changes the Shunemite's status from a sister of millions, to a Shulamite, a mother of millions.

groans with mankind (המו) literally; "groans-with-mankind."

The Hebrew word *ha-mah* (המה) is generally translated as "groaning, or raging." Since our word is close, it's easy to understand why many translators lean in that direction, but since this verse connects with So 7:2, they're wrong.

When we translate, at the letter level, we get something very close, but the final *vov* (ו) carries the additional idea of, "mankind." Further, the context tells us she has been transformed, granted an elevated status, sealed. (Re 7:2-4) So, as the new mother to mankind, we have to let context take its course.

The same thing happened to a prior matriarch, Rebekah. "And the children struggled together within her. And she said, If it be so, wherefore do I live? And she went to inquire of Jehovah." –*Ge 25:22* Rebekah's womb groaned with twins. Now, the Shulamite's womb groans with mankind.

Before our very eyes, we are watching a Shunemite become a Shulamite. In the twinkling of an eye, she is being transformed from a virgin (who has not known a man) to the mother of a great crowd, which no man was able to number. (Re 7:9) In that instant, how should her womb feel? (Ge 25:22) It "groans with mankind."

5 [EARTHLY SHUNEMITE:] I arose to open for my beloved, and my hands were purified by myrrh, my fingers with overflowing myrrh, on the recesses of the lock.	קמתי אני לפתח לדודי וידי נטפו־מור ואצבעתי מור עבר על כפות המנעול:

5 *to open* (לִפְתֹּחַ) literally; "to-open."

A feature of "the time of the end" is the "standing up" of the Messiah. The Messiah was to stand up in the final part of the days. (Da 8:8-25) The symbolism of Da 8:8-25 connects to this verse. This former Shunemite has been selected to become a co-ruler. Like her lord and king, she too must stand up.

Feeling the call is one thing, but responding is quite another. This Shunemite is finally reacting to the call. She has risen and is about to "open" a door to a one-way journey. What she is feeling and experiencing cannot be understood by anyone except herself and her beloved. She must go to him.

The Shunemite knows the consequences of both going, and staying. Thus, she leaves—her hands still dripping with "myrrh." Myrrh is one of the ingredients used to prepare the dead. (Mt 2:11) If she goes through that door, she knows she is going to her heavenly calling.

Brides who keep one foot in their mother's household and another in her husband's household never learn the fundamentals of marriage. (Ge 2:24) There is no difference in discipleship or marriage, when it comes to covenants.

the recesses of the lock (כפות המנעול) literally; "palm-of the-lock."

The Hebrew word *kaf* (#H3709 כף) means "the hollow of the hand, the palm, bowl." The "palm" hints at getting wonderful things. So, this lock contains the promise of good things to come.

The Hebrew word *man-ool* (#H4514 מנעול) means "a locking bolt, that can be pushed open with the palm of their hand." It represents something that separates us from what we want. There is a "lock" between them. Yet, a calling has been made. Her response is required.

Whatever obstacles, impediments, or locks, between her and her responsibilities are her's to remove. They must be removed by her own hand.

Have you removed all the barriers between you and your husband? Too many couples go to their graves with monumental expectations and all the resulting revenges for mates who don't deliver them. Let it go. A whole other life is waiting for you. Drop the expectations and jump in with both feet.

6 [EARTHLY SHUNEMITE:] I'm out, my beloved . . . but my beloved has left. He journeyed on. My soul went out to speak to him. I looked for him, but didn't find him. I called him, but he didn't answer.	פתחתי אני לדודי ודודי חמק עבר נפשי יצאה בדברו בקשתיהו ולא מצאתיהו קראתיו ולא ענני:

6 ***I am out*** (פתחתי אני) literally; "let-go I."

The Hebrew word *paw-thakh* (#H6605 פתח) means "to open wide, appear, draw out, free, ungird." The Shulamite has responded to the first obstacle, but what will she do next? "If then the son may make you free, in reality ye shall be free." – *Joh 8:36*

has left. He journeyed on. (חמק עבר) literally; "he-left he-journeyed-on."

These words have a way of following the Heavenly Solomon. Christians teach that Jesus (in his pre-human existence) was likely one of the three persons who appeared to Abraham. In that "theophony," Abraham implored the three to eat, before they journeyed on [עבר]. (Ge 18:5) Abraham recognized that this third person was on a journey [עבר], and the Shulamite recognized that Solomon was on a journey [עבר]. To Christians, Jesus is a busy person with many important things to do. She must find him.

    I looked for him (בקשתיהו) literally; "I-looked-for-him."

At So 1:7, and at So 3:1-2, the Shunemite had looked for Solomon. Her search had been relentless, even while her character was forming. Now that her character has been found worthy, he found her.

    I called him (קראתיו) literally; "I-called-him."
Why is she "calling him?" Why didn't she leave with him? Because, she delayed! The Heavenly Solomon knows where she is, who she is, and hears what she says. It's the former Shunemite who is puzzled—not the Messiah.

    Consider the contrast: when Rebekah was "called" for marriage, her family asked for a delay in departure. Abraham's servant, said "No." Since Rebekah departed promptly, she rode in style, atop a parade of camels.

    This new Shulamite is no Rebekah. Because of this delay, she must go trotting off behind her man. No parade of camels for this slowpoke.

    In an ideal marriage, there is no "looking" or "calling." Keep your head in the game. Saddle the stinking camels—even if your lazy husband sits and picks his teeth. Stay ahead of the game. Drop the "chasing." Drop the "searching." Drop the "trying." Be pro-active.

7 [EARTHLY SHUNEMITE:] The watchers found me, as they made their rounds in the city. They struck me. They bruised me. They took away MY WRAP, those watchers of the walls.	מצאני השמרים הסבבים בעיר הכוני פצעוני נשאו את־רדידי מעלי שמרי החמות:

7 *The watchers* (השמרים) literally; "the-men-watching."

From a Christian perspective, this verse was already anticipated. At Mt 13:39 the angels were referred to as "reapers." "And the harvest comes at the end of the Satan's reign; and the reapers are angels." –*Mt 13:39* The Father selects the brides; the angels reap from the Shunemites; the son marries them. Those "reapers" have come to harvest her.

made their rounds (הסבבים) literally; "the-ones-going-round."

These "watchers" are not in Heavenly Jerusalem. These angels are wandering the streets of earthly Zion. (Jer 31:10-12)

These appointed watchers know where they can find the true Earthly Brothers and the true Earthly Shunemites. In fact, that's why they were standing guard in Zion. "The burden of Dumah [ceremonial death]. One calleth unto me out of Seir [tempest (reference to So 2:11)], Watchman, what of the night? Watchman, what of the night? The watchman said, The morning cometh, and also the night: if ye will inquire, inquire ye: turn ye, come.'" –*Is 21:11-12* She returned.

they struck me (הכוני) literally; "they-struck-me."

Since all mankind were brought forth "with error" and conceived "in sin," direction must be administered which is symbolized by the rod. Therefore, this earthly child must be "struck" with death, yet again. (Ps 51:5)

The former Shunemite would not be surprised that she was struck. She went there expecting to be struck. It was the same with her beloved. (Pr 23:35) "And the men that held [Jesus] mocked him, and beat him. And they blindfolded him, and asked him, saying, Prophesy: who is he that struck thee?" *–Lk 22:63-64* These "watchers" were not evil. They struck the Shunemite because they are dutiful workers. They are harvesting souls.

MY WRAP (את־רדידי) literally; "wrap-of-me."

The definition of the Hebrew word used here, is unknown. It may mean many things. When compared to what her beloved wears (כתנת), her wrap (רדיד) resembles the Hebrew word "beloved" (דוד). This hints at what she has "wrapped" herself in—a lifetime of romantic hopes for her beloved. She wants to dwell where dreams are born—with her beloved.

One thing is certain: the flesh she wears must be removed—for her own good. She is on her way to the symbolic dinner. (Re 19:7-10) As a participant of this celebratory dinner, the angels must attend to her decorum. They are obligated to remove inappropriate dress. (Mt 22:11) A fleshly "wrap" is not appropriate to wear in Heaven. Like a lost child, she will be given a new robe, seal ring, and a festive meal.

"Now this I say, brethren, that flesh and blood cannot inherit the kingdom of God; neither doth corruption inherit incorruption. Behold, I tell you a mystery: We all shall not sleep, but we shall all be changed, in a moment, in the twinkling of an eye, at the last trump: for the trumpet shall sound, and the dead shall be raised incorruptible, and we shall be changed. For this corruptible must put on incorruption, and this mortal must put on immortality." *–1Cor 15:50-53*

8 [EARTHLY SHUNEMITE:] The pleadings of mine for you, daughters at Jerusalem, if you find MY BELOVED, what will you tell him? Tell him "I'm faint with love."	הִשְׁבַּעְתִּי אֶתְכֶם בְּנוֹת יְרוּשָׁלִַם אִם־תִּמְצְאוּ אֶת־דּוֹדִי מַה־תַּגִּידוּ לוֹ שֶׁחוֹלַת אַהֲבָה אָנִי:

    8 *The pleadings of mine for you* (השבעתי אתכם) literally; "The-entreaties-of-me you-for."

    In prior entreaties, the Shunemite pled for her Earthly Brothers. (So 2:7 and So 3:5) Now, she pleads for herself. She wants only one thing: to be with her beloved, at any cost.

    In Hebrew, "pleading" (שבעה) can sometimes be, proclaiming, or victoriously reiterate the terms of the completed assignment. The Shunemite isn't avoiding an obligation, rather, announcing her success at completing one.

    The sour whine has wisely been eliminated from her character. Self-pity drains the spirits of anyone standing nearby.

    "Self-pity is our worst enemy and if we yield to it, we can never do anything wise in this world." –*Helen Keller* This is the proclamation of a successful steward, not a sniveling foot dragger.

    if you find (אם־תמצאו) literally; "if you-find."
    Why does this new Shulamite think the daughters at Jerusalem know where her messiah is? God's people have a tradition of spirit creatures knowing how to access other spirit creatures. "See that ye despise not one of these little ones; for I say unto you, that in Heaven their angels do always behold the face of my Father who is in Heaven." –*Mt 18:10* These "daughters at Jerusalem" (her new sisters) have already ascended and descended Jacob's ladder many times. They have access. Their Angelic Brothers have access.

I'm faint (שֲחוֹלָה) literally; "that-one-being-faint-of."

So, why is this new Shulamite "faint?" The answer is so simple it's often overlooked. Solomon knocked, but she didn't open. "Behold, I stand at the door and knock: if any man hear my voice and open the door, I will come in to him, and will sup with him, and he with me." –*Re 3:20*

She responded to his knock after he departed. (So 5:2-6) She missed her supper. Divine love (אהבה) is food for someone about to enter the realm of Heaven. The Shulamites' prospects are improving, but she must locate her "beloved" fast.

The musical classic, *Tell Him* encapsulates her longing. "Tell him, tell him that the sun and moon rise in his eyes; Reach out to him; And whisper tender words so soft and sweet; I'll hold him close to feel his heart beat; Love will be the gift you give yourself; Touch him with the gentleness you feel inside, I feel it; Your love can't be denied, the truth will set you free; You'll have what's meant to be, all in time you'll see." –*Afanasieff, Walter, Foster, David; Thompson, Linda D*

9 [HEAVENLY SHULAMITE:] How is your beloved better than the beloved of others, most beautiful of women? How is your beloved better than the beloved of others, that you plead with us so?	מה־דודך מדוד היפה בנשים מה־דודך מדוד שככה השבעתנו׃

9 ***better than the beloved*** (מדוד) literally: "better-than-the-beloved."

Within one verse, we have a quick repeat of four "beloveds." Four conveys the idea of conversion. The way she answers this question may decide whether, or not, she will be accepted as a Shulamite. Does she adore him because everyone adores him, or for the right reasons? Which begs the question: What do you want?

The world is full of men adored by "fans." They may be recipients of: Oscars, Grammies, NBA trophies, Nobel Peace Prizes, Bronze Stars, fiefdoms, and kingships.

Women, without godly standards, chase such men and dishonor themselves. It was never difficult for Pilate to find adoring women. Even Hitler was surrounded by women anxious to make his acquaintance. It seems there is a never-ending supply of those kinds of women.

It should be the goal of every matriarch-to-be to emulate the two qualities of Israel's original matriarch, Sarah. First, Sarah sought nothing more than being the mother of God's people. (Is 51:2) Second, Sarah never sought the attention of men in power. (Ge 12:19) Sarah was re-named, "princess." (Ge17:15) She behaved accordingly.

"I am ashamed to think how easily we capitulate to badges and names, to large societies and dead institutions. Every decent and well-spoken individual affects and sways me more than is right." –*Ralph Waldo Emerson*

What's the nature of this Shulamite's admiration? What does she admire? Who else emulates those qualities? Even the Satan attracted a third of the angels from Heaven. (Re 12:4) Is it popularity that influences this Shulamite?

10 [EARTHLY SHUNEMITE:] My beloved is radiant and ruddy, <u>outstanding</u> among 10,000.	דודי צח ואדום דגול מרבבה:

10 *outstanding* (דגול) literally; "being-outstanding."

It's important to compare this word "outstanding" (דגול) to the word "banner" (דגל). This former Shunemite was clever enough to make the connection.

Banners of Israel's patriarchs were displayed to help a person find their proper place in the camp. (Nu 2:2) This new Shulamite knows where she belongs. Israel's camp was orderly. Under this theocratic arrangement, chiefs were appointed over 10's, 50's, 100's, and 1,000's. These were "capable men, fearing God, trustworthy men, hating unjust profit." (Ex 18:21; De 1:15) This former Shunemite gravitated toward "trustworthy men."

Here, begins the upbeat descriptions of her "outstanding" husband-to-be. He has journeyed on, but there is no complaint in her voice. With our mother, there is no self-pity. Self-pity is one of the most destructive forces we indulge in. It drives a wedge between those who practice it, and those who observe it.

11 [EARTHLY SHUNEMITE:] His head is purest gold. His hair is wavy, and black as a raven.	ראשו כתם פז קוצותיו תלתלים שחרות כעורב:

11 ***His head*** (רֹאשׁוֹ) literally; "head-of-him."

The head, as the governing member of the body, was also used to represent headship. His leadership is "golden." The Messiah's having "nowhere to lay down his head" meant he had no wife, or offspring that he could call his own. (Mt 8:20) That sad picture is reversed when she claims his head of "gold" as hers. Gold represents heavenly qualities. His wisdom is from the Heavens . . . she is saying.

A man can get discouraged many times, without being a failure. Only when he dumps his responsibility on another does he truly forfeit leadership. David was a great leader, because he accepted his failures, and persevered. He described discipline as "oil that his head would not want to refuse." (Ps 141:5) David's wisdom was also from the Heavens.

His hair (קוּצּוֹתיו) literally; "hair-of-him."

Israelite men were forbidden to cut the extremities of their hair. Therefore, although ordinary in appearance, he was not regarded by this former Shunemite as common, or out of style. Rather, she respected the reason for his ordinary appearance. His appearance conformed to Jehovah's standards, and she admired that.

Sarah saw kings with shaved heads. They were dressed with the best clothing, but they did not conform to Jehovah's standards. Sarah chose Abraham, instead of them. Like Sarah, the former Shunemite knew what her man should look like.

Since his hair was anointed with oil, it would have the shiny appearance of raven's wings. Since the Messiah was purposeful, his hurried steps would blow his hair back, giving the appearance of a raven's flapping wings. Again, it's not the appearance itself, but how he self-identifies. It's the *reason* for his appearance that makes him so attractive. This new Shulamite knows to whom she belongs—and why.

All matriarchs have a story. Your marriage has a story. "I've found 94% of the time that couples who put a positive spin on their marital history are likely to have a happy future as well." *–John M. Gottman / Professor of Psychology*

NUMERICS: *black* (שחר) literally; "black, early dawn, dark part of the morning." This is the final of four uses. At the *remez* level, the number four demonstrates conversion. The fourth letter of the Hebrew alphabet is *dalet* (ד). It hints at conversion within the words it appears in: The word *debash* (דבש) = honey (converted from pollen); the word *dayah* (דע) = knowledge (converts experience into knowledge); the word *dardah* (דרדע) = pearl of knowledge (converts plain knowledge into superlative knowledge); etc. In this verse, "black" encapsulates the harbinger of death—the raven. The new Shulamite and her beloved have, at one time, died. This new Shulamite and her beloved have, have now been resurrected to a superlative life.

12 [EARTHLY SHUNEMITE:] His eyes are like doves, by the water streams, washed in milk, mounted like jewels.	עיניו כיונים על־אפיקי מים רחצות בחלב ישבות על־מלאת:

12 *mounted* (יֹשְׁבוֹת) literally; "ones-being-mounted."

Again, Hebrews rarely give physical descriptions, but instead provide comparative analogies. Doves mate for life. If his eyes are like doves, then they are not wandering. A Hebrew describes qualities, rather than appearance.

Precious jewels are carefully set, because of their great value. Jehovah set His eyes toward our good. "Who holdeth our soul in life, And suffereth not our feet to be moved. For thou, O God, hast proved us: Thou hast tried us, as silver is tried." –*Ps 66:9-10* The former Shunemite now shares Jehovah's same vision . . . just as your family should.

13 [EARTHLY SHUNEMITE:] His cheeks are like beds of spice, yielding perfume. His lips are like lilies, dripping with myrrh.	לחיו כערוגת הבשם מגדלות מרקחים שפתותיו שושנים נטפות מור עבר:

13 *His cheeks* (לְחָיָו) literally; "cheeks-of-him."

A messiah does more than teach his disciples, he becomes their example: "You heard that it was said, 'Eye for eye and tooth for tooth.' However, I say to you: Do not resist him that is wicked; but whoever slaps you on your right cheek, turn the other also to him." (Mt 5:38-39)

In this example, Jesus was not teaching pacifism or denying the right of self-defense. He was teaching his disciples how to stop quarrels. A slap on the cheek is not intended to kill or injure, but only to insult. Mature marriages learn to hold their tongues. What Jesus meant, it's within your power to de-escalate an argument.

If rulership were based on kindness, instead of intimidation, her Messiah would have ruled earth long ago. The former Shunemite's heart is with the innocent. The former Shunemite would never side with a "slapper" just because they had more power than the weak. Solomon is the perfect king for the Shunemite, whether anyone else thinks so or not.

His lips (שׁפתותיו) literally; "lips-of-him."

Moses tried to excuse himself from speaking to Pharaoh. He claimed to be "uncircumcised in lips." (Ex 6:12, 30) Isaiah lamented that he was "unclean in lips." God then caused Isaiah's lips to be cleansed. (Is 6:5-7) The Heavenly Solomon's lips, however, are flowing with godly speech.

Prophecy exhorts disciples to offer God "the fruit of lips which make public declaration to his name." (Heb 13:15) The new Shulamite promotes this family trait. She knows to whom she belongs—and doesn't hesitate to tell others.

Showing all your cards might be foolish in poker, but in relationships you can't go wrong with total honesty and full disclosure.

14 [EARTHLY SHUNEMITE:] His arms are rods of gold, set in Tarshish. His body is like polished ivory, decorated with sapphires.	ידיו גלילי זהב ממלאים בתרשיש מעיו עשת שן מעלפת ספירים:

14 ***in Tarshish*** (בתרשיש) literally; "in-Tarshish."

If "rods" represent discipline, why would the great Messiah plunge his arms into Tarshish? If "arms" represent strength, why would the great Messiah plunge his arms into Tarshish? What does Tarshish mean? Where do typhoons emanate from? Where were demon angels cast down to? Who do these same demons stir up? (Is 24:21-23)[24]

At the story level, Tarshish is an intriguing word parallel with 1Pe 3:19-20. There we find a similar Greek word, "Tartarus." One is a Hebrew word and the other is a Greek word. Still, the phonetics should not be ignored.

No wonder Jonah believed God would not be in Tarshish (תרשיש). Not because it was far from Jerusalem, but because did not reside in Tarshish. (Is 14:12-16)

Tarshish was the symbolic prison for demon angels. Just as Zion was earth's new symbolic capital city, Tarshish was the symbolic capitol city from which the Satan ruled over a world alienated from God.

The new Shulamite advocates that the strong arms of her messiah should reach down to the very source of mankind's problems. The new Shulamite never had an interest in earth's political solutions. Her citizenship was always in Heaven—the Jerusalem Above. The former Shunemite always knew her king would one day depose the god of this earthly kingdom. (2Cor 4:4)

| 15 [EARTHLY SHUNEMITE:] His legs are pillars of marble, set on bases of pure gold. His appearance is like Lebanon, choice as its cedars. | שוקיו עמודי שש מיסדים על־אדני־פז מראהו כלבנון בחור כארזים: |

15 *His legs* (שׁוֹקָיו) literally; "legs-of-him."

There is a metaphor that's almost lost among Westerners. Legs are what we stand on. To a Hebrew, legs are a metaphor for "understanding." Even though Solomon hears what is said to him, understanding goes beyond simple awareness. Understanding means that he, and his brides, can makes application of Jehovah's messages.

Eve left God. People who leave God lose an important source for important decisions. (Job 34:27) When people reject God's values, they are left to sort through inferior ideologies, thus forfeiting "understanding." (Ps 36:1-4)

16 [EARTHLY SHUNEMITE:] His mouth is sweetness itself. He is altogether lovely. This is my beloved. This is my friend—daughters at Jerusalem.	חכו ממתקים וכלו מחמדים זה דודי וזה רעי בנות ירושלם:

16 ***His mouth*** (חכו) literally; "mouth-of-him."
As Jesus himself said, "Out of the abundance of the heart the mouth speaks." (Mt 12:34) Judging by the things Jesus spoke during his visit in the flesh, we can conclude his family was close to his heart.

What comes from her mouth is proof. Small deeds done are better than exaggerated deeds planned. She may have delayed in opening her door, but she remains positive. Compliments for her husband continue to pour from her mouth.

Solomon's character speaks to the daughters of Heaven in ways no other song can.

He is altogether lovely (וכלו מחמדים) literally; "and-all-of-him lovely-ones."
It's a Muslim teaching that this verse connects to Muhammad, in symbolic ways. The Hebrew word used in this verse, is *mukhammadim* (מחמדים). In the *Authorized Version* of the Bible, however, this word is rendered, "The Praised One." In Arabic, "Muhammad" means "the one who is most praised."

my friend (רעי) literally; "friend-of-me."

The Hebrew word *ray-ah* (#H7453 רֵעַ) means "associate, friend, companion, fellow." This Messiah has yet to dialogue with the new Shulamite. For this new Shulamite, she was separated from Solomon all her life. Yet, somehow, she responded when he called.

The Shulamite loves what the Messiah loves. She embraces his community. By claiming to be his "friend," she is claiming she's fond of his core beliefs.

Let me end the chapter with this story: In the movie *A.I. (Artificial Intelligence)*, aliens searched the universe for meaning. They discover David, an android, from the broken remains of Planet Earth.

Before the failure of earth, they had a saying: "You can't program love." But, David was earth's best effort. For that reason, the aliens greet David with awe and reverence.

"David," they said, "you are the enduring memory of the human race—the most lasting proof of their genius."

David had all the sweet, vulnerable, and endearing, features common to children. David was specifically programmed for love, to fill the void of a grieving mother. The aliens were deeply moved by his sincerity, and unfailing kindness. They wanted, above all, to make David happy.

Since they asked what they could do for David, he requested they bring back the human mother who rejected him, centuries earlier.

It's a common refrain. There is something irresistible about replaying our tragic melodies until we get them right. David convinced the aliens that she would not reject him, this time.

Reluctantly, the aliens recreated a facsimile of David's estranged mother. That was the ultimate moment David had hoped for.

In this alien version of reality, his mother told him that she loved him, and always would. That fulfilled every circuit in the little robot's body. With that, David was finally able to bond with his flesh-mother—just as he was programmed to do.

As his mother ended her day with human sleep, for the first time ever, David and his mother slept a sleep from which they would never awaken. David drifted into the world where dreams are born—but it wasn't an earth world.

The aliens continued their search, hoping to discover another David.

This Hollywood story ended, revealing everyone's insurmountable expectations. David wanted more than his flesh-mother could give, and the aliens wanted more than this little android could give.

Even in a future world the important questions are still the painful ones: What's real love? What do we owe others? Can we repair our failed melodies? Where does love's music come from? How do we keep the music playing? In the end, where are dreams born? Did the little android achieve transcendence, or simply stop trying?

Chapter 6:25
Solomon Inspects Graveyards

In matters of true love, old age is never a problem—it's a crown of beauty. Even when reduced to mere dust among flowers, the most valuable part of us can still be retrieved. Love always brings us back. True love is like a spiral. It has its bumps and detours, but never ends.

Human relationships are steppingstones to divine love. Death may be stronger than life, but love is stronger than death. As Robert Browning wrote: "Grow old with me, the best is yet to be."

6 [HEAVENLY BROTHERS:] Where has your beloved gone, most beautiful of women? To where did your beloved slip away that we may seek him with you?	ו אנה הלך דודך היפה בנשים אנה פנה דודך ונבקשנו עמך:

1 Where (אנה) literally; "to-where."

I have some terrible news for you, dear daughter. This generation, this society, this culture, doesn't place a high value on older women. Grow old at your own peril.

Choose carefully who you grow old with. How fortunate for you that God laces *Song of Songs* with values to aspire to. Have you chosen a man who embraces His ideals?

Unlike today's Hollywood culture, the coming Messiah has a preference for the aged. The Shulamite's beloved has gone down to his "garden," (*sheol*) to pick lilies. The book of *Ezekiel* describes Solomon's grizzly "garden." "'There is Edom, her kings and all her princes, who in their might are laid with them that are slain by the sword: they shall lie with the uncircumcised, and with them that go down to the pit. There are the princes of the north, all of them, and all the Sidonians, who are gone down with the slain; in the terror which they caused by their might they are put to shame; and they lie uncircumcised with them that are slain by the sword, and bear their shame with them that go down to the pit. Pharaoh shall see them, and shall be comforted over all his multitude, even Pharaoh and all his army, slain by the sword, saith the Lord Jehovah. For I have put his terror in the land of the living; and he shall be laid in the midst of the uncircumcised, with them that are slain by the sword, even Pharaoh and all his multitude, saith the Lord Jehovah!" *–Ezk 32:29-32*

Where is this garden, and why does it cause "shame?" The garden is *sheol*, the common grave of mankind. Death is mankind's shame.

A woman, such as yourself, needs a safe place to live, love, lounge, and learn. Despite America's endless lectures, despite government's mandated sensitivity training, despite federal laws prohibiting age discrimination, we now throw our elderly away without a twinge of regret.

Male, or female, society's elders are treated with shameful neglect. In Costa Rica, local hospitals see a 20% increase of families dumping the elderly around Christmas time. The explanations are startling. "People want to be in peace, with liberty to enjoy their festivities."[26] In New York, local hospitals have also seen a jump in families dumping their elderly. "According to their administrators, hospitals are increasingly used as receptacles. Too many of the community's hospitals, are now faced with another challenge: The abandonment of the elderly in parking lots and emergency rooms."[27]

You *have* chosen an honorable man. You have chosen a man who appreciates Abrahamic values. He resists the values society tries to impose on him. On any given day, he is surrounded by people who wear a variety of "cause" ribbons, who walk past elderly people unable to negotiate a tall step. "Cause-proclaimers" seldom offer the elderly assistance. You and your husband live in an age when it's more *chic* to rescue a dog than grandparents. In an ideal world, "family" means no one gets left behind. Unlike the "world," our messianic father comes back for his elderly.

most beautiful of women (היפה בנשים) literally; "the-beautiful-one among-the-women."

What makes the Shulamite beautiful? She has been recreated in a spectacular way. (So 6:12) It's her appearance. It's her adherence to Abrahamic ideologies. It's her personality which conforms to messianic principles. Compare that to "cause-proclaimers," who are notoriously seasonal.

This generation, for example, has targeted "dead-beat dads," but are oblivious to "dead-beat kids." Abrahamic values, by contrast, are consistent. Abraham was good to his wife, dad, son, nephew, neighbor, and God.

Do you know the difference between adhesive tape and cohesive tape? Adhesive tape is sticky on one side. Cohesive tape is sticky on both sides. Healthy families should be "cohesive." The young should be as concerned for their elders as their elders were for them—cohesive.

It wasn't so long ago that households had several generations under one roof. Every age-category suffers a time of disfavor. Yet, every age category always has something to contribute to the family. In the Messiah's family, we neither fear inexperience, nor old age. The world-to-come embraces both, and it will be a safe place for a woman to grow old, with loved ones nearby.

NUMERICS: *seek* (בקש) literally; "seek, look, search, strive." This is the last of five uses. At the *remez* level, five hints at judgment with a view to salvation. The Heavenly Shulamite has been tested, quantified, and found worthy. Her new Brothers (Heavenly) will help her "seek" the king (Heavenly) who will validate her salvation.

2 [HEAVENLY SHULAMITE:] My beloved came down to his garden, to the beds of spices, to inspect in the gardens, and to gather lilies.	דודי ירד לגנו לערוגות הבשם לרעות בגנים וללקט שושנים:

2 came down (ירד) literally; "he-went-down."
History testifies that our messiah never descends, or goes "down," without an important reason—love. He went "down" to earth to die. (1Pe 1:10-12) Look what they did to him. He went "down" to Sheol to fulfill prophecy. (Mt 12:40) Yet, few people noticed or cared.

This Solomon-like messiah isn't coming down to retrieve Abishag-like fashion models. He's coming "down" to retrieve 144,000 qualified leaders. (Lk 22:29-30)

Despite others taking no notice of the injustices done to the former Shunemite, their Messiah noticed—and cared. The first duty of love is to listen. This kind of partner is someone she can grow old with—someone she can trust. He returned when everyone else forgot her name.

"(Now this, He ascended, what is it but that he also descended into the lower parts of the earth? He that descended is the same also that ascended far above all the Heavens, that he might fill all things.)" –*Eph 4:9-10*

What do "spices" have in common with graves? In Israel, when you open a grave, you are guaranteed to find two things: (1) A dead body. (2) Spices. Consider how the body of Jesus was prepared: "And when the sabbath was past, Mary Magdalene, and Mary the [mother] of James, and Salome, bought spices, that they might come and anoint him." –*Mk 16:1* This Solomon is inspecting graves.

Where are your elderly?

Hopefully, they're not cleaning a house that no one will visit. Hopefully, theyre not shaving and dressing, but no one comes. Hopefully, they're not throwing out goodies, because their grandchildren never came.

This messianic Solomon watched at a respectful distance as his loyal servants drew their last breath. He knows. He saw. He cared. He will soon reassure the forgotten—the marginalized.

The coming Messiah has a decided preference for maturity. His heart may break many times for his lonely bride-to-be, but he had to wait for them to prove faithful . . . to the end.

The elderly die so absolutely alone. After everyone else has moved on with their busy lives, this Solomon-like messiah tenderly planted them in his garden, waiting for the proper season, when he could return and harvest them.

Make your home a haven for every generation, unlike this heartless Western culture. It may sound like bad math, but the math of love is: one plus one equals everything. Two minus one equals nothing.

Loneliness was the first thing that alarmed Jehovah, in the book of *Genesis*. (Ge 2:18) Jehovah noticed. The Messiah will notice. You should too. Bring lonely family into your home—as long as they do no harm to the innocent. Who knows? They might alleviate your emptiness, too.

to inspect (לרעוֹת) literally; "to-browse."

Hebrew poetry loves progressive word pictures. From a Hebrew root word meaning "shepherd," we are gradually informed that this Solomon-like Messiah intends to shepherd the deceased children of Abraham from the most inaccessible place on earth—*sheol*. *Sheol* is the pit this metaphorical ewe fell into. (Mt 12:11)

Gardens were commonly used as burial places. Manasseh and his son, Amon, were buried in the garden of Uzza. (2Ki 21:18, 25-26) Gardens hide a harsh reality. The gruesome reality is, the Heavenly Solomon is browsing through such a garden—filled with dead Shunemites.

Character isn't something you were born with. Character isn't something that rubs off just because you attend church. A beautiful child is a biological accident. A beautiful old person is a well-crafted piece of fine art.

In the end, character is the deciding factor that Jehovh uses to choose His son's 144,000 wives. (Mt 20:23)

Fear not. This is a joyful inspection. This Solomon-like Messiah is anxious to awaken his old friends who expired clinging to the tenents of his new covenant. The standards that shape your boundaries, and your courage to enforce them, all go a long way to make the beautiful soul this Messiah is searching for.

It's a human compulsion to hide or ignore death. We seldom give thought to all the death beneath our feet, but there is no section of earth that's not digesting the life that once walked on its surface.

For thousands of years many children of Abraham have lead beautiful lives of selfless service. Look what this life did to them. The coming Messiah intends to shepherd every past generation out of death, but only a small flock for Heaven. (compare Lk 12:32 to Joh 10:16)

and to gather lilies (וללקט שושנים) literally; "and-to-gather lilies."

Many have wondered why there are so many references to lilies. "Lilies" appear frequently in superscripts all through the *Psalms*. (Ps 45, 60, 69 and 80) The superscript at Ps 45 reads, "To the director upon The Lilies. Of the sons of Korah Maskil. A song of the beloved women." Who are the "beloved women?" Are these "lilies" our prophetic Shulamites?

They probably are. The root word of lily is the number, six (שש). The mathematician, Stan Tenen, has broken down the first verse of *Genesis* into a lily-like geometric form. "Both the 3, 10 torus knot and the Shushon Flower [lily] are mathematical arrangements of '6-around-1.'"[28]

Mr. Tenen observed that the lily fits well within the mathematical metaphor of Dini's surface. "Dini's surface also helps us to see why Jewish descent must be from the mother. Well before a female fetus is born it contains, fully formed, all of its eggs for the next generation. The female line connects back to the origin directly, umbilus to umbilus, and egg to egg—directly back to the origin. All future eggs for all future generations exist potentially within the first egg."[29]

All that being said, the lily has always played a significant role in Hebrew writing that goes ignored by today's Bible scholars—but not Jesus. "Consider the lilies of the field, how they grow; they toil not, neither do they spin: yet I say unto you, that even Solomon in all his glory was not arrayed like one of these. But if God doth so clothe the grass of the field, which to-day is, and to-morrow is cast into the oven, [shall he] not much more [clothe] you, O ye of little faith?" –*Mt 6:28-30*

3 [HEAVENLY SHULAMITE:] I am my beloved's, and my beloved is mine. He quantifies among the lilies.	אני לדודי ודודי לי הרעה בשושנים: ס

3   *He quantifies* (הרעה) literally; "the-one-examining."

Hebrew poetry loves progressive word pictures. At So 2:16 this same word (הרעה) was translated as "He nourishes." It contains the untranslated idea of shepherding. Bear in mind, this is the last Shulamite, the final lily to retrieve.

He is "browsing," but what's lost in the English translation is, his "purposeful browsing." He is not selecting every flower from this garden, nor every lily. Using Abrahamic standards, Solomon is *quantifying*.

These rare lilies are measured by the "measuring reed" of God. (Mt 20:23) That's what אהבה (divine love) requires. "I know also, my God, that thou triest [quantifies] the heart, and hast pleasure in uprightness. As for me, in the uprightness of my heart I have willingly offered all these things: and now have I seen with joy thy people, that are present here, offer willingly unto thee." *–1Ch 29:17*

Jehovah recognizes the best lilies, because those lilies do not demand special attention. They do not expect special treatment that places them above the authority of non-Shunemite elders.[30] They humbly recall that some chosen men in the first century did not qualify to serve as elders, or ministerial servants. (1Tim 3:1-13; Tit 1:5-9; Jam 3:1) Some chosen disciples were even spiritual failures. (2Th 3:14)

All the earth, Shunemite or not, must stay busy teaching others about this kingdom that solves mankind's problems. The "quantified" lilies are content to work among the other disciples, as long as God wills it. (Ac 2:17)

This new Shulamite has come to life, along with her character. The musical classic, *I Swear* encapsulates the Abrahamic principles of her special relationship. "And when there's silver in your hair; Won't have to ask if I still care; 'Cause as time turns the page; My love won't age at all; I swear; By the moon and the stars in the sky; I'll be there; I swear; Like a shadow that's by your side; I'll be there; For better or worse; Till death do us part; I'll love you with every beat of my heart; I swear." *–Baker, Gary, Myers, Frank J*

BROTHERS: At this point (in *Song of Songs*), there are no remaining Earthly Shunemites. All that remains, on earth, are the Earthly Brothers. "After these things I saw, and behold, a great multitude, which no man could number, out of every nation and of [all] tribes and peoples and tongues, standing before the throne and before the Lamb, arrayed in white robes, and palms in their hands; and they cry with a great voice, saying, Salvation unto our God who sitteth on the throne, and unto the Lamb. And all the angels were standing round about the throne, and [about] the elders and the four living creatures; and they fell before the throne on their faces, and worshipped God, saying, Amen: Blessing, and glory, and wisdom, and thanksgiving, and honor, and power, and might, [be] unto our God for ever and ever. Amen. And one of the elders answered, saying unto me, These that are arrayed in white robes, who are they, and whence came they? And I say unto him, My lord, thou knowest. And he said to me, These are they that come of the great tribulation," –Re 7:9-14

Before the tribulation, however, some Brothers who do not respect her heavenly calling are described later, at So 6:13.

4 [HEAVENLY SOLOMON:] You are beautiful, my commandress, as Tirzah, lovely as Jerusalem, terrific as those with banners.	יפה את רעיתי כתרצה נאוה כירושלם אימה כנדגלות:

4 **commandress** (רעי) literally; "commandress, shepherdess, director."

The Heavenly Solomon speaks for the first time, in this chapter. Consider carefully who he is speaking to. He speaks to the former Shunemite, who was resurrected and rescued from the ravages of old age, because she courageously stood her ground.

What a refreshing victory when love survives, after the other charms have withered away. The sweetest love is what remains. I encourage you to grow old with your husband—even when everything and everyone around you is failing.

as Tirzah (כתרצה) literally; "like-Tirzah."

Tirzah was rendered as a place name, but Tirzah literally means, "delight exits." How fitting. She's leaving earth, because she proved delightful to Jehovah. (So 6:12)

Despite Tirzah's connection to a death exit, it was also described as one of the fairest cities of the land. Now, the earth is losing one of the most beautiful people who ever walked its surface—this new Shulamite.

as those with banners (כנדגלוֹה) literally; "as-the-ones-having-banners."

This frail Shulamite has become like one of the mighty warriors, mentioned earlier, at So 3:8. The reference will occur again, at So 6:10. She is "terrific," and as never before, she inspires "terror." At the same time she is wonderful—inspiring wonder.

The adjective "terrific" (#H367 אימה) is used in a calculated way. The Shulamite is a newly transformed creature that deserves fearful, terrifying, respect. After all, who is her new Father? (Ps 111:10)

In her former life, she was not so beautiful, nor was she terrific. In her former life, she was stripped of everything—everything. These rich contrasts only deepen her appreciation for Solomon's kind reception.

Banners are lofty signal-flags, not usually carried about, but stationary. Banners were usually erected atop a great city. (So 7:13)

When viewed from afar, such a lofty city was a "terrific" sight and gave pause to anyone considering attacking such a majestic city.

Yet, when seen by their own citizens, the sight encouraged them, made them feel safe. (Is 11:12; 13:2; Jer 4:6, 21) Those who stand in the shadow of God's "banners" would be wise to submit and pay tribute. (Ps 2)

5 [HEAVENLY SOLOMON:] Avert your eyes from me—they embolden me. Your hair is like a flock of goats, descending from Gilead.	הסבי עיניך מנגדי שהם הרהיבני שערך כעדר העזים שגלשו מן־הגלעד:

5 *they embolden me* (הרהיבני) literally; "they-embolden-me."

This phrase is a bridge back to So 4:9. Although, when this book repeats, it still moves the narrative forward. What she once overheard as a Shunemite, is now being directed at her—as a new Shulamite. How should we interpret the way Solomon has used this word, "embolden" (רהב)?

A verse from *Psalms* helps to clarify the proper translation. "In the day that I called thou answeredst me, Thou didst encourage [תרהבני = you-made-bold-me] me with strength in my soul." –*Ps 138:3* How many times have we heard stories of someone near death, rally, because they were strengthened by a memory?

What's vitally important, yet un-translated, is this word's (they-embolden-me) relation to rahab (רהב). Both words have the same letters, just a different pronunciation. Rahab (רהב) means "storming, or thundering."

The final Shulamite's arrival may explain the mysterious passage in *Revelation*, "And when the seven *thunders* uttered [their voices], I was about to write: and I heard a voice from Heaven saying, Seal up the things which the seven *thunders* uttered, and write them not.'" –*Re 10:4*.

Could So 6:5 be related to Re 10:4? There are several locations in this song that directly deciphers the mystery of Re 10:4-6: So 6:5; 7:9; 7:13; and 8:5. The time-line seems to match, but for some reason, the *Revelation* Messiah wanted her words to be hidden—concealed for a future time.

Could your love embolden others? I hope so. Love changes us, if we allow it to work on us. True love (אהבה) strengthens. The Heavenly Solomon knows that he will kill for this Shulamite, just as the original Solomon was emboldened to kill for Abishag—the Shunemite. (1Ki 2:24)

> **HEAVENLY SHULAMITE:** The handy-work of God overwhelmed Adam when he first saw Eve. (Ge 2:23) The handy-work of God overwhelmed John when he first saw Jesus. (Re 1:17) No wonder this Solomon-like Messiah was overwhelmed as he inspects this new Shulamite. He too is encountering the finished product of his Father's handy work. (So 6:4-9) That was the sentiment behind Adam's poetic description of Eve. "Alas, bone of my bone, flesh of my flesh."

descending from Gilead (שגלשו מנ־הגלעד) literally; "that-they-descend from Gilead."

Manasseh represents the land of those with a heavenly hope. Gilead (גלעד) is another way to describe the means by which they ascend and descend. *Gil* (גל), as in *galal* (גלל) means "to roll, or turn." If we had to describe their descending Jacob's spiral staircase, this would be the perfect Hebrew word to use. The remainder of this compound word, "עד" could mean "go on." Gilead could mean "turning ever onward—as in a spiral staircase." So, again, it's easy to connect Jacob's ladder to this word (Gilead).

Hebrew poetry loves progressive word pictures. You can't appreciate the full import of goat's hair unless you revisit Ex 25:4 and Ex 35:26. There, we learn how goat's hair was used in preparing the tabernacle (the mobile house of God) for holy service.

God presumes the reader has mastered all previous holy books. All the symbolisms, from *Genesis* to *Revelation*, are important tools to understand *Song of Songs*.

Hebrew poetry loves progressive word pictures. If Ephraim represents those with an earthly hope (Re 20:12) and Manasseh represents those with a heavenly hope (Re 21:2), then the reference to "Gilead" is an important connection between the two. (Ge 28:11-17) Manasseh owns Gilead. "And there fell ten parts to Manasseh, besides the land of Gilead and Bashan, which is beyond the Jordan." *–Jos 17:5*

If she descends from Gilead, this verse is describing her descent on Jacob's ladder. So, maybe one of the most beautiful features of the Shulamite's hair is where it descends from: Manasseh—or the Jerusalem Above.

6 [HEAVENLY SOLOMON:] Your teeth are like a flock of ewes, coming up from the wash. Each has its twin, and not one of them is alone.	שניך כעדר הרחלים שעלו מן־הרחצה שכלם מתאימות ושכלה אין בהם:

6 *Your teeth* (שניך) literally; "teeth-of-you."

This phrase is a bridge back to So 4:2. What a Shunemite once overheard for another, is now being addressed to her, as a new Shulamite. It wasn't very long ago that this Shulamite lost her teeth, due to old age. She remembers those unfortunate times. She appreciates her new body and rejoices over her new teeth. These teeth are better than any teeth shehad on earth.

This verse would be difficult to understand if you didn't understand the significance of "teeth." "Arise, O Jehovah; Save me, O my God: For thou hast smitten all mine enemies upon the cheek bone; Thou hast broken the teeth of the wicked." –*Ps 3:7*

Broken teeth can symbolize the defeated enemies of God. Having a complete set of beautiful teeth symbolizes someone protected by God.

If twin (or two) portends potential for good or bad, then maybe her teeth will accomplish both. If "teeth" are used to symbolize the ability to devour another, then the enemies of the messianic kingdom should be terrified that the combination of upper and lower teeth will devour the Satan and his attempt to undermine theocratic rulership.

That's bad for God's enemies, but good for His children.

7 [HEAVENLY SOLOMON:] Like the section of a pomegranate is your sternum, behind your veil.	כפלח הרמון רקתך מבעד לצמתך:

7 *Like the section of a pomegranate* (כפלח הרמון) literally; "like-segment-of-the-pomegranate."

This phrase is a bridge to So 4:3. What a Shunemite once overheard for another, is now being addressed to her—as a new Shulamite. The "v" between your neck and chest looks like a section of the pomegranate. Let us start with this understanding: The explanation of this verse will have very little to do with a "pomegranate," but much to do with "section."

In Hebrew culture, making a covenant always involves blood. This is where the term "cut a deal" comes from. So, severing an animal, in pieces, was legal term that any Hebrew could relate to. She was not sectioned, but the implements of her covenant were sectioned. In Hebrew *khaw-tsoth* (#H2677 חצות) means "half/section." The first time "half/section" (*khaw-tsoth*) is used in holy text, is at Ex 24:6.

Ex 24:6 is where Moses sprinkled blood on the two parties of the covenant: Moses sprinkled "half" the blood on the implements of the tabernacle and sprinkled the other "half" on the Israelites.

Now, what has that got to do with a pomegranate and the Heavenly Shulamite's sternum? The blood Moses sprinkled, looked "like" pomegranate seeds—directly over her heart.

your sternum (רקתך) literally; "flattened-shingle-of-you."

This word "thinness, as on the side of the head" (#H7541 רקה) is commonly translated as "Temple." But, that does not work in this case. The pattern, here, is one of descent: eyes first, teeth second, and then sternum. To jump back up to the Temples is a non sequitur.

The Hebrew word *rak-kath* (#H7557 רקח) means "diffusing, a beach [in the sense, a beach is where land flattens out before reaching the water's edge], expanded shingle). Between her teeth and breasts, there is only one flattened area. The Hebrew word *rak* (#H7534 רק) means "emaciated, flattened out." The flattened part of the chest where the "v" of the chest looks like a section of a halved pomegranate—the sternum.

Like ancient Israel, the Shulamite is beginning the ceremony of a covenant marriage. Only when the sacrificial blood is sprinkled, and the 10 vows are completed, will she be escorted up to her husband's house—the Jerusalem Above.

behind your veil (מבעד לצמתך) literally; "at-behind to-veil-of-you."

Where did the high priest sprinkle blood on the Ark of the Covenant? Behind the woven curtain which separated the holy from the most holy. That tabernacle curtain was "like" the woven veil described in this verse. "And behold, the veil [curtain] of the Temple was rent in two from the top to the bottom." –*Mt 27:51*

8 [HEAVENLY SOLOMON:] Sixty queens there may be, and eighty concubines, and maidens beyond number,	ששים המה מלכות ושמנים פילגשים ועלמות אין מספר:

8 *Sixty* (ששים) literally; "sixty."

Verse eight is describing earthly women—not the Heavenly Shulamite. The root word for lily (שׁוֹשַׁן) is the number, six (שׁשׁ). Not all lilies were selected to become heavenly lilies.

Although 60 could represent a human family. Here, it indicates a reoccurrence of a family-type. This is covered in more detail in the commentary back at So 3:11.

Again, the divine author plays with sequential contrasts. Queens are in a higher position, but are in lower numbers. Maidens are in the lowest position, but are in higher numbers. Solomon is comparing the 144,000 to the 288,000, and finally, to the Great Crowd which could not be numbered.

Like a pomegranate, the earth will be divided into many sections, during the millennial reign. "And Jesus said unto them, 'Verily I say unto you, that ye who have followed me, in the regeneration when the Son of man shall sit on the throne of his glory, ye also shall sit upon twelve thrones, judging the twelve tribes of Israel.'" –*Mt 19:28* "And I saw thrones, and they sat upon them, and judgment was given unto them: and [I saw] the souls of them that had been beheaded for the testimony of Jesus, and for the word of God, and such as worshipped not the beast, neither his image, and received not the mark upon their forehead and upon their hand; and they lived, and reigned with Christ a thousand years." –Re 20:4

  queens (מלכות) literally; "subordinate king-like rulers."

These are earthly queens, not heavenly queens—the 288,000. The proof is, these queens will defer to the new Shulamite, in verse nine. These may be the highest ranking on earth, but not Heaven. This word (queens מלכות) is never used for the wives of Judean, or Israelite kings (מלכים). Thus, we can be certain these queens do not come from Earthly Jerusalem or Heavenly Jerusalem.

The new Shulamite is likely to recognize these women of nobility, but these earthly queens are not likely to recognize her. This Shulamite's origins were modest. This Shulamite's life was far removed from their celebrated lives.

"For behold your calling, brethren, that not many wise after the flesh, not many mighty, not many noble, [are called]: but God chose the foolish things of the world, that he might put to shame them that are wise; and God chose the weak things of the world, that he might put to shame the things that are strong; and the base things of the world, and the things that are despised, did God choose, [yea] and the things that are not, that he might bring to nought the things that are: that no flesh should glory before God." –1Cor 1:26-29

  eighty (שמנים) literally; "eighty."

Eighty symbolizes the beginning of a new family. That thinking is based (in part) on the principle of: If seven concludes the full week, then the eighth day symbolizes the beginning of a new week. "And Moses was fourscore years old [80], and Aaron fourscore and three years old [83], when they spake unto Pharaoh." –*Ex 7:7* Why does holy text mention that Moses was "80" years old? At 80 years Moses (like this new Shulamite) was leaving Egypt and embarking on the birth of a new nation—a new age.

In any case, by invoking the number "80," it's easy to make the numeric connection that these concubines come from "the world-to-come." These "queens" will be resurrected into the Messiah's earthly Zion—not Heaven. They will be resurrected into a new cycle of family headship, as opposed to kingdom rulership, which would be characterized by four digits (1,000 for example).

concubines (פילגשים) literally; "half-wives."
For Hebrews, a concubine is referred to by the Hebrew word *pil-e-gesh* (#H6370 פילגש). Although lexicons seldom venture into the origins of this word (פילגש), it's closely related to the Aramaic word *palga-isha*, meaning "half-wife." A cognate term later appeared in Greek, as a loan word, *pallax-pallakis*, meaning "half-wife." This is also a clever and poetic connection to verse seven.

The word "concubine" is largely misunderstood by modern scholars. Israelite men were quick to acknowledge their concubine's legal rights, and concubines enjoyed the same rights as "full" wives. (Jg 20:3-5) The principal difference between a "wife" and a "concubine" is that a full-wife was bought with a bride price, while a concubine cost the husband nothing.

Yet, the earthly concubine was due the same respect and inviolability as the "full" wife. It was a dishonor, and illegal, for another man to lay hands on a concubine. David, for example, was fully dishonored when Absalom forced sex on his concubines. (2Sa 16:20-22) The point is: David was not "half" dishonored.

It was regarded as a direct blessing from God to have many children. The greatest curse was to have no children. No children equals, no matriarch. "Full" wives occasionally gave their hand maidens (as half-wives) to their husbands to overcome their own lack of children, as Leah did with Zilpah, or, Rachel did with Bilhah. (Ge 30:9; Ge 30:4) The children of these concubines, however, had equal rights with those of the "full" wife. For example: Bilhah (Jacob's concubine) gave birth to Dan and Naphtali. Zilpah (Jacob's other concubine) gave birth to Gad and Asher. Which tribe was illegitimate?

9 [HEAVENLY SOLOMON:] but my dove, my perfect one, is unique— the only daughter of her mother, the favorite of the one who bore her. [EARTHLY BROTHERS:] The maidens saw her, and called her blessed. The queens/concubines praised her.	אחת היא יונתי תמתי אחת היא לאמה ברה היא ליולדתה ראוה בנות ויאשרוה מלכות ופילגשים ויהללוה: ס

9 *unique* (אחת) literally: "unique."

This entire verse is a testimony to the uniqueness of this new Shulamite. Never before has there been such a creation, and never again will there be such a creation (as far as I know). "Having been begotten again, not of corruptible seed, but of incorruptible, through the word of God, which liveth and abideth." *–1Pe 1:23* All previous angels were male. Never had there been any daughters in Heaven—until now.

only daughter of her mother (אחת היא לאמה) literally; "only she to-mother-of-her."

Who is her heavenly mother? "The woman" gave birth to a son. (Re 12:1-2) Now, "the woman" gives birth to the entire Bride Class, who will reside with her, as "daughters."

Previously, all angels were described as male. There are no exceptions in your Bible. The only female in Heaven is the Shulamite's mother—the woman. This verse is a subtle hint of what will happen, later, at So 8:5.

It should be obvious that "the woman's" daughters are symbolized by the 12 divisions of stars, mentioned at Re 12:1.

queens/concubines (מלכות ופילגשים) literally; "queens/concubines."

These are earth's administrators—the 288,000—who are speaking, but they also praise the Shulamite (the 144,000). There is no jealousy—only love and admiration.

Queens/concubines have been noted for their beauty through the ages. The most powerful men with the greatest resources select and maintain these women, allowing them to indulge their beauty regimen. Yet, these pampered 288,000 praise the Heavenly Shulamite.

This new Shulamite did not come from such pampered ones.

> *Samuel Clemens carved this over the grave of his beloved daughter.*
>
> *Warm summer sun; shine kindly here; warm southern wind; blow softly here; green sod above; lie light, lie light; good night, dear heart; good night, good night.*
> *–Robert Richardson*

As a former Shunemite, she spent sleepless nights worrying about life's necessities, and about the welfare of her children. There was never enough. Her life was anything but a life of ease.

10 [EARTHLY BROTHERS:] Who is this that appears like the dawn, beautiful like the moon's glow, pure like the sun's radiation, terrific like the luminaries' parade?	מי־זאת הנשקפה כמו־שחר יפה כלבנה ברה כחמה אימה כנדגלות: ס

10 ***Who is this*** (מי־זאת) literally; "who this."

This verse takes us back to So 1:5. In the first chapter, the Earthly Shunemite was wandering in the cold darkness of dawn. As a new Shulamite, she now radiates warmth and life-giving light to the Earthly Brothers.

This verse is spoken by the Earthly Brothers—not the Heavenly Brothers. She has yet to ascend to Heaven. You may remember, Jesus took 40 days before he ascended to Heaven.

Note that these words parallel So 8:5. Like a divine hand-off, the new Shulamite utters these same words, "Who is this?" to a future un-named woman. Just as this verse applies to the new Shulamite, these same words will soon apply to her new mother, at So 8:5.

Song of Songs forces us to know the difference between the Daughters at Zion, and the Daughters at Jerusalem; the Earthly Brothers, and the Heavenly Brothers; the mother of the great crowd, and the mother of the Jerusalem Above.

There are many mysteries that are yet to unfold. She is not the moon—but like the moon's glow. She is not the sun—but like the sun's radiation. She is not the luminaries—but like the luminaries' parade.

It's fairly easy to identify the person in question. The word "moon" (ירח) is not in this Hebrew verse. Instead, the divine author uses the word, "moon's glow" (כלבנה). The root word *la-bon-ah* (לבנה) is the feminine form of *laban*. So, we know this can't be the masculine Solomon. The person addressed in this verse would have to be female.

Also, the Hebrew word *labonah* (לבנה) connects this Shulamite to the six original matriarchs of Israel: Sarah, Rebekah, Rachel, Leah, Zilpah, and Bilhah. All six matriarchs are connected by one Bible character, Laban (לבנ). Laban means "white" as in the "white" glow of the moon (לבנה). Laban was the nephew of Sarah; the brother of Rebekah; the father of Rachel and Leah. Laban also provided his daughters with their own slaves (Zilpah and Bilhah).

So, by calling the Shulamite *labanah* (לבנה), this connected the Shulamite to the house of Laban. The divine author forces the connection.

luminaries parade (כנדגלוֹת) literally; "like-the-ones-proceeding."

The word "stars" (#H3556 כוֹכב) is not present in this Hebrew text, yet many translations include "stars." They shouldn't, since prophetic time is part of the subtext. Prophetic time is calculated by lunar (luminary) cycles—not "stars." Angels are referred to as "stars." (Jg 5:20) The Angelic Brothers who came to fetch her (So 5:7) strike terror, like "stars," but angels are not "luminaries." Angels are stars.

This new Shulamite is also an angel. She too is terrific, like "stars," yet, she was never described as a "star." She was described as someone "like" the moon (לבנה). In Joseph's dream, his brothers symbolized the 12 tribes of Israel who would one day bow down to a greater Joseph. (Ge 37:9-10)

Joseph's son, Manasseh, was the son with the smaller numbers—as the queens were described with the smaller numbers—as Jesus described a "little flock" with smaller numbers. Is it all beginning to connect yet? Shulamites are few in number—rare. (Lk 12:32; Re 14:1)

The Heavenly Shulamite carries herself like the luminaries on parade. Some women carry themselves so flawlessly and effortlessly that outsiders forget how their mannerisms were formed.

No one is born with a regal disposition. The cruelties of elementary school quickly does away with that. No, if a woman has retained her elegance and charm beyond elementary school, it can only be attributed to her rejection of today's Western "culture." She deliberately re-designed herself by some other set of standards—regal standards.

NUMERICS: *sun's radiation* (חמה) literally; "heat, radiation, warmth of this raised (resurrected) woman." (Ps 19:6) This is the first and only use in *Song of Songs*. At the *remez* level, one points to something that emanates from Jehovah. (De 6:4) Now, Jehovah is her eternal Father. That will transform her into the sister of Solomon. Now, she fits the description of "sister bride."

11 [HEAVENLY SHULAMITE:] I went down to the grove of nut trees to look at the new growth of the valley, to see if the vines had budded, or if the pomegranates were in bloom.	אל־גנת אגוז ירדתי לראות באבי הנחל לראות הפרחה הגפן הנצו הרמנים:

11 *nut trees* (אגוֹז) literally; "nut-tree."

Post-biblical Hebrew would translate אגוֹז as "walnut tree." These trees may well have been walnut trees, but that word is not explicitly stated. Walnut trees are currently cultivated in Galilee, Lebanon and Mount Hermon. The Jewish historian, Josephus, said walnut trees grew in abundance around the Sea of Galilee, in the first century A.D.[31]

The walnut is an attractive tree that serves many functions. The walnut's fragrant leaves provide excellent shade. The wood is tightly-grained and prized by cabinet makers. The fruit of the walnut tree is encased in a husk containing tannic acid. When boiled, tanic acid produces a rich-brown dye. The nutmeats are delicious and can be pressed to produce a quality oil nearly equal to olive oil.

The more we describe this tree, the more we recognize these qualities are also human characteristics. We should all watch God's creation and find parallel characteristics.

Like Jesus who remained on earth for 40 days before ascending to Heaven, she is still on earth. Now that she has been resurrected, shouldn't her first words be, "Thank you."? Instead, her first concern was for her new children.

Had her first words been, "Thank you," then we would see where her real priorities were. Her focus was not on garnering compliments, but on her children who have also been discarded, marginalized, and demeaned. Are they blossoming? The words that were concealed earlier may have been thundering cries of concern for her babies—The Great Corwd, which no man was able to number. (Re 7:9)

There is no other event on earth worth her attention. Her thoughts are with you—children of the kingdom.

new growth of (באבי) literally; "at-new-growths-of."

Jesus also spent 40 days examining and encouraging the earthly church—before ascending to Heaven. Obviously, he too was interested in the "new growth." (Ac 1:9-11) Since father (אבא), spring (אביב) and new growth (באבי) are all grammatically related, the implication seems to be how the Father's teachings are sprouting among his children who were like nut trees.

Like her new husband's Father, the new Shulamite is keenly interested in earth's "new growth." Notice what Jesus said after he had ascended to Heaven. "But the eleven disciples went into Galilee, unto the mountain where Jesus had appointed them. And when they saw him, they worshipped

[him]; but some doubted. And Jesus came to them and spake unto them, saying, All authority hath been given unto me in Heaven and on earth. Go ye therefore, and make disciples of all the nations, baptizing them into the name of the Father and of the Son and of the Holy Spirit.'" –*Mt 28:16-20* (compare Mt 28:16-20 to Eph 1:20-21)

Again, as an appointed king, in the year 33 A.D., King Jesus was ready to start taking wives which would form the Jerusalem Above. (Mt 28:18) And based on this, Paul claimed Christ's brides already existed in his day. (Gal 4:26)

The identity of this hard-working "daughter" is not new information—just overlooked information. "'And behold, I send forth the promise of my Father upon you: but tarry ye in the city, until ye be clothed with power from on high. And he led them out until [they were] over against Bethany: and he lifted up his hands, and blessed them. And it came to pass, while he blessed them, he parted from them, and was carried up into Heaven." –*Lk 24:49-51*

Why did Jesus lead these Earthly Shunemites to Bethany? The Hebrew word *bethany* (בת אני) means "I am the daughter." So, as he ascended, he looked down at those standing at, "I am the daughter." As we learned a few verses back, at verse nine, the Heavenly Shulamite is "the only daughter of her mother."

The Shunemite was always a potential daughter. How appropriate on three counts: (1) A Shulamite would be the only full-daughter. (2) Lazarus was the first person resurrected by Jesus. Lazarus was from Bethany. (3) Jesus sent the message for potential "daughters" to remain there (on earth), until they are "clothed with power."

As the above examples demonstrate, the Heavenly Shulamite and Jesus share a common interest: The growth of their religious family. So, like Jesus, this "sister bride" lingers to admire the "new growth" before ascending to Heaven.

the valley (הנחל) literally; "the-valley."

A dark valley may be rich with grass, but it also depends on the care of a shepherd. It's a sad truth, earth's Brotherly leadership is painfully neglectful of those who fall behind, due to health and old age.

Nothing displeases Solomon more. Abandoned by Mother Israel, David was faced with this same darkness. David found security in the knowledge that he had a fine shepherd. David declared: "Yea, though I walk through the valley of the shadow of death, I will fear no evil; for thou art with me; Thy rod and thy staff, they comfort me." –*Ps 23: 4*

Those who are no longer producing in the congregation are too often marginalized and forgotten. I have seen it.

12 [HEAVENLY SHULAMITE:] I do not know this soul. My spiritual name qualifies me to be among the royal chariots of my prince.	לא ידעתי נפשי שמתני מרכבות עמי־נדיב:

12 ***not know this soul*** (לא ידעתי נפשי) literally; "no know-my soul-of-me."

This sentence is commonly mistranslated as, "Before I realized it." Yet, we find something very close at Job 9:21, נפשי לא אדע which other translations render as, "not know my soul." How odd that the words from Job 9:21 are rendered differently here, by most translators. They ignore context.

The Shulamite has just been resurrected. She is dumfounded by her new soul (נפש). Only moments before (So 5:7) she was a human soul—flesh and blood. How else could a new spirit person describe themselves? They are a new creation. (Is 66:18-22)

No matter. The royal chariots convey the idea that she will now be carted away from the sad life she once knew on earth. The royal chariots are part of her thrilling escort to the "new Heavens"—the Jerusalem Above. (Gal 4:25-26)

My spiritual name (שמתני) literally; "name-connected-to-me."

This word is unknown to Hebrew translators. A similar Hebrew word *shoo-maw-thee* (#H8126 שמתי) means "patron." It comes from an unused word that means "garlic smell." Our word, however, is a compound word, *shoo-maw-than-ee* (שמתני). The additional Hebrew letter *nun* (נ) adds the idea of a connection. Connection to what? Her new family "name" (שם).

An additional problem for translators is, there is no biblical Hebrew word for "spiritual." In modern Israel, the word *ruakh-ani-yut* was coined to create an equivalent for the English word, "spiritual." An ancient Israelite would have to create a physical equivalent to something invisible, but blatantly present to the other senses.

No other commentary supports this conclusion, however. I've concluded this, because she has already employed a vocabulary of non-visual metaphors in earlier texts, at So 2:13, 3:6, 5:5, and 5:13.

What I am about to say may be the most important point found in *Song of Songs*. The last Shulamite has taken Solomon's name, and she knows what that means. Most Christians don't know what that means—and I can prove it: What did Jesus mean when he instructed his disciples to pray in his name?

Listen to any Christian prayer. They routinely conclude with: "We say this in the name of Jesus. Amen." Is that what Jesus meant? Not one Christian prayer in the four gospels ends with "Amen." Not even the Lord's Model Prayer ends with "amen." Not one prayer in the entire Bible ends with "in the name of Jesus. Amen." Did every Bible character get it wrong?

Taking the name of your husband should be life altering. Maybe this, "not knowing" the Hebrew meaning of "name" has spilled over to our generation in the form of Christian divorces. The very same people who end their prayers with, "in the name of Jesus" are divorcing in the same percentages as the non-religious.

The Shulamite has gained her new credentials by embracing, and living faithfully, in the root of Solomon's name: *shalom*. Peace means building bridges. Peace means adopting his ideology, and embracing his family—and his family values.

If wives do this properly, people will see that their lives are different, superior to their former life. (Lk 15:8-10) Her quiet but powerful example began with Abraham and Sarah, and will end with the coming Messiah and his Shulamites.

Now, the Shulamite belongs to Solomon (*shlomo* שלמו). Thus, her related name "Shulamite" (שולמית).

However we render this verse, the Heavenly Solomon gave her a new name, unknown to anyone else—until now. "He that hath an ear, let him hear what the Spirit saith to the churches. To him that overcometh, to him will I give of the hidden manna, and I will give him a white stone, and upon the stone a new name written, which no one knoweth but he that receiveth it." –*Re 2:17* It's not what we end our prayers with that's important, it's whether we conform to the "name" of this divine family.

13 [EARTHLY BROTHERS:] Come back, come back, Shulamite. Come back, come back, that we may gaze upon you! [HEAVENLY SOLOMON:] Why? Would you gaze upon the Shulamite, as on the dance of sickness at the Mahanaim?	שובי שובי השולמית שובי שובי ונחזה־בך מה־תחזו בשולמית כמחלת המחנים:

13 *Come back* (שׁוּבִי) literally; "come-back."

Given Solomon's open invitation at So 5:1, the Earthly Brothers' response seems oddly inappropriate. Why would her former Earthly Brothers ask her to "come back" . . . twice?

If two denotes potential for good, or bad, then beware! If the Shulamite turns back, she will become as double-minded as Lot's wife. All we need to do is remind ourselves why Jeroboam, an Ephraimite, made two golden calves. Jeroboam was the first king of the ten-tribe nation. But, his two Temples were invalid. (1Ki 12:27-28) "Come back, come back," Jeroboam was saying.

Jesus responded in the negative, but as politely as he could, at Joh 4:22.

If these Earthly Brothers celebrated her wedding as they should, why stop the wedding parade, or create "doubt" in the bride? The phrase, "come back," is an improper request to a bride. But, since this phrase is repeated four times (in the original Hebrew), what does "four" mean?

Delta (Δ) is the fourth letter in the Greek alphabet. Like the Hebrew *dalet* (ד), the Greek *delta* (Δ) conveys the same idea of displacement, or conversion (review your physics). *Delta* (Δ) even looks like the crystal prism Isaac Newton used to "convert" sunlight into a rainbow. He also took a second prism and "converted" the rainbow back into a single shaft of white light.

But what about Hebrew numbers? The idea of "conversion" stays with *dalet* (ד). For example: When you walk through your door (דלה pronounced, *dalet*), you are "converted" from outside to inside, or inside to outside. (Mt 7:7-8; Re 3:20)

This small group of Earthly Brothers don't like her conversion. You may be surprised that many such Earthly Brothers are hiding among us (rather than working among us). They use "church" the way the ancient Israelites used the Ark of the Covenant against the Philistines.

Those Israelites cheapened its value by using it as a good-luck charm. The ploy was so offensive that God had them soundly defeated, their High Priest killed, and the Ark of the Covenant stolen. (1Sa 4:1-3) All that, because they were fraudulent "Brothers" hiding within God's family. In this verse, these are so-called "Brothers" hiding within God's family—brothers in name only.

So, why would these so-called "Brothers" not want her to go away? They would be losing a follower, a contributor to their household. For some, the church is the be-all and end-all. They commit an idolatry of religion over their religion's God.

Would you gaze (תחזו) literally; "would-you-gaze."

The Hebrew word *te-khe-zoo* (תחזו) "would-you-gaze," is a masculine plural. This indicates the speaker is Solomon and he is speaking to Earthly Brothers. This compound word is constructed on top of *khaw-zaw* (#H2372 חזה). *Khaw-zaw* (חזה) means "gaze, contemplate, have a vision, prophecy."

If idolatry means giving something, or someone, a prominence they don't deserve, then these Earthly Brothers have a problem. Not only are they over estimating the role of church membership in God's arrangement, but they are looking "back" while God's heavenly organization is moving forward. (2Cor 3:12-15)

Moving forward is difficult for some. Jesus met with the same resistance as a human. "And Peter took him, and began to rebuke him, saying, 'Be it far from thee, Lord: this shall never be unto thee. But he turned, and said unto Peter, 'Get thee behind me, Satan: thou art a stumbling-block unto me: for thou mindest not the things of God, but the things of men.'" – *Mt 16:22-23* Avoid pointless debates when Earthly Brothers have neither the wit to speak with precision, nor the discretion to hold their tongue.

Lack of appreciation is one thing, but idolatry is quite another. Don't lose that role that sings in God's big family. To delay the bride for any reason is worse than rude, it would be a sin against the Holy Spirit. In the future, these Heavenly Shulamites may re-visit these Earthly Brothers in the future, but the Earthly Brothers must never interfere with the duties of this bride. It was healthy that you left our family for your husband. Likewise, it's healthy for these two groups to part.

dance of sickness (מחלת) literally; "dance-of-sickness."
The Heavenly Solomon doesn't like these Earthly Brothers' response. In the Old Testament, several expressions are translated as "dancing." The Hebrew verb *khool* (#H2342 חול), which basically means "whirl; turn," is also rendered "dance." *Ma-khole* (#H4234 מחול), means "dance." *Mek-o-law* (#H4246 מחלה), means "circle dance."

Verse 13, however, uses none of these Hebrew words. Our Hebrew word is *makh-al-ath* (#H4257 מחלת) which means "sickness, probably (as some commentators have said) the title of a popular song." Context, however, blends both ideas. Whether they mourn her, or not, this is still an inappropriate mourning. "Inappropriate" may not go far enough—it's sick. (Joh 3:29)

Mahanaim (המחנים) literally; "the two-camps."
Mahanaim is a location on the other side of the Jordan. Crossing the river Jordan has long been a metaphor for going to Heaven. After Jacob parted company with Laban (and before he crossed back over into the Promised Land), he encountered a company of angels. Jacob then called the place "Mahanaim." (Ge 32:1-2)

We too are on a Jacob-like journey, on the verge of the Promised Land. "Two Camps" may allude to a human camp and an angelic camp.

If Manasseh represents the heavenly class and Ephraim represents the earthly class (two camps), it's interesting that the first group of sisters to own property in Beersheba were from the tribe of Manasseh.

One of those sisters was Mahlah. Did Mahlah dance when her sisters were granted property rights? Who can say? Holy text is silent on the matter, but the root word has been invoked by the divine author, for some reason.

The Jewish sage, Maimonides stated, "A dance of the two companies' alludes to the joy of the theophany in Mount Sinai in which both the camp of Israel and the camp of God is intimated in the two following verses: 'Moses brought forth the people out of the camp to meet God' (Ex 19:17), and 'The chariots of God are myriads, even thousands upon thousands; the Lord is among them, as in Sinai, in holiness' (Ps 68:18)"[32]

Any time the camp of man joins with the camp of God, a divine intervention is about to take place, and that's something these so-called "Brothers" should *not* interfere with.

Let me end this chapter with a story. A young, frazzled, mother closed her bedroom door, seeking a few minutes of solitude. Anxious for her mother's company, the daughter slipped inside. To keep her daughter occupied, the mother picked up a magazine, and found a picture of the Planet Earth. She tore the picture into 40 tiny squares.

"Here, put this puzzle of earth back together." The mother's plan to preoccupy her daughter lasted only seconds. The mother couldn't believe how quickly her daughter reassembled the complicated picture.

"It was easy," explained the young girl. "There was a little girl's face on the back side. When I put her together, the whole world came together."

Chapter 7:33
Final Parade to Heaven

Picture the rambunctious, lighthearted, trip back to the groom's house. That describes chapter seven. You will hear compliments, promises, and plans that are common wedding banter. This is an ecstatic couple being escorted by some very joyous angels. These Angelic Brothers are well-intended, but not sure how they can help. Listen to their confusion.

7 [HEAVENLY BROTHERS:] How beautiful your feet in sandals, daughter of a noble one! Your graceful legs are like jewels, from the hands of an expert.	ז מה־יפו פעמיך בנעלים בת־נדיב חמוקי ירכיך כמו חלאים מעשה ידי אמן:

    1 ***feet in sandals*** (פעמיך בנעלים) literally; "feet-of-you in-the-sandals."
    Before you say "I do," there's something you must know: Most women can survive an insult, but not many can keep their equilibrium after a compliment. A woman of class will.
    The Shulamite's grasp of the big picture remains intact, despite this shower of compliments. Compliments can sway allegiances. Never forget your number-one loyalty. This new Shulamite is still puzzling over her new "soul," that she does not recognize. (So 6:12) While the new Shulamite comes to terms with her new self, she is showered with compliments.
    Yet, this new bride never breaks formation. She didn't let her Earthly Brothers delay her, neither will she let her Angelic Brothers delay her. She was formed from the "crucible of suffering," which anchors her in humility.

What does a "sandal" mean, to a Hebrew? Under Hebrew law, a widow without children had no right to property. Without a son, she couldn't secure her deceased husband's property rights. She could, however, obtain a son through brother-in-law marriage. If the brother-in-law refused, she would ceremonially remove his sandal . . . and slap his face with it. (De 25:9-10) Removing the sandal relates to an inheritance dispute. (Ru 4:7-10)

The new Shulamite's feet, however, are snugly placed within her "sandals." She is no widow. She has many children, and her property is well secured.

The direction of the Heavenly Brothers' praise goes from the bottom of her feet to the top of her head. Notice the path: feet and legs (verse one); navel and waist (verse two); breasts (verse three); neck, eyes and nose (verse four); head and hair (verse five). Their compliments are ascending—which is a big clue, as to the direction they are traveling.

daughter of a noble one (בת־נדיב) literally; "daughter noble-one."

The previous chapter informed us that the Shulamite is an "only daughter." Now, we are progressively informed that she is the daughter of a "noble." The Hebrew word *naw-deeb* (#H5081 נדיב) means "noble, magnanimous; willing one, generous one." This same Hebrew word is properly translated elsewhere as "noble." At Nu 21:18 נדיב = noble; at Ps 83:11 נדיב = noble; at Pr 8:16 נדיב = noble; at Is 13:3 נדיב = noble; and many other texts.

Truly, *Song of Songs* is a book for daughters. She is the daughter of a royal couple, but being their child requires noble behavior. Nobles (נדיב) take the wisdom of Heaven to show us how to walk it, on plain soil.

With the same regal behavior of her husband, she walks the walk. She is a daughter with a clear destination. This is further proof that she has mastered the song.

hands of an expert (ידי אמן) literally; "hand-of-me an-expert."

This verse expands on the commentary back at So 4:1 and So 6:9. How appropriate, since this new Shulamite is about to meet her "noble" parents, in chapter eight.

The Hebrew word *khaw-rawsh* (#H2796 חרש) is most frequently translated as "craftsman," but that's *not* our word. The Hebrew word in this verse, is *aw-mawn* (#H542 אמן). It means "an expert, cunning workman." The Heavenly Solomon has already seen this "expert" at work. In his pre-human existence, Jesus served an apprenticeship with this "expert."

That apprenticeship is detailed in *Proverbs*: "Before the mountains were settled, Before the hills was I brought forth; While as yet he had not made the earth, nor the fields, Nor the beginning of the dust of the world. When he established the Heavens, I was there: When he set a circle upon the face of the deep, When he made firm the skies above, When the fountains of the deep became strong, When he gave to the sea its bound, That the waters should not transgress his commandment, When he marked out the foundations of the earth; Then I was by him, [as] a master workman [אמון]." –*Pr 8:25-30*

2 [HEAVENLY BROTHERS:] Your insides are a rounded goblet that never lacks blended wine. Your waist is a bundling of wheat, encircled by lilies.	שררך אגן הסהר אל־יחסר המזג בטנך ערמת חטים סוגה בשושנים:

2 ***Your insides*** (שררך) literally; "insides-of-you."

The "insides" being discussed is not her stomach, but her womb. This thought is a progressive connection to So 5:4 where her "womb groans with mankind." This verse is also connected to So 1:4. We learned that a vineyard could be fine citizens of the kingdom. Wine, that comes from this vineyard, symbolizes highly developed children of the kingdom. "Blended wine," however, was served in the courts of royalty or the powerful—a likely reference to the 288,000. This also hints at another form of wealth: children. (see "wealth" So 8:7)

Incorporating the word, "inside" was deliberate. How appropriate that the first matriarch's name meant, "princess." "And Sarah [princess] laughed *within* herself, saying, After I am waxed old shall I have pleasure, my lord being old also?" – *Ge 18:13* "Inside" Sarah was the rootstock of "Israel."

encircled by lilies (סוגה בשושנים) literally; "being-encircled in-lilies."

"Rounded" (אגן) and "encircled" (סוגה) appears nowhere else in the Bible. This Shulamite is just as rare. Within the Hebrew letter, *gimmel* (ג), is a hidden idea that conveys precious cargo. This *gimmel* (ג) appears in both words.

As you recall from earlier chapters, the Heavenly Solomon only selects "rare" lilies. Rare in what way? The lilies Solomon selects will be like the solitary "sheaf" in Josheph's dream. Joseph's symbolic sheaf stood erect, and his brothers *"encircled"* the sheaf, and bowed down.

This Shulamite was also like the "moon" in Joseph's second dream. The moon not only *circles* the earth, but as earth follows the sun, that journeys deeper into the universe, the moon's orbit appears to *spiral* like a grape vine. In the second dream, the sun, moon, and 11 stars, bowed down to Joseph. (Ge 37:5-11: Mt 28:16)

3 [HEAVENLY BROTHERS:] Your two breasts are like two fawns, twins of a gazelle.	שני שדיך כשני עפרים תאמי צביה:

3 ***breasts are like*** (שדיך) literally; "breasts-like."

She needs to give the milk of truth, and her children need to partake. Otherwise, her children will succumb to the dangers that lie ahead. Notice how quickly three references are made to, "two." Two is a potentially bad number, to a Hebrew. Remember, two has the potential of good and bad.

Did Aaron's son, Nadab, sin when he offered an extra (second) sacrifice? If one sacrifice is good, isn't two better? "And Nadab and Abihu, the sons of Aaron, took each of them his censer, and put fire therein, and laid incense thereon, and offered strange fire before Jehovah, which he had not commanded them. And there came forth fire from before Jehovah, and devoured them, and they died before Jehovah." – *Le 10:1-2*

The two aspects of her breasts are not responsible for the entire growth process of her earth children. Milk is only prescribed for a brief period of time. Good mothers never permit "milk" to become the primary source of her children's education.

gazelle (צביה) literally; "gazelle."

Fawns (עפרים) and gazelles (צביה) are mentioned in quick succession. Yet, fawns are rarely mentioned in the Bible. Gazelle is the more common description for a small antelope. The gazelle that Israelites were most familiar with was, the fawn-colored, Gazelle Arabica.

Those who take milk from this mountain-dwelling Shulamite are taking the same nourishment she has taken from her mother—the woman. (Re 12:6)

Beware Earthly Shunemite! If you claim you are the source of scriptural milk, you will be every bit as guilty as Moses when he struck the rock, twice, and claimed that *he* (Moses) gave them water. Scriptural milk is from "the woman," not the Shunemite.

4 [HEAVENLY BROTHERS:] Your neck is like an ivory tower. Your eyes are the pools of Heshbon, by the gate of Bath Rabbim. Your nose is like the tower of Lebanon, facing toward Damascus.	צוארך כמגדל השן עיניך ברכות בחשבון על־שער בת־רבים אפך כמגדל הלבנון צופה פני דמשק:

4 *ivory tower* (כמגדל השן) literally; "the-ivory like-tower-of."

The Hebrew word for "ivory" is *shen* (#H8127 שן) and *shen-hab-beem* (#H8143 שן הבים). The latter means "teeth." Though hard, ivory is highly elastic and easily carved. Although hard, its fine grain makes it pleasing to the touch and has a finish that's remarkably durable.

Ancient earthly Israel was described as a hardheaded wife. (Ezk 3:7) The angelic Brothers are praising this Shulamite as someone teachable—not someone with a head like flint that cannot be inscribed.

The Shulamite has received a protective mark, etched on her forehead. When wives make their minds like flint, the name of God cannot be etched on their forehead.

The mention of "ivory" continues the theme of wealth. Ivory has long been associated with the luxuries of life—fine art, elegant furnishings, treasured riches. Solomon's ships brought ivory, once every three years. (1Ki 10:22; 2Ch 9:21) Befitting his glory and greatness, Solomon "made a great ivory throne." (1Ki 10:18; 2Ch 9:17)

Psalms mentions "the grand ivory palace" in connection with stringed instruments of music. (Ps 45:8) King Ahab built a palace with it, creating a veritable "house of ivory." (1Ki 22:39) In the days of Amos, wealthy homes and extravagant couches were constructed with ivory. (Am 3:15; 6:4) Ivory conveys one of the Shulamite's royal qualities.

Heshbon (בחשבון) literally; "in intelligence." Heshbon is a city in Israel, about 12 miles southwest of Amman. The Hebrew word *khesh-bone* (#H2808 חשבן) means "intelligence, reason, devise." It connects to verse one of this chapter. In verse one, we discovered where she learned her cleverness. She was formed by Amman (an expert). "Hands of an expert," *aw-mawn* (#H542 אמן) identifies who made her.

By looking into the Shulamite's eyes, her angelic Brothers could see the depth of her intelligence. (So 4:9) That's an important asset during her husband's millennial reign, when she helps to bring her children (those from her "insides") back to perfection.

Bath Rabbim (בת־רבים) literally; "daughter of-leaders."

Bath-rabbim is also the name of a gate in Heshbon. By no coincidence, it faces toward the city of Amman. There are many hidden messages in this verse. The word "gate" portends death. Simon states, "We do not find the image of a gate with reference to the land of living, but only with reference to the land of the dead."[34]

How did this Shulamite become a "daughter?" She had to die. Her dying and going to Heaven must have something to do with "apple." (So 2:3; 8:5) Read on. It's coming.

Lebanon (הלבנון) literally; "the-whiteness-connecting-man."

The six founding matriarchs (Sarah, Rebekah, Leah, Rachel, Bilhah, and Zilpah) were all from Haran. These white mountains of Lebanon stood between Jerusalem and Haran.

The same verse incorporates the word "nose." In ancient times the punishment for adulteresses was, cutting off the offenders "nose." Oholibah [אהליבה = my-shunned-tabernacle] was the name used to symbolize the adulterous two-tribe kingdom of Israel. Like an outraged husband, Jehovah severed Israel's nose—Israel's anointed kings (who were like the "very breath of our nostrils"). (Lam 4:20) By contrast, Jehovah has a long nose. (Ex 4:6-17)

Not only was the beautiful "nose" of this Shulamite intact, but she had it turned toward Lebanon (north/heavenward). All direction references in the Bible, assume you are standing in Jerusalem. So, north is up (on a map), symbolically heavenward.

5 [HEAVENLY BROTHERS:] Your head crowns you, like Mount Carmel. Your hair is like royal weaving. The king is held captive by its tresses.	ראשך עליך ככרמל ודלת ראשך כארגמן מלך אסור ברהטים:

5 *like Mount Carmel* (ככרמל) literally; "like-crimson."

The entire range measures about 30 miles, stretching from the Mediterranean across to the Plain of Dothan. But, where did it get its personality from? Was it the physical attributes of the range, or did its personality come from the people from Carmel?

Nabal's wife (Abigail the Carmelitess) used her wisdom to restrain David from bloodguilt. (1Sa 25:2-35) Abigail later became David's wife. (1Sa 25:36-42) Elijah's successor, Elisha, was at Mount Carmel when a woman of Shunem (a Shunemite) came seeking his help for her dead child. (2Ki 4:8, 20, 25) See a theme?

Elisha dutifully resurrected this faithful Shunemite's child. Armageddon is so much more than killing the evil sons of the Satan. It's also about resurrecting the legitimate sons of the Messiah, and his Shulamite. The history of Mount Carmel helps us to understand why it was placed in this verse. Its history fits the story line.

like royal weaving (כארגמן מלך) literally; "like-the-weaving king."

David commented on this "royal weaving" before *Song of Songs* was ever written. "For thou didst form my inward parts: Thou didst cover me [תסכני] in my mother's womb." –*Ps 139:13*

The Hebrew word *tah-skon-ee* (תסכני) literally means "you-knit-me-together." What was translated above as, "cover me" is actually, תסכני (you-knit-me-together). A more literal translation would be, "For you created the inmost being of me. You knit me together in the womb of my mother. I praise you because, in a terrific way, I was awesomely made in a terrific way, as my soul knows well." Like David, the Shulamite was "woven" into creation by an expert creator. (So 7:1)

tresses (ברהטים) literally; "by-the-tresses."

A comparable use of "tresses" (דלה) can be found at Is 38:12. "Tresses" comes from the Hebrew root word meaning "to hang down" (דלל). The fabric described in *Isaiah* has yet to be woven into a garment. So, it hangs off to the side, waiting for the weaver to create something terrific.

What does "hair" mean? Job cut his hair to symbolize his desolate condition. He lost his children and property. So, he cut his hair. (Job 1:20) This new Shulamite is not desolate and had so many children that no man was able to number them. (Re 7:9) Her hair was long, and hung luxuriantly. No wonder these angels are impressed with her prospects.

Ezekiel cut his hair to symbolize the Job-like tragedies that would befall Israel. (Ezk 5:1-13) The hair of ancient Israel was a pathetic sight at her death, in 70 A.D. In contrast, this Shulamite has stunning hair, and her faithful children will be the new custodians of the earth. (Ge 1:28)

6 [HEAVENLY SOLOMON:] How beautiful you are, and how pleasing, O love, with your delights!	מה־יפית ומה־נעמת אהבה בתענוגים:

6 *love* (אהבה) literally; "divine-love."

What enables disciples to endure severe trials? Love. Such love goes beyond just giving up material advantages. It keeps pace with the ever-evolving family needs. (Lk 9:24-25)

When you read holy text, it presumes your knowledge of previously text. For instance: Many foolish disciples equate love with the degree of heat in their relationship. Will that be the standard? I hope not. It wasn't that way with Sarah.

What happens when one of you is no longer "hot" looking? In that case, foolish mates might feel justified to end a marriage. Their love for an outsider may generate more "heat." Those types abandon marriage mates, disrupt the lives of their children, and ignore the commands of God, on the strength of an abortifacient (*notice the big word?*) feeling.

That kind of love is not principled love. That's not deep-rooted divine love (אהבה). That type of love may feel "hot," but it's counterfeit. Would you applaud a friend who left her husband? What if she boasted that she "found someone new who finally appreciates her."? The matriarchs would never condone such a behavior.

No emotion is permanent, nor is emotion a standard to build a life on. (Pr 28:26) There will be times when you will fall out of love. The good news is, that too is temporary.

To succeed in marriage requires falling in and out of love many times—but always with the same person. You must develop the patience and motivation to fall back in love. Behavior first, emotions follow thereafter. I'm not asking you to do anything you haven't already done for your religion. Your religious commitment also requires re-motivation—even temporary pretending. Does it not?

"And this is love, that we should walk after his commandments. This is the commandment, even as ye heard from the beginning, that ye should walk in it." –2Joh 6 This verse tells Christians that when they no longer "feel it," keep walking.

Some inappropriate forms of love get out of control and become an idolatry of desire over good. A flock of birds can be a great example of group wisdom. We marvel when we see a flock weave through the sky, in and out of geometric order. Yet, beyond their conformity is a bigger mission.

From one part of the world to another, the flock works in unity for the greater good. "Flocking" is a temporary vehicle. Groups (social, professional, or kingdom) are never permanent. (1Cor 15:22-28) They simply get us from one place to another, but all of us are alone with God, in-between.

So, always be teaching your children to be independent, responsible, adults—yet shrewd enough to utilize the benefits of a "flock."

with your delights (בתענוגים) literally; "with-your-delights."

True happiness does not come from wealth or power—at least that's what Solomon's God taught him. No one who loves money ever has enough. (Ec 5:9)

Hard work contributes to family happiness, but sacrifice, growth from God's correction, and discipline makes the sage. The truly happy person trusts in God (Pr 16:20), delights in His law (Ps 112:1), and invites re-adjustment by God's holy word (Ps 128:1).

7 [HEAVENLY SOLOMON:] Your stature is likened to that of the palm, and your breasts likened to clusters of fruit.	זאת קומתך דמתה לתמר ושדיך לאשכלות׃

7 *to the palm* (לתמר) literally; "to-palm."

One Hebrew word for palm is *taw-mar* (#H8558 תמר). Palms are often markers of a hidden oases. A welcome sight for desert travelers. (Ex 15:27) The long taproot enables the palm to reach deep water, unreachable by other plants. So, the palm can exist in a seemingly waterless region.

That's a fitting description for the Shulamite. How did she attain her stature? From an unseen source of water. While others were dying of thirst, she was drawing deep truths from holy text, that no one else could see.

The offering of lofty palm fronds to the Messiah evidently symbolized that he walked in elevated places. It also symbolized the crowd's submission to his elevated position. The "great crowd" (non-Shulamites) of Re 7:9-10 are likewise pictured with palm branches in their hands, for the Lamb.

clusters of fruit (לאשכלות) literally; "to-clusters-of-fruit."

The Hebrew word for cluster is *esh-kole* (#H811 אשכול). It means "to bunch, as in bunching a number of dates." The vital point is, she transformed the water into fruit. The second point is its location. The fruitage of her breasts are elevated. In a previous commentary (So 7:3) we learned her children must climb to her food, or do without.

8 [HEAVENLY SOLOMON:] I said, "I will climb the palm tree; I will take hold of its fruit." May your breasts be like the clusters of the vine, the fragrance of your breath, like apples,	אמרתי אעלה בתמר אחזה בסנסניו ויהיו־נא שדיך כאשכלות הגפן וריח אפך כתפוחים:

8 *I will climb* (אעלה) literally; "I-will-climb."

This is a reference to the final verse in *Song of Songs* (So 8:14). The Heavenly Solomon regularly goes away and regularly comes back to his Shulamite. If she will wait, he will return. If she visits earth, he will climb down Jacob's ladder. If she waits in Heaven, he will climb up Jacob's ladder.

He claims, before all, that he will make the effort. She demands, before all (So 8:14), that he make the effort. She tests his claim, at So 8:14. "Be like a gazelle."

In the Bible, there is a reward at the end of every sentence. It may take you decades to deduce its wisdom, but it's worth the wait. Your marriage is the same way. A wife who masters patience, masters everything.

its fruit (בסנסניו) literally; "of-fruits-of-him."

It's important to acknowledge where these fruits of the spirit come from. That insight will teach us which qualities make the Shulamite desirable. "But the fruit of the Spirit is love, joy, peace, longsuffering, kindness, goodness, faithfulness, meekness, self-control; against such there is no law." –*Ga 5:22-23*

Godly love is a fruit that cannot exist apart from knowledge and service to God. Godly love cannot exist without meditation, or without living a life of appreciation. (Ps 77:11; Eph 5:1-2; Ro 12:2)

A woman of dignity doesn't indulge in self-promotion. Self-promotion is an idolatry of self, over courtesy. She would rather be a slave, under the foot of love than be a tyrant with love under-foot. Condescension, one-upmanship, are not for her household—ever.

fragrance of you (וריח) literally; "and-fragrance-of."

As we learned back at So 1:3, 3:6, and 6:12, the Bible has no Hebrew word for "spiritual." So, non-physical qualities are conveyed through non-physical expressions such as "wind, taste, and smell."

This couple values the quiet fruits of holy spirit. They are attracted to one another by what's obliquely described as, "fragrance." The Heavenly Solomon locates her by her invisible "aroma," which is covered in detail back at So 1:12.

like apples (כתפוחים) literally; "like-apples."
This is an obvious reference to So 2:3 and So 8:5. It reminds us of the location, the gateway, through which this new daughter must travel to reach her new parents. (So 8:5) It also reminds us of the non-physical senses she must employ, that Solomon is using the same senses to find her.

The word "apple," indicates that which is distinguished by its *fragrance,* or *scent*. It comes from the root *naw-fakh*, (#H5301 נפח) meaning "blow; pant; struggle for breath." (Ge 2:7; Jer 15:9) It's a combination of נפש (soul) and רוח (spirit).

What fitting symbolisms. Since these Hebrew words are connected, it's extremely important that the reader connect "spirit" to "apple." It's also important to make the connection to "daughter" (בה), since daughters are affectionately called "apple of my eye" in Hebrew. If you miss those connections, you'll completely miss the hidden lesson, at So 8:5.

NUMERICS: *arise/climb* (קוּמ) literally; "arise, resurrect, ascending, climb." This is the last of four uses. At the *remez* level, the number four hints at a conversion, because of the Earthly Shunemite's conversion to the spirit realm.

9 [HEAVENLY SOLOMON:] and your mouth multiplies the best wine. [HEAVENLY SHULAMITE:] May the wine be straight ones, to my beloved, flowing gently over his lips and teeth.	וחכך כיין הטוב הולך לדודי למישרים דובב שפתי ישנים:

9 and your mouth (וחכך) literally: "and-mouth-of-you."

This is an unusual mix of two words that could easily be misunderstood, if context was ignored. We have already learned the meaning of "mouth," at So 1:2. As Ro 10:10 teaches us, "For with the heart one exercises faith for righteousness, but with the mouth one makes public declaration for salvation." We learned the meaning of "wine," at So 1:2. So, the teachings from the Shulamite's mouth will do more than save—they will "multiply" her children.

Opening the palm (*kuf* / כ) portends a thriving population, within the kingdom. The Hebrew letter *kuf* (כ) appears in front of the word, "wine" (יין). So, its exponential growth is further emphasized with the word, "multiplies."

Expanding Solomon's borders was responsible for the population growth, described at Re 7:9. By using her "mouth" wisely, her family becomes elevated, educated, and inspired.

Abraham was wise to find Rebekah for Isaac. Rebekah saved Jacob, from Esau. Solomon's wise Shulamite will teach us how to prosper. (Is 65:8)

be straight (למישרים) literally; "as-straight-ones."

No word is wasted in holy text, not even a letter. Therefore, expect this Hebrew word (straight) to teach us something hidden in the text. "And Eleazar the priest shall take of her blood with his finger, and sprinkle her blood toward the front of the tent of meeting seven times." –*Nu 19:4*

It's nothing but my speculation, but based on Nu 19:4, this may be teaching us Solomon has already made six journeys to gather his lilies. Now (on this symbolic seventh day), he will make seven, additional, journeys (in one day) to gather the full, and final, number to complete his Bride Class.

There are several locations in this song that seem to help us decipher the mystery of Re 10:4-6: Compare So 6:5; 7:9; 7:13; and 8:5.

"And when the seven thunders uttered [their voices], I was about to write: and I heard a voice from Heaven saying, Seal up the things which the seven thunders uttered, and write them not. And the angel that I saw standing upon the sea and upon the earth lifted up his right hand to Heaven, and sware by him that liveth for ever and ever, who created the Heaven and the things that are therein, and the earth and the things that are therein, and the sea and the things that are therein, that there shall be delay no longer.'" –*Re 10:4-6*

In English, the word "lady" is a feminized derivative of "lord." So, it's easy to see how proper it is to address the Shulamite as "lady," or yourself, as the "lady" of the house.

Lords and ladies are known for their *straight* conduct. There is honesty at the tip of a lady's tongue, but not at the expense of others. The Shulamite's goal is the building-up of her household—not tearing it down. (Pr 14:1)

lips and teeth (שפתי ישנים) literally; "lips-of your-teeth."

The Hebrew word for "lips" is *sef-eth* (#H8193 שׂפה). It carries the idea of a termination, or an outer margin. It's used for brim, edge, bank, or border. In this text, it describes the boundaries to inside, compared to outside. What wells up within us, will eventually pour through our "lips." That works in reverse too. What's outside must be kosher before we permit it inside, over our "lips."

The Hebrew word for "teeth" has already been discussed at So 6:6. This phrase connects to So 4:2, in the sense that both references have to do with being clean. At So 4:2, the ewes were just washed. In this verse, what passes over his teeth is straight, kosher, or clean to God.

10 [HEAVENLY SHULAMITE:] I am my beloved's, and his longing is for me.	אני לדודי ועלי תשוקתו: ס

10 *longing is for me* (תְּשׁוּקָתוֹ) literally; "desire-of-him."

This "longing" is the kind of desire that impels one to action. A Shulamite has many admirers, but she wants a man-of-action.

How ironic, the first earthly daughter craved her husband, Adam. The first heavenly daughter craves her husband, Jesus. Longing *tashookah* (#H8669 תְּשׁוּקָה) is derived from *shook* (#H7783 שׁוּק), which means: craving, running after, stretching after. This same Hebrew word was used to describe Eve's longing for Adam, at Ge 3:16 and Ge 4:7.

When we learn to crave what's good, we harness our desires. Jehovah thought that to His wife. "And thou shalt love Jehovah thy God with all thy heart, and with all thy soul, and with all thy might. And these words, which I command thee this day, shall be upon thy heart; and thou shalt teach them diligently unto thy children, and shalt talk of them when thou sittest in thy house, and when thou walkest by the way, and when thou liest down, and when thou risest up." –De 6:5-7

"Thou shalt love"?

What gall! Is God brazen enough to demand a feeling? Yes! Jehovah operates from the position that humans can, and must, cultivate proper desires. God has never hesitated to hold His people accountable for neglecting this principle. The Hebrew words for love are all verbs, thus connecting love to actions. By doing certain behaviors, we create loving feelings. It may not match the thinking of the West, but God believes humans are perfectly capable of controlling their feelings. (1Joh 5:3)

11 [HEAVENLY SHULAMITE:] Come, my beloved, let's go to the woman of the house, let's spend the night within their community.	לכה דודי נצא השדה נלינה בכפרים:

11 ***the woman of the house*** (השדה) literally; "the-lady-of-the-house."

The Hebrew word *shid-ah* (#H7705 שׁדה) means "wife, mistress of the house, or musical instrument." Since the person speaking is the Shulamite, we know the other person is "the woman." The Shulamite seems to know who this other "woman of the house" is, and where she is. It's her goal to go there, first thing in the morning.

Hebrew poetry loves progressive word pictures. Since the secondary meaning of *shid-ah* (שׁדה) is "musical instrument," this word (שׁדה) may be directing us to one of the sources of this very song (*Song of Songs*), which is the same song that the brideclass must master in *Revelation*. (Re 14:3 not to be confused with Re 15:3)

Is it possible that the greatest song of all time has, at its origin, this "woman," waiting at the Shulamite's final destination? Who could she be? The final chapter will tell us. Read on.

within their community (בכפרים) literally; "in-the-villages."

Translators have had a difficult time making sense of this Hebrew word, but if they gave it a little thought, it contains a very common word. It's a word often used in connection to the tabernacle. The word *kaw-far* (#H3722 כפר) means "to cover, atone, forgive." It was also used to describe the lid on the Ark of the Covenant. Most translators would accept, בכפרים as meaning "covered village, protected village." It boils down to a difference in pronunciation.

In this verse, it may mean a little of both. Since this word is a plural, it may be referring to the greatness of this community—this is a city of redemption. This new Shulamite wants to go to this woman's house, because she seems to think it will bring both of them some measure of security.

We are forced to ask a very important question: "Who could bring relief to the commander of Armageddon, and an immortal Shulamite? Who is this other "woman?" She must be a very special "woman."

A waiter, an usher, a parking-lot attendant, all have some authority. How do you treat these hard-working people, and what do your children learn by watching your example?

When you show respect for all levels of authority, you lay a fine foundation for honor, in general. That foundation is where you want your children's values to take root.

At So 7:1, the Shulamite could have let flattery go to her head. In this verse, however, we see proof of her humility. Royalty strengthens their own position when they show honor to others in relative positions of authority. (2Sa 9:1-13)

12 [HEAVENLY SHULAMITE:] Let's agree to go out early to the vineyards, to see if the vines have budded, if He opened the blossoms, and if the pomegranates are in bloom—there I will give to MY BELOVED the mandrakes.	נשכימה לכרמים נראה אם פרחה הגפן פתח הסמדר הנצו הרמונים שם אתן את־דדי לך:

12 *Let us agree to go out early* (נשכימה) literally; "let-us-go-early."

The new Shulamite introduces two different destinations. The first destination, at So 7:11, is "the woman of the house." The second destination, on the following day, at So 7:12, is the "vineyards." "The woman's" house is in Heaven, but the "vineyards" are on earth.

All that remains, is for the reader to calculate the departure time. The Hebrew word *shaw-kam* (#H7925 שכמ) means "incline the shoulder to a burden," in other words, "to start early in the morning." It's a Hebrew idiom.

There isn't much flexibility with this word. The Shulamite has designated this trip to the "vineyard" as the task on the following day.

Obviously, there are additional Hebrew letters, other than the root שׁכמ. With the additional *nun* (נ) and *hay* (ה), the divine author forces additional thoughts, beyond the time of day. Therefore, this translation adds "agree" and "out." The translation method is found in, *The Meaning of Hebrew Letters*.[35]

budded (פרחה) literally; "she-budded."

Within this compound Hebrew word is the root *paw-roo-akh* (#H6515 פרוח). It means "blossomed." It's a feminine (or subordinate) term. So, it may hint the the master will call for this blossoming, that is, call for Earthly Brothers.

The full number of Shulamites has already been satisfied, and now, the Heavenly Shulamite has an interest in seeing her budding children, on earth.

the mandrakes (הרמונים) literally; "the-mandrakes."

I have inserted this word (mandrakes) at the end of this verse by taking it from the beginning of the next verse. Otherwise, the English becomes absurd. Let me emphasize: There was no need to revise the Hebrew.

This is the only place in *Song of Songs* where "mandrakes" are mentioned. It seems to invoke the same intentions of the matriarch, Leah. "And Reuben went in the days of wheat harvest, and found mandrakes in the field, and brought them unto his mother Leah. Then Rachel said to Leah, 'Give me, I pray thee, of thy son's mandrakes.' And she said unto her, 'Is it a small matter that thou hast taken away my husband? and wouldest thou take away my son's mandrakes also?' And Rachel said, 'Therefore he shall lie with thee tonight for thy son's mandrakes.' And Jacob came from the field in the evening, and Leah went out to meet him, and said,

'Thou must come in unto me; for I have surely hired thee with my son's mandrakes.' And he lay with her that night." –*Ge 30:14-16*

Much has been made of this word (mandrakes), but maybe an examination of the Hebrew will demystify the many misunderstandings that seem to be floating around, causing people to draw some very crazy conclusions. In the Hebrew *doo-dah-ee* (דוּדִי) means "mandrake." Notice how close "mandrake" (דוּדִי) is to the word we have been translating as "my beloved" (דוֹדִי). Same letters, with a slightly different pronunciation.

Ancient Hebrews were not using mandrakes as aphrodisiacs. They simply gifted these flowers, with a name, that very closely resembled the Hebrew word "beloved." The plant (mandrake) was simply a love message, much like a valentine that pagans send to their love interest.

A valentine is not an aphrodisiac. It's an icon to express loving intentions. The mandrake is the icon for love (to a Hebrew). It's that simple.

What an interesting way to end the verse: "There I will give to MY BELOVED [דוֹדִי] the mandrakes [דוּדִי]." For all the negative and nasty things said about earth, this verse makes a dramatic point. It was on earth that all the proofs of love (or lack of love) were made.

The proof of no love: (1) The Satan called God a liar. (Ge 3:4) (2) Adam and Eve agreed with the Satan. (Ge 3:6) (3) A third of the angels agreed with the Satan. (Jud 6)

The proof of godly love: (1) Abraham became God's friend. (Is 41:8) (2) David became a man after God's own heart. (Ac 13:22) (3) Jesus died for his Father. (Mt 22:37-39)

13 [HEAVENLY SHULAMITE:] They send out their fragrance. At our entrance are all the eminent ones, new ones, also old ones, who have been waiting for you, my beloved.	הדודאים נתנו־ריח ועל־פתחינו כל־מגדים חדשים גם־ישנים דודי צפנתי לך:

    13 *fragrance* (ריח) literally; "fragrance." Speaking of similarities, notice how close it is to the word commonly translated for "spirit" (#H7307 רוח). The Hebrew word for "fragrance" (#H7381 ריח) means "savour, scent, smell." This word also invokes, spirit (רוח). The mandrake plant has 55 principle odoriferous constituents. This invisible attention-getter (scent) makes the mandrake romantic.

    Love is traditionally identified with the 13th chapter of 1Cor. But, Paul begins at 1Cor 12:1, and concludes at 1Cor 13:13. This time, just read those two verses. You will discover the answer to a very important question that Solomon's Father will ask in chapter eight.

    at our entrance (ועל־פתחינו) literally; "and-at entrance-of-us."

    The Hebrew word *peh-thakh* (#H6607 פתח) means "an opening, door, gate, entrance way, entrance." The typical word for "door" is *deh-leth* (#H1817 דלת). "Door" is *not* used nor intended. This word has to do with the grand entrance of a patriarch, or matriarch. (So 6:4)

    Don't forget her itinerary. She is describing her return to earth. (Ge 28:12) Messianic rule, as we have already learned, emanates from the Jerusalem Above, but is dispensed through earthly Zion. (So 3:11; Re 14:1) Logic and holy text informs us where she is coming from, and where she is going to. She will be coming from Heaven, and going back to earthly Zion.

After spending all day with "the woman," she is anticipating returning to earth. She intends to make a meaningful entrance, through a portal (Jacob's ladder).

The same Hebrew word is used in a prophecy. "And I will give her her vineyards from thence, and the valley of Achor [עכור/trouble] for a door [פתח] of hope; and she shall make answer there, as in the days of her youth, and as in the day when she came up out of the land of Egypt." –Ho 2:15

The American classic, *Just In Time* encapsulates her state of mind. "Just in time you've found me just in time; Before you came my time was running low; I was lost the losing dice were tossed; My bridges all were crossed nowhere to go; Now you're here, now I know just where I'm going; No more doubt or fear, I've found my way; For love came just in time; You've found me just in time; And changed my lonely nights [Passover time]; Just in time." –*Jule Styne, Adolph Green, Betty Comden*

eminent ones (מגדים) literally; "eminent-ones."

The Hebrew word *meh-ghed* (#H4022 מגד) means "to be eminent, distinguished, valuable." Given the time period, it's worth noting the close connection to the Hebrew word *meg-id-do* (#H4023 מגדו). Many use this word (מגדו) as the Mountain of Megiddo, or Armageddon.

Uh-oh.

Previously, Solomon/Jesus mentioned Mt. Amana, Mt. Senir. But, Hebrew poetry loves progressive word pictures. Now, she uses this word (מגדים) to infer Mt. Megiddo. So, pay close attention to the prophetic time period. They will come in the name of love. They have come and gone, up and down Jacob's ladder, but now they arrive for justice, riding horses of war, to house and educate children, in His name of love.

Like Israel's entrance into the promised land, our priests will make its seven marches around Jericho. After that event, this bride and groom will instruct their earthly 288,000 administrators (eminent/*meh-ged* ones), then return home to their heavenly family, Jehovah, the woman, and their angelic brothers (eminent/*meh-ged* ones). The Heavenly Shulamite is describing Armageddon.

Like Jacob's prophetic ladder, Jericho has been dropped into an ongoing time-loop. Maybe the seven marches around the city brought Heaven to earth. The name "Jericho" means "moon city." (Re 10:4-6: Compare So 6:5; 7:9; 7:13; and 8:5)

Again, who are these eminent ones? The symbolic group of 288,000 who David selected to administrate over Israel. (Acts 24:15) The eminant ones of Heaven, however, will be addressed in more detail, in chapter eight.

new ones also old ones (חדשים גם־יישנים) literally; "new-ones also old-ones."

The newly-minted Shulamites/144,000 will be presented to the ancient of days, Jehovah, as well as those faithful ones who died without receiving the promises. (Heb 11:13) This sounds very much like a scene from the book of *Revelation*. "And I saw, and behold, the Lamb standing on the mount Zion, and with him a hundred and forty and four thousand, having his name, and the name of his Father, written on their foreheads. And I heard a voice from Heaven, as the voice of many waters, and as the voice of a great thunder: and the voice which I heard [was] as [the voice] of harpers harping with their harps: and they sing as it were a new song before the throne, and before the four living creatures and the elders: and no man could learn the song save the hundred and forty and four thousand, [even] they that had been purchased out of the earth." –*Re 14:1-3*

Let me end the chapter with this story: Will you come back for your husband? Do you, at least, have the loyalty of a goose? By flying in unison, in a "V" formation, geese can fly 71% further than they could as an individual.

That's the advantage of community. For all the toes that get stepped on, there are still definite advantages for working in groups. Geese in the rear will even honk to encourage those taking the wind resistance, up front.

When a goose gets sick, or injured, and falls out of formation, two other geese follow it down. They will protect and assist the weaker goose until it's able to fly . . . or dies. Only then, will the two remaining geese resume their journey by seeking another formation of geese, at least until they can locate their own family group.

When done the right way, we don't lose ourselves in a marriage. When we become parents, we are no less for it. To the contrary, we often grow into a better person. When marriage is done the right way, our community will benefit, our children will benefit, our partner will benefit, and best of all—you will benefit.

Humans don't always show as much wisdom as a goose. Wherever we find wisdom, we should seize it. Where we find wisdom is less important than finding it.

Chapter 8:[36]
Last Shulamite Meets Her Mother

Her shame is gone. Now that the last Shunemite has been resurrected to Heaven, she has a heavenly body like the other Shulamites. She can openly embrace Solomon.

In ancient times, Abishag had a parallel story that unfolded in Zion. In her time of widowhood (after king David's death), Abishag could show *no* interest in Solomon. After her mourning period was over, neither family nor citizen could challenge Abishag's love for Solomon.

8 [HEAVENLY SHULAMITE:] Who made you like my brother? Who nursed you at my mother's breasts? When I find you outside, I will kiss you, and no one will despise me.	ח מי יתנך כאח לי יונק שדי אמי אמצאך בחוץ אשקך גם לא־ יבוזו לי:

MEDITATE ON THIS TEXT WHILE LISTENING TO DEMO 81

    1 *made you like my brother* (יתנך כאח) literally; "he-could-make-you-like-brother."

    My beloved daughter, I have a confession: You are not who you think you are. You were placed in my care, temporarily. That "care" was the best job I ever had. I would gladly repeat it. I may be your dad, but Jesus is your eternal father, and Jehovah is your Grandfather.

    Like your search for identity, this Shulamite also wants to know who she is. *Who made me like your sister?* the new Shulamite wonders.

    Jesus' Father made her that way—with "the woman." Like the Heavenly Solomon, this new Shulamite was re-birthed (into Heaven). "And a great sign was seen in Heaven: a woman arrayed with the sun, and the moon under her feet, and upon her head a crown of twelve stars; and she was [with] child; and she crieth out, travailing in birth, and in pain to be delivered." –*Re 12:1-2*

That same "woman" gives birth to more than this one son, however. She will later give birth to 144,000 daughters, symbolized by the 12 stars in her crown. (Re 21:9-11)

when I find you (אֶמְצָאֲךָ) literally; "should-I-find-you."

The Hebrew word *maw-tsaw* (#H4672 מצא) is a far-ranging word. *Strong's* states, "to come forth to, i.e. appear or exist; to attain, find or acquire; meet or be present, be able, befall, being, catch, certainly, deliver, be enough, cause to find, get hold upon, be here, light upon, meet with, take hold on."

Where else will you find this word in holy text? "A worthy woman who can find [מצא]? For her price is far above rubies." –*Pr 31:10*

NUMERICS: ***find*** (מצא) literally; "find." This is the final of eight uses. At the *remez* level, eight conveys starting over. If seven completes the week, then the eighth day is the beginning of a *new* week. Jesus (the Heavenly Solomon) is a *new* king and *new* husband, the Shulamite is a *new* sister and *new* bride, in a *new* family. She has found herself in this *new* position, beginning a *new* life.

outside (בַחוּץ) literally; "at-the-outer."

The Hebrew word *khoots* (#H2351 חוּץ) means "sever, separate by a wall." Her outside will always be in relation to the walls of her residence (the Jerusalem Above). So, where is her "outside?" The Shulamite is not the only person in Heaven. Her new mother is "the woman." (Re 12:5-6; Ge 3:15) Her children will be on earth. (Joh 14:1-3 compare Lk 12:32-35) So, with the exception of her husband, most creatures (spirit and flesh) are "outside" the walls of Jerusalem.

The Shulamite's marriage to Solomon will be a heavenly event—not earthly. But, wherever the Shulamite goes—in Heaven or earth—there will be no shame in kissing her new husband. Above or below, they will be celebrated.

In that *new* age, their Father will proclaim, "Serve Jehovah with fear, And rejoice with trembling. Kiss the son, lest he be angry, and ye perish in the way, For his wrath will soon be kindled. Blessed are all they that take refuge in him." –*Ps 2:11-12*

In *Song of Songs*, Solomon repeatedly uses a phrase "sister bride," because the Heavenly Solomon was born from the same "woman." The Heavenly Shulamite is his sister, the same way Israelite citizens were brothers and sisters.

The first chapter of *Song of Songs* starts off with Solomon kissing the first Shulamite, and now the final chapter concludes with the last Shulamite kissing Solomon. Remember the geometry of Hebrew. This scroll was designed to fold in half—the first half kissing the last half.

NUMERICS: *kiss* (נשק) literally; "kiss." This is the final of three uses. At the *remez* level, three portends life eternal. Her "kiss," unlike Rachel's, will require the stairs from Jacob's dream. "And Jacob kissed Rachel, and lifted up his voice, and wept. And Jacob told Rachel that he was her father's brother, and that he was Rebekah's son. And she ran and told her father. And it came to pass, when Laban heard the tidings of Jacob his sister's son, that he ran to meet him, and embraced him, and kissed him, and brought him to his house. And he told Laban all these things." –*Ge 29:11-13*

2 [HEAVENLY SHULAMITE:] I will lead you and bring you to my mother's house. She, who will teach me. I will give you spiced wine to drink, the nectar of my pomegranates.	אנהגך אביאך אל־בית אמי תלמדני אשקך מיין הרקח מעסיס רמני:

MEDITATE ON THIS TEXT WHILE LISTENING TO DEMO 82

2 ***mother's house*** (בית אמי) literally; "house mother-of-me."

This verse is nothing like So 3:4. Forget the Earthly Shunemite, and forget the Shunemite's earthly mother. Instead, focus on the Heavenly Shulamite, and the Shulamite's heavenly mother.

Heavenly Jerusalem has a specific purpose and a specific location. The Shulamite's city can be specifically measured, with a golden reed. (Re 21:15) Not so, with the Shulamite's mother's ("the woman's") house. "The woman's" house lies beyond Heavenly Jerusalem, in the infinite Heavens, which cannot be measured.

Consider what the Earthly Solomon said about "the woman's" husband, Jehovah. "But will God in very deed dwell on the earth? behold, Heaven and the Heaven of Heavens cannot contain thee; how much less this house that I have builded!" –*1Ki 8:27* Obviously, we are dealing with two different heavenly mothers (the Shulamite and "the woman") and two different houses.

Again, "the mother" in this verse cannot be the Shulamite, because the Shulamite is the wife of Solomon—not his mother. The Shulamite cannot be her own mother, and the Messiah ("the seed") cannot be his own Father.

When two verbs appear, side-by-side (אנהגך אביאך = lead you and bring you) it indicates extra determination. This Shulamite will be impossible to stop. She is determined to bring her *new* husband to the house of her *new* mother.

she who will teach me (תלמדני) literally; "she-teach-me."

This is a *new* daughter who is determined to learn. We already know there are regular meetings that take place in Heaven. (1Ki 22:21) At those meetings, information was presented and explained. "Now it came to pass on the day when the sons of God came to present themselves before Jehovah, that Satan also came among them." –*Job 1:6*

By Christian definition, when she was on earth (as an Earthly Shunemite), Jesus was her eternal father. When she was chosen, and resurrected (as a Shulamite), her *new* eternal Father became Jehovah. Her *new* eternal mother would be Jehovah's heavenly wife, "the woman."

Forgive me for repeating myself, but this is an important distinction that must be understood. This was the same "woman" who gave birth to the "seed" (Jesus). (Re 12:5-6) During the Shulamite's *new* birth to this *new* Father and mother, Jesus becomes the Shulamite's *new* Brother. Now you know who made Solomon like her brother: Jehovah.

The Shulamite graciously submits to her matriarch. Honor is the glue that holds a family together. In a very beautiful way, our family links us to our past, and our future.

So, "the woman" would have the duty to teach her *new* daughter. She would welcome her the way any loving mother would welcome a *new* daughter. The Shulamite's *new* family (*new* mother; *new* Father; *new* Brothers; *new* husband) is a loving, nurturing family.

spiced wine (מיין הרקח) literally; "from-wine the-spice." Wine can be made from many juices—not just grape juice. Some wines add juices, some add spices. A clever wife made "spiced wine" for her family's table. "Wisdom hath builded her house; She hath hewn out her seven pillars: She hath killed her beasts; She hath mingled her wine; She hath also furnished her table." –*Pr 9:1-2*

Pomegranates generally symbolize a fruitful womb. Today, new Jewish families still plant pomegranate trees to symbolize their hope for a fruitful family. Verse 12 will demonstrate the symbolic bounty of the Shulamite's womb, below. The variety of wine indicates the variety of children.

NUMERICS: *wine* (יין) literally; "effervesce, wine." This is the final of eight uses. At the *remez* level, the number eight describes starting over. If seven completes the week, then the eighth day is the beginning of a *new* week.

We have already learned that wine symbolizes refined children. "And it shall come to pass in that day, that the mountains shall drop down sweet wine, and the hills shall flow with milk, and all the brooks of Judah shall flow with waters; and a fountain shall come forth from the house of Jehovah, and shall water the valley of Shittim. Egypt shall be a desolation, and Edom shall be a desolate wilderness, for the violence done to the children of Judah, because they have shed innocent blood in their land. But Judah shall abide for ever, and Jerusalem from generation to generation. And I will cleanse their blood, that I have not cleansed: for Jehovah dwelleth in Zion."
–Joe 3:18-21

This *new* family is correcting their old tragedies and starting over.

3 [HEAVENLY SHULAMITE:] His left arm is under my head, and his right arm embraces me.	שמאלו תחת ראשי וימינו תחבקני:

MEDITATE ON THIS TEXT WHILE LISTENING TO DEMO 83

3 *His left arm* (שמאלו) literally; "left-arm-of-him."

This is the second time these words have been spoken. The first time was at So 2:6. This last Shulamite is being transported by the fine shepherd. Solomon is her shepherd. His left arm is under her chin, and his right arm wraps around her hind quarters. "Fear not, little flock; for it is your Father's good pleasure to give you the kingdom." –*Lk 12:32*

his right arm (רימינו) literally; "and-right-arm-of-him."
"Then shall the King say unto them on his right hand, Come, ye blessed of my Father, inherit the kingdom prepared for you from the foundation of the world.'" –*Mt 25:34*

4 [HEAVENLY SHULAMITE:] Daughters at Jerusalem, what [about] these pleadings of mine? "Don't arouse the watchers, or awaken LOVE, until He wills it so."?	השבעתי אתכם בנות ירושלם מה־תעירו ׀ ומה־תעררו את־האהבה עד שתחפץ: ס

MEDITATE ON THIS TEXT WHILE LISTENING TO DEMO 84

NUMERICS: *Daughter* (בה) literally; "daughter, or apple branch." This is the last of 12 uses. At the *remez* level, the number 12 locates a specific position on earth. To start, you need six Cartesian coordinates. So, to show a relocation (from six Cartesian coordinates to another six Cartesian coordinates) you need a total of 12 Cartesian coordinates. The number 12 symbolizes, relocation. As the 12 stars (on "the woman's" crown) hinted, her daughters have been relocated from earth to Heaven. Finally, the *new* Shulamite makes her last pleading from Heaven.

4 *the pleadings of mine* (השבעתי) literally; "the-entreaties-of-me."

Despite her resurrection to Heaven, she still implores the *other* daughters at Jerusalem. When we are young "please" seems like a magic word that will open doors and get us what we want. When we are wiser, we pray that God will protect us from what we want.

Immature "wants" can destroy a family—or an entire world, for that matter. As a wife of Solomon, the peace of the world does not rest on her shoulders. The peace of the world depends on what her *new* Father wants.

"Pray for the peace of Jerusalem: They shall prosper that love thee. Peace be within thy walls, And prosperity within thy palaces. For my brethren and companions' sakes, I will now say, Peace be within thee.'" *–Ps 122:6-8*

Is something missing? Previous refrains contain the phrase, "are on the gazelles and on the does of the field." (So 2:7; 3:5)

Nothing is missing.

To the contrary, finally, she's got it right. When these specific words are used in this specific word-order, God's holy name clicks into place, starting at the sixth word, skipping every five letters.

Now, she needs no delivery service (gazelles and does). She is there—in Heaven. Twice in the *Torah* God instructed us to love humans. (Le 19:18, 34) Not only are we witnessing the gradual enlightenment of the *new* Shulamite, but we also see the trigger phrase that awakens her *new* Father, Jehovah. (Is 51:9-15)

Suddenly, our *new* Shulamite is less anxious for human opportunity and more anxious for her Father to enforce her husband's dominion. Possibly she realizes kingdom enforcement would create safety for her *new* children, below.

Notice also that a new word, *mah* (מה), was added. It means "why or what." In this instance, its use is emphatic. So, it's translated as "what [about]." Not only has her intensity changed, but her former demands have turned into a question.

What a dramatic change in tone. What a dramatic change in emphasis. What a dramatic change for earth.

The *new* Shulamite has made the transition. The Shulamite is no longer in darkness. She knows. Finally, she speaks as an enlightened matriarch.

Suddenly, she realizes, humanity has had ample opportunity to flee to the mountain of God. "For the time past may suffice to have wrought the desire of the Gentiles, and to have walked in lasciviousness, lusts, winebibbings, revellings, carousings, and abominable idolatries." *–1Pe 4:3*

The musical classic, *The Prayer*, encapsulates her transition: "I pray you'll be our eyes; And watch us where we go; And help us to be wise; In times when we don't know; Let this be our prayer; As we go our way; Lead us to a place; Guide us with your grace; To a place where we'll be safe." *–Carole Bayer Sager and David Foster*

NUMERICS: *Jerusalem* (ירושלם) literally, "two hills, foundation of peace." This is the final of eight uses. At the *remez* level, the number eight describes starting over. If seven completes the week, then the eighth day is the beginning of a *new* week. This is not ancient Jerusalem. This is the *new* Jerusalem, the Jerusalem Above. Invoking "eight" helps to further that point.

NUMERICS: *pleading* (שבע) literally; "to seven, repeat a declaration, prophetic week." This is the final of five uses. At the *remez* level, the number five portends judgment, with potential salvation. This will be the last request for patience. It's time for the doors to close. For earth below, it's time for salvation—or no salvation. "LOVE" will finally be awakened in the next verse, five.

arouse the watchers (תעירו) literally; "arouse (by implication: city-watchers)."

A prophetic execution is looming far below this heavenly city. There are four angels holding back the four winds of destruction. (Re 7:1) The *new* Shulamite now views the "sheep of another fold" (Earthly Brothers) as her children. (Joh 10:16; Re 7:9) She questions her former requests. She knows the time for patience is over.

> **NUMERICS:** *arouse* (#H5892 עיר) literally; "arouse (by implication: arouse city watchers, angels, guards of Heavenly Jerusalem)." This is the final of five uses. At the *remez* level, five portends judgment, with a potential for salvation. It means, salvation awaits the righteous, but punishment awaits the wicked. There will be no more requests for patience from this final Shulamite.

LOVE (אהבה) literally; "DIVINE-LOVE."

God is love. (De 7:13; 1Joh 4:16-17) And He will be arriving in the following verse. God help whoever underestimated His love for His son. Any non-members of the messianic family will "awaken" a fury of retribution.

A further aspect to Jehovah's superlative love is His passionate desire for justice. Real justice requires strict adherence to His son's right to rule. (Ps 2) This was prefigured by David's slaughter of foreigners, to establish his son's (Solomon's) reign of peace.

"Therefore thus saith the Lord Jehovah, Behold, I lay in Zion for a foundation, a stone, a tried stone, a precious corner-[stone] of sure foundation: he that believeth shall not be in haste. And I will make justice the line, and righteousness the plummet; and the hail shall sweep away the refuge of lies, and the waters shall overflow the hiding-place.'" –*Is 28:16-17*

This citation (Is 28:16-17) is describing the way divine love
(אהבה) will remove His son's opposition.

He is, now, awake.

> **PUZZLE:** The God you worship enjoys weaving additional messages beneath the surface message. These puzzle-like Bible codes hide beneath the text, the way a watermak hides beneath a handwritten letter.
>
> That's what separates holy text from Jewish newspapers. The Hebrew language doesn't weave these messages, naturally. It takes the mind (and deft hands) of God.
>
> This *new* Shulamite divinely decodes the holy language. Starting in the sixth word and the third letter, you will find letter skips of five that will spell out God's holy name. Suddenly, she speaks mathematical Hebrew—Bible code.

5 [HEAVENLY SHULAMITE:] Who is this coming up from the wilderness, leaning on her beloved? [JEHOVAH:] Under the apple tree I resurrected you. There your mother conceived you. There, she who was in labor, gave your birth.	מִי זֹאת עֹלָה מִן־ הַמִּדְבָּר מִתְרַפֶּקֶת עַל־ דּוֹדָהּ תַּחַת הַתַּפּוּחַ עוֹרַרְתִּיךָ מָה חִבְּלַתְךָ אִמֶּךָ שָׁמָּה חִבְּלָה יְלָדַתְךָ:

MEDITATE ON THIS TEXT WHILE LISTENING TO DEMO 85

5 *Who is this* (מי זאה) literally; "who this."
Two important thoughts must be considered while dissecting this verse: (1) Since this Hebrew has all masculine endings, it's an irrefutable fact that the Shulamite is speaking to a man. This is the *new* Shulamite speaking to her *new* husband—the

Heavenly Solomon. (2) Since the Heavenly Solomon is with the Shulamite, she must be speaking of some other couple—besides themselves. Who?

The Shulamite sees a couple (other than themselves) approaching in the distance. It's Jehovah and "the woman." Her "seed" was to crush the serpent's head, the same serpent who severed Adam's divine relationship, thus all of mankind's relationship.

This "woman" is described further in the 12th chapter of *Revelation*. She is described as bringing forth a son from this heavenly family, a ruler who is to "shepherd all the nations with an iron rod." (Ps 2:6-9) Today, the only way to re-connect to Jehovah is through adoption, by His son.

wilderness (מדבר) literally; "wilderness."

The wilderness of Heaven is not the same as the wilderness on earth. This "woman" has been secluded in some remote part of Heaven for a long period of time, for a very specific purpose. (Re 12:6)

Well, she's back!

Since this is Heaven, obviously, we are dealing with metaphors. Yet, understanding the origins of "wilderness" (*mid-bawr* מדבר) will help us to understand why Jesus went into the "wilderness" for 40 days to meditate. Being in the "wilderness" is a deliberate method of surrounding yourself with creations from the mind of God.

His creations speak to us, helping us to straighten out our crooked thoughts. His creations speak to us, helping us to align our limited thoughts with the limitless mind of God. (Ro 1:20) That's where "the woman" has been hidden for 1,260 (symbolic) days. (Re 12:6) She's revealing herself to the Shulamite. *The Shulamite is looking right at her!*

leaning on her beloved (מתרפקת על־דודה) literally; "leaning on beloved-of-her."

Here, we are given a word that appears nowhere else in the Bible. The word *raw-fak* (#H7514 רפק) means "leaning." "Leaning" in no way implies weakness, or exhaustion. It simply informs us of her familiarity with Jehovah, her husband.

We are being shown the mother and Father of the Heavenly Solomon, and the 144,000 Shulamites. We are witnessing Jehovah escorting His heavenly wife back from the wilderness, as described at Re 12:6. This "woman" is the *new* mother of this *new* Shulamite, and the grandmother of us Earthly Brothers.

"The woman" is also the "musical instrument" referred to earlier, at So 7:11, in the sense that she accompanies her daughters with the *new* song they have mastered.

the apple tree (התפוח) literally; "the-apple-tree."

This is the first time Jehovah, speaks. He will only speak again, at verse seven. Why would He mention "the apple tree?" Pay close attention: "Apple tree" equals the "gate" between Heaven and earth. What's my proof? There was a city in Israel, *En Tappuah* (עין תפוח/spring of the apple tree).

This city (*En Tappuah*) was used as a boundary marker between the tribe of Manasseh and Ephraim. "And the border of Manasseh was from Asher to Michmethath, which is before Shechem; and the border went along to the right hand, unto the inhabitants of En-tappuah. The land of Tappuah belonged to Manasseh; but Tappuah on the border of Manasseh belonged to the children of Ephraim." –*Jos 17:7-8*

How does this prove the "apple tree" is the "gate" between Heaven and earth? If Joseph's son, Manasseh, symbolizes the heavenly class and Ephraim symbolizes the earthly class, then going to Heaven (Manasseh) from earth (Ephraim) would begin at their symbolic boundary marker—the apple tree (*En Tappuah*). (Jos 17:7-8)

This same word (apple tree) is also connected to the seven occurrences of the word "daughter" (female child, apple branch). Only when we connect this verse to So 1:5; 2:2; 2:7; 3:5; 3:10; 7:1 and 8:4 does the proper meaning begin to emerge.

It's no accident that the fruit of the apple tree is red. If you recall, the Earthly Shunemite stained herself with the henna plant. (So 1:14) That red stain has many meanings.

The Tabernacle, for example, was constructed from skins dyed, red. (Ex 39:33-34) So, if the tabernacle represents the body of the Messiah, that explains why the Messiah's wife stained herself with henna, at So 1:14.

NUMERICS: *apple* (תפוח) literally; "apple; blow; breathe; kindle." This is the last of five uses. At the *remez* level, the number five portends judgment, with a potential for salvation. It means salvation for the righteous, but punishment for the wicked. Here, we discover the Shulamite's reward. She gets to speak directly with Jehovah, Himself.

NUMERICS: *resurrected* (עור) literally; "awakening (or by implication: resurrect)." This is the final of seven uses. At the *remez* level, seven describes a messianic finality. The Father's messianic prophecy is complete. He provided a messiah to redeem mankind, and messianic wives for His messianic son.

The Father reminds this heavenly couple, "I resurrected you." but what lies beneath the surface translation is the fury behind His words. The Father really loves them in a protective way. The Father is furious at the injustice done to His son and daughter. The Father seems to have heard, and registered, His daughters' request for "revenge." (Re 6:10)   He's back! And He's enraged!

As a side note: There are several locations in this song that deciphers the mystery of Re 10:4-6. Compare that with, So 6:5; 7:9; 7:13; and 8:5.

6 [JEHOVAH:] Place me like a seal over your heart, like a seal over your arm, for divine love is strong, like death, its jealousy unyielding as the grave. It burns like blazing fire, like a mighty flame of Jah.	שִׂימֵנִי כַחוֹתָם עַל־לִבֶּךָ כַּחוֹתָם עַל־זְרוֹעֶךָ כִּי־ עַזָּה כַמָּוֶת אַהֲבָה קָשָׁה כִשְׁאוֹל קִנְאָה רְשָׁפֶיהָ רִשְׁפֵּי אֵשׁ שַׁלְהֶבֶתְיָה׃

MEDITATE ON THIS TEXT WHILE LISTENING TO DEMO 86

6 *like a seal* (כחותם) literally; "like-seal."

The Hebrew word for seal is *kho-thawm* (#H2368 חותם). "Seal" is a highly flexible word. It can mean "signature-ring, seal, signet." The way Jehovah uses this word in previous text provides the basis for a number of figurative expressions. "Seal" implies authority, given by a higher authority. Jer 22:24 shows us that Jehovah removed that seal, from Jehoiachin.

Joseph was given the "seal" of Pharaoh, for his hand, because the Pharaoh authorized Joseph to work in his behalf. (Ge 41:42) Jehovah gives authority to this couple (Solomon and the Shulamite). Solomon and the Shulamite are given authority to manage Jehovah's earthly household.

What does that "seal" get the Shulamite? Family. I'm reminded of the author Pearl S. Buck, who expresses this sentiment better than I can: "The lack of emotional security of our American young people is due, I believe, to their isolation from the larger family unit. No two people—no mere father and mother—as I have often said, are enough to provide emotional security for a child. A child needs a world of kinfolk, persons of different ages, temperaments, allied by an indissoluble bonds which cannot be broken."

Call it family or tribe, either way—you need one.

unyielding as the grave (קָשָׁה כִשְׁאוֹל) literally; "unyielding as-sheol."

With the Father's seal of approval, no outsider can sever her marital bond. City, County, State, nor Federal law, has jurisdiction over death. Government agencies can't get a court order to reverse death. The Shulamite's marital covenant is as impervious as death.

Only one person has the "keys" to reverse death. The Messiah was given "the keys of death and of Hades." (Re 1:18) "Do not marvel at this," Jesus reminded the crowds to whom he preached, "because the hour is coming in which all those in the memorial tombs will hear his voice and come out." (Joh 5:28-30) The word connection allows the resurrected earthly sons to join this loving family covenant.

I'm sure that you too have envisioned an ideal environment for your family. Your eternal father isn't so different from you. The repurchaser of mankind has set his terms for resurrection into his family. "And there shall in no wise enter into it anything unclean, or he that maketh an abomination and a lie: but only they that are written in the Lamb's book of life." –*Re 21:27*

Like yourself, the Messiah is concerned about placing his children in a safe place. After all is said and done, our Messiah is about family. After all is said and done, his Father, Jehovah, is about family.

fire (אֵשׁ) literally; "fire."

This Hebrew word for "fire" (*ash* אֵשׁ) sounds like the Hebrew word "husband" (*aysh* אִישׁ). That's either a pleasant coincidence, or a significant hint as to the nature of the

Shulamite's husband. It has been said before, "His eyes were as a flame of fire." (Re 19:12)

Fire is used for testing, refining, purifying. "The messenger of the covenant" is compared to a refiner's fire, a fire used in purifying gold and silver. If you are part of his family, you might be suffering from his refining process as you read this. Suffering for righteousness benefits the sufferer—it refines the sufferer. Paul says: "Tribulation produces endurance." (Ro 5:3) Family who successfully pass through a difficult "burning" trial are stronger, as a result. (Ac 14:22; Ro 12:12)

> *Of all the haunting moments of fatherhood, few rank with hearing your own words come out of your daughter's mouth.*
> *–Vic Secunda*

You may face a marital trial that takes years to work out. Gandhi was middle-aged when he was struck with the epiphany that he was guilty of oppressing his wife. It took decades of complaints before it clicked. It took years before Gandhi's wife saw him at his best. The point is, she waited.

To Gandhi's credit, he worked hard to eliminate his oppressive behaviors. Afterwords, Gandhi advocated kindness toward all women, throughout India.

Women were so appreciative, and responded so well, that millions of women became enthusiastic supporters. That was the turning point for India to become a free nation. World liberation starts in the family. All husbands need to love their wife.

In his autobiography, Gandhi confessed, "All the sorrows I have given to my wife due to my stringent lifestyle and the torments I've made her go through; I will never be able to forgive myself for that."

This is hopeful news for wives with immature husbands. Gandhi, Jacob, and Abraham, improved themselves by expressing proper shame for their failures. All the while, their wives endured their youth and inexperience. (Jas 5:7-9)

like a mighty flame of Jah (שלהיבמתיה) literally; "flame-of-Jah."

This is the only place in *Song of Songs* where the holy name of God (abbreviated, or not) appears. He does, however, weave it, in mathematical patterns (Bible codes), throughout.

> **PUZZLE:** The God you worship enjoys weaving additional messages beneath the surface message (Bible codes). That's what separates holy text from Jewish newspapers. The Hebrew language doesn't weave these messages, naturally. It takes the mind (and deft hands) of God.
>
> This *new* Shulamite continues to decode the holy language. She too enjoys the multi-dimensional messages that praise the holy name of God. Starting in the eighth word and the second letter, you too can find letter skips of three that spell out the holy name of God.

7 [JEHOVAH:] Many waters cannot quench THE LOVE, and rivers cannot wash it away. If one were to give ALL the wealth of his house for love, he would be utterly scorned.	מים רבים לא יוכלו לכבות את־האהבה ונהרות לא ישטפוה אם־יתן איש את־כל־הון ביתו באהבה בוז יבוזו לו: ס

MEDITATE ON THIS TEXT WHILE LISTENING TO DEMO 87

7 *Many waters* (מים רבים) literally; "waters many-of."

This is the last time Jehovah speaks, but His final words quickly sum up the entire fall, and restoration, of mankind.

Jehovah has already repaired the damage done in Heaven (by ousting Satan and his kind). Now His son and *new* daughter must repair the earth. His reference to "waters," has two applications: (1) The Satan's concentrated attack on God's family. (2) Time. Because time is symbolized by a "river."

Consider the proof texts: "And when the dragon saw that he was cast down to the earth, he persecuted the woman that brought forth the man [child]. And there were given to the woman the two wings of the great eagle, that she might fly into the wilderness unto her place, where she is nourished for a time, and times, and half a time, from the face of the serpent. And the serpent cast out of his mouth after the woman water as a river, that he might cause her to be carried away by the stream." –*Re 12:13-16*

Does earth have a mouth? Of course. What is the "mouth" for? Back at So 1:2 we learned, "with the mouth one makes public declaration for salvation." –*Ro 10:10* It's the goal of the Satan to dilute what came from the mouth of our king—the kingdom message.

The Satan intends to drown out the kingdom message—over time by eliminating its messengers. By proclaiming the coming messianic kingdom, we share in overcoming the Satan's attempt to dilute the memory of the Messiah "the woman" gave birth to. "And this gospel of the kingdom shall be preached in the whole world for a testimony unto all the nations; and then shall the end come." –*Mt 24:14*

Notice also, the Satan has a "mouth." His public declaration, however, is a refutation (a dilution) of our public declaration. "And no marvel; for even Satan fashioneth himself into an angel of light. It is no great thing therefore if his ministers also fashion themselves as ministers of righteousness, whose end shall be according to their works." –*2Cor 11:14-15*

Like our message, the Satan's message proceeds as a river. "River," is just a metaphor for, time. Both parties are conducting a campaign that transpires over a long river of "time."

So 8:7 sums it all up. Recounting the difficult path that brought them to this moment is cathartic. The Heavenly Shulamite is asked to reflect on humanity's exile from the Garden of Eden, the exile from Israel, and the dispersement of the disciples of Jesus throughout the world. At long last, her children are safe, and well on their way to being repaired.

NUMERICS: *love* (אהבה) literally; "divine love, godly attraction, desired." This is the final of 17 uses. At the *remez* level, the number 17 invokes the age of Joseph (the father of Manasseh and Ephraim) when he was sold into Egypt. Joseph's undying love re-united his family. (Ge 45:3-8)

When you read holy text, it presumes your knowledge to previously written text. For instance: the ultimate form of love for many (including some believers) is the mistaken belief in *unconditional love*.

Some go too far, demanding *unconditional forgiveness* for any, and all, transgressions. They seek relationships without consequences. What if their mate believes in molesting children? Does our God believe in unconditional forgiveness? No. There are boundaries in love—walls that must be maintained.

Jehovah advocates *accountability* in love. Let me give you one example: "All their wickedness is in Gilgal; for there I hated them: because of the wickedness of their doings I will drive them out of my house; I will love them no more; all their princes are revolters." –*Ho 9:15*

Some degraded forms of love become an idolatry of desire over fact. Idolatry means giving something, or someone, a prominence they don't deserve.

and rivers (וּנְהָרוֹת) literally; "and-rivers."

"River" is a metaphor for "time." The Satan's goal was to dilute the Messiah's kingdom message, and he has used every means at his disposal. Whether through culture, science, politics, economic, or religious schemes, the Satan hoped that with time he could alienate humanity to discredit our Messiah. (2Cor 2:8-11)

Despite the Satan's continuous opposition, the Earthly Shunemites, the Earthly Brothers kept the Messiah's kingdom message alive. In this verse, the heavenly family acknowledges the many obstacles their earthly family overcame, despite satanic opposition.

"Jehovah hath done great things for us, [Whereof] we are glad. Turn again our captivity, O Jehovah, As the streams in the south. They that sow in tears shall reap in joy. He that goeth forth and weepeth, bearing seed for sowing, Shall doubtless come again with joy, bringing his sheaves [with him]." –Ps 126:3-6   What are His "sheaves?" (see So 7:2)

The lesson for married couples is, don't be afraid to let go of the life you romanticized. Concede to the reality of setbacks, but use the down-time as an opportunity to deepen your family's roots. Always do something. Never stop helping each other get back up.

wealth (הוֹן) literally; "satisfied."

This Hebrew word for wealth is *hone* (#H1952 הוֹן). It means "satisfaction from overflowing, surfeited, wealth, substance, riches."

What God considers wealth and what humanity considers wealth has always been at odds. Jehovah considers "family" as His wealth. The Satan abandoned that family—Jehovah's family—for prestige. The Satan "utterly scorned" the most precious thing to Jehovah.

What do you consider wealth? Marital love is the sweetest thing this earth has to offer—and all other family relationships are calibrated from that. But, anything worth having comes at a cost.

Humans go to great lengths to avoid giving of themselves. According to her Father's standards, the best investment she could make (in her husband's absence) was to look after the children of Jesus. (So 1:6)

We can all participate in that facet of family life. Just because you don't have authority doesn't mean you can't be a leader. Anyone can encourage disciples of Jesus . . . if they have a strong sense of family loyalty.

utterly scorned (בּוֹז יָבוּזוּ) literally; "scorn they-would-scorn."

The Hebrew word for scorned is *booz* (#H936 בּוּז). It means "to disrespect, condemn, despise—utterly." Notice the quick doubling of the word "scorned." You won't see it in the English, but in the Hebrew, it's there. Two always hints at potential badness. When our weaker members stop respecting family, they too have scorned what the Father values.

That was the public scorn she received at So 1:6. There is a saying: "A man is never a failure . . . until his family thinks so." Her family thought so. Yet, she plowed on.

At what point will you let go of your husband? Every family comes with some measure of shame. When Sarah chose Abraham, instead of the wealthy Pharaoh who wanted her, she passed up a glorious life. Instead, she opted for the life of a sojourner, trusting in God's promise to her husband.

Likewise, Jesus, accepted his assignment to leave Heaven, becoming lower than the angels. That choice made the Satan scornful. (Heb 2:7) The Satan's low estimation of God's family was displayed when he offered Jesus all the wealth and glory of earth. (Lk 4:3-6)

To the fallen angels, it was as if Jesus had sacrificed his dignity, and position, for unworthy humans. Jesus gave everything for his Father's human family. (Pr 8:30-31) To his credit, Jesus scorned the Satan's scorn.

> **NUMERICS:** *angry* (בּוֹז) literally; "angry, scorning." This is the final of three uses. At the *remez* level, three is a very important number. On the third day, God created the seed-within-the-seed; recursive life; life in perpetuity. Some measure of "scorn" was prophesied. "For you therefore that believe is the preciousness: but for such as disbelieve, The stone which the builders *rejected*, The same was made the head of the corner; and, A stone of *stumbling*, and a rock of *offence*; for they *stumble* at the word, being disobedient: whereunto also they were appointed. But ye are an elect race, a royal priesthood, a holy nation, a people for [God's] own possession, that ye may show forth the excellencies of him who called you out of darkness into his marvellous light. –1Pe 2:7-9

8 [HEAVENLY BROTHERS:] Our sister is young, and without breasts. What can we do for our sister, in the day he calls for her?	אחות לנו קטנה ושדים אין לה מה־נעשה לאחתנו ביום שידבר־בה׃

MEDITATE ON THIS TEXT WHILE LISTENING TO DEMO 88

8 young (קטנה) literally; "young."

The speaker is definitely the Shulamite's Heavenly Brother (an angel), but this is not one of the angels who escorted her to Heaven. This angel is one of those who greeted her, on arrival. He is unaware of her rapid growth, during the trip.

His sour observation is permitted, but is it welcomed? Plain talk exists in Heaven, too. Family is a place where epiphanies are hammered and honed, on the anvil of everyday dialogue.

Like all of us, angels have much to learn about the *new* Shulamites. "Searching what [time] or what manner of time the Spirit of Christ which was in them did point unto, when it testified beforehand the sufferings of Christ, and the glories that should follow them. To whom it was revealed, that not unto themselves, but unto you, did they minister these things, which now have been announced unto you through them that preached the gospel unto you by the Holy Spirit sent forth from Heaven; *which things angel desire to look into.*" *–1Pe 1:11-12* Angels have a lot to learn, and what's more, they are curious to "look into" this new development in Heaven.

Sarah, Rebekah, Leah, and the former Shunemite made many mistakes, but unlike them, this group of Heavenly Shulamites (144,000) has reached their full number. In fact, she is the *last* Shulamite.

Before the victory at Jericho, God ordered 13 marches around Jericho. The majority (seven) of those marches happened on the very last day. Maybe the Shulamites' full number happened suddenly—without some angels realizing the Shulamite had reached her full number. Still, after 2,000 years, the *new* Shulamite's house was immature. She is *new*. Her family is *new*.

The early Jewish Brothers also puzzled over what to do with gentile Christians. (Ac 5:34-42) Likewise, Heaven has never seen anything like these Shulamites—former humans, now living in Heaven. Their Angelic Brothers are stunned. "For neither is circumcision anything, nor uncircumcision, but a *new* creature." –Gal 6:15

What can we do (מה־נעשׂה) literally; "what shall-we-do."

Can angels be ignorant? Of course. Why else would they ask "What can we do?" Abraham did not know how to describe Sarah. So, Pharaohs did not understand (or respect) Sarah's marital status. Hagar underestimated Sarah's role. This Heavenly Shulamite is greater than Sarah.

Whatever awkwardness or confusion that began at their meeting should not be interpreted as malice. The angels who had remained with God, share His high regard for faithful humans. Remember who spoke earlier: Jehovah. These Angelic Brothers are simply anxious to help Jehovah. The Heavenly Shulamite's husband will instruct these angels on what they can do. Jesus has seen this problem before.

The Messiah advises his Angelic Brothers wisely: Be fair; be kind; be loving; love your neighbor as yourself. She is their new neighbor. "And the multitudes asked him, saying, 'What then must we do?' And he answered and said unto them, 'He that hath two coats, let him impart to him that hath none; and he that hath food, let him do likewise.' And there came also publicans to be baptized, and they said unto him, 'Teacher, what must we do?' And he said unto them, 'Extort no more than that which is appointed you.' And soldiers also asked him, saying, 'And we, what must we do?' And he said unto them, 'Extort from no man by violence, neither accuse [any one] wrongfully; and be content with your wages.'" –Lk 3:10-14

The thinking of Jesus has not changed, not for man nor angel.

NUMERICS: *sister* (אָחוֹת) literally; "sister." This is the final of seven uses. At the *remez* level, seven describes a messianic finality. Jehovah's messianic prophecy is complete. He provided 144,000 messianic "sisters" to help the Messiah restore mankind. Her Angelic Brothers are anxious to help their new "spirit sister."

9 [HEAVENLY BROTHERS:] If she is a wall, we will build turrets of silver on her. If she is a door, we will engrave her panels of cedar.	אִם־חוֹמָה הִיא נִבְנֶה עָלֶיהָ טִירַת כָּסֶף וְאִם־דֶּלֶת הִיא נָצוּר עָלֶיהָ לוּחַ אָרֶז׃

MEDITATE ON THIS TEXT WHILE LISTENING TO DEMO 89

9 *If* (אִם) literally; "If" [or *"mother"*?].

This word appears twice in this verse, and at first glance, it would be easy to draw a different conclusion on how best to translate. That too is interesting. A different translator might translate this word as *ame* (#H517 אֵם) which means "mother." The commonly accepted translation is *eem* (#H518 אִם) which means "if, whether, although, when, since, etc."

The letters are exactly the same, but the pronounciation could result in wildly different translations. It could also change who is speaking. To make this translation more complicated, אִמּ has already been translated as "mother," at So 8:5. You be the judge.

If the speaker was calling her "mother," that would make the speaker the Earthly Brothers (since the Jerusalem Above is their mother). Traditionally, verse nine is translated as "if." I have opted for "if" because these persons offer to "build turrets of silver on her." It seems, to me, they would have to reside in Heaven to do that type of construction.

Since it would also translate well as "mother," I am admitting that I could be wrong about which class of Brothers are speaking. Verse nine is a dilemma. I have given my best. You decide.

silver (כסף) literally: "silver."

The first-person plural, ensures that the Brothers are speaking. I am assuming it's her Heavenly Brothers. Immediately, her *new* Brothers express their support. Silver and cedar is their first offering, but these items are not defenses against assault. They are decorative. More precisely, in this highly symbolic song, they are decorative metaphors on top of function metaphors.

The Hebrew word *tee-rawth* (טירה) has been translated as "turrets." By definition, turrets are not as tall as a tower, yet rise above the walls of a castle. This will help you to understand why the Heavenly Shulamite sternly replies, "my breasts are like towers [#H4026 מגדלות]." The Heavenly Shulamite refuses to use her Brothers' word, "turrets (טירה)."

The root of *tee-rawth* (טירה) is *tee-raw* (טירה #H2918) which is commonly translated as "some type of row, turrets, a row of dwellings forming an outer-city defense, or a row of stones." At Ezk 46:23, *tee-rath* conveys the idea of a "row of upper stones." Ezekiel wasn't describing just a defense system. He was describing buildings, where sacrifices were boiled for food. Yet, those extra buildings also served as the castle's turrets, an architectural device for a defense battle.

Silver symbolizes death—because it tarnishes. To equate silver, or flammable cedar, as some form of protection would be quite a stretch of logic. The take-away lesson is this: her Angelic Brothers are not adding to the strength of the city, they are simply contributing decorations that proclaim her dramatic story, and how she got there. Often, gifts with a message were given to royalty. The wise men brought message-charged gifts to the young Jesus. (Mt 2:11)

Through symbolism (silver) they are telling onlookers how the Shulamite came to her *new* home. Both her and her husband had to die to inhabit this dwelling. Silver symbolizes death, because silver tarnishes.

"The holy city, New Jerusalem," which comes down out of Heaven, already has "a great and lofty wall" of jasper, the height of which is 144 cubits/maidens. (Re 21:2, 12, 14, 17-19) Again, "protection" is not a factor in Heaven. The Satan and his angelic followers have already been kicked out. Who else in Heaven wants to attack the Shulamite?

door (דלת) literally; "door."

Humans will not be resurrected to paradise as ready-made citizens. Therefore, earth's resurrected foreigners may be marking up her symbolic "door" with an adoption ceremony. This may sound un-achievable for an earthly person, but within the following words you will realize it's quite possible—when you know the true nature of this "door."

Let me explain: In Israel, when a slave loved the family he sold himself to, and didn't want to leave, God required that the slave perform a ritual *adoption process*. "And it hath been, when he saith unto thee, I go not out from thee—because he hath loved thee, and thy house, because [it is] good for him with thee—then thou hast taken the awl, and hast put [it] through his ear, and through the door, and he hath been to thee a servant age-during; and also to thy handmaid thou dost do so." –*De 15:16-17* That explains why mankind is willing to impale themselves to join this *new* family. (Gal 2:20)

we will engrave her (נצור) literally; "we-will-mark-her."

The translation of, צור is not easy to translate, nor is there any consensus. The Jewish translators of the *Septuagint* viewed this word as a "delineation," something "marked off," or "engraved." (Ex 32:4; 1Ki 7:15)

Maybe this engraving is simply a connection to Re 21:17 and De 15:16-17. Each of those citations seem to indicate inscribing, or a marking. Possibly the Angelic Brothers were offering to be the ones who pierce the ears of the resurrected foreigners who want to, symbolically, attach themselves to this happy household—the Jerusalem Above.

During the 1,000-year reign, resurrected foreigners must accept, or reject, this messianic household. Since the Satan will be released after the 1,000-year reign, possibly these doors of opportunity will be bloodied with awl marks, where the *newly* baptized have voluntarily attached themselves (by piercing their ears) to the Heavenly Shulamite's household. (Re 20:1-3)

10 [HEAVENLY SHULAMITE:] I'm a wall, and my breasts are like towers. At this juncture, in his eyes, I'm one bringing peace.	אני חומה ושדי כמגדלות אז הייתי בעיניו כמוצאת שלום: פ

MEDITATE ON THIS TEXT WHILE LISTENING TO DEMO 810

10 *wall* (#H2346 חומה) literally; "wall."

The sassy response of the Shulamite (to her Angelic Brothers) may sound flippant, but it's accurate. It carries the sternness of royalty. She is not the "door." She shrewdly declines the title reserved for her husband. Her husband is the "door." "I am the door; by me if any man enter in, he shall be saved, and shall go in and go out, and shall find pasture." –*Joh 10:9*

It's an old problem: her Brothers (earthly and heavenly) occasionally forget that she is a married woman, and the matriarch of an esteemed household—thus her sharp-tongued response. She has boundaries, and must repudiate any perceived slight to her husband's household.

Song of Songs is not the only place that describes heavenly "engraving" or "inscribing." "Having a wall great and high; having twelve gates, and at the gates twelve angels; and names written thereon, which are [the names] of the twelve tribes of the children of Israel." "And the wall of the city had twelve foundations, and on them, twelve names of the twelve apostles of the Lamb." –*Re 21:12, 14*

The walls of ancient Jerusalem were destroyed in 70 A.D. by the Romans. The Shulamite's walls, however, surround a city that will never be brought to ruin. (Da 2:44) To answer Jehovah's question (in verse seven), her walls, are one of her more valuable assets.

"And he measured the wall thereof, a hundred and forty and four cubits, [according to] the measure of a man, that is, of an angel. And the building of the wall thereof was jasper: and the city was pure gold, like unto pure glass. The foundations of the wall of the city were adorned with all manner of precious stones. The first foundation was jasper; the second, sapphire; the third, chalcedony; the fourth, emerald." –*Re 21:17-19*

As a wife, you have a duty to set limits for outsiders who approach you. Immodesty and unenforced boundaries are contrary to the holy covenant of marriage. The only grounds for a legal divorce, according to Jesus, is adultery. (Mt19:9) Israel's divorce was from her lack of boundaries. (Is 50:1)

like towers (כמגדלוֹת) literally; "like-towers."

In these modern times, it's hard to appreciate what towers meant to ancient cultures. The historian, Josephus, relates the thinking of Rome when they destroyed ancient Jerusalem's walls.

"Now as soon as the army had no more people to slay or plunder, because there remained none to be the objects of their fury (for they would not have spared any, had there remained any other work to be done), [Titus] Caesar gave orders that they should now demolish the entire city, and Temple, but should leave as many of the towers standing as they were of the greatest eminence; that is, Phasaelus, and Hippicus, and Mariamne; and so much of the wall that enclosed the city on the west side. This wall was spared, in order to afford a camp for such as were to lie in garrison [in the Upper City], as were the towers [the three forts] also spared, in order to demonstrate to posterity what kind of city it was, and how well fortified, which the Roman valor had subdued."[37]

> *Suspend the sigh, dear Sir, and check the groan, divinely bright your daughter's virtues shone: How free from scornful pride her gentle mind, which never its aid to indigence declined! Expanding free, it sought the means to prove unfailing charity, unbounded love! She unreluctant flies to see no more her dear loved parents on earth's dusky shore: Impatient Heavens resplendent goal to gain, where grief subsides, where changes are no more, and life's tumultuous billows cease to roar; she leaves her earthly mansion for the skies, where new creations feast her wondering eyes.*
> *–Phillis Wheatley*

It's an inescapable conclusion: milk, alone, cannot bring peace. If you will go back and review the earlier definition we established for "milk," at So 4:11, you will understand that the Heavenly Shulamite's breasts were filled with the kingdom basics, which is only the first stage of peace.

This was what Jehovah had in mind when He called the promised land "a land flowing with milk and honey." (Ex 3:8) Simply inhabiting this land was not enough. The God of Israel required—demanded—that His people mature. "Milk and honey" was not the destination, but a fuel to launch a nation.

like one bringing peace (כמוצאת שלום) literally; "like-one-bringing peace."

As Josephus wrote, a wall is the difference between extinction or survival. The moral boundaries you set for your household will equal your family's security, or destruction.

The Hebrew word *mo-tsaw* (#H4161 מוֹצָא) means "a going forth, an exit, exportation, vein." Basically, it's the way, or the source by which something is brought. In this case, "peace" is the thing being delivered—and the Shulamites are the 144,000 veins (*mo-tsaw* מוֹצָא) delivering that peace.

Every child begins with the weight of history within them. Ancestors prowl the attic of your mind. It's the commission of the Shulamites to create the human family. It's her duty to weave mankind's ancestry into a peace that will last an eternity.

Can she do it? Can you help?

11 [HEAVENLY BROTHERS:] Solomon had a vineyard. This husband of the multitude gave THE VINEYARD to those given to him. Each would bring, for its fruit, 1,000 pieces of silver.	כרם היה לשלמה בבעל המון נתן את־הכרם לנטרים איש יבא בפריו אלף כסף:

MEDITATE ON THIS TEXT WHILE LISTENING TO DEMO 811

11 ***Solomon had a vineyard*** (כרם היה לשלמה) literally; "vineyard he-was to-Solomon."

Rebuffed by the stern Shulamite, her Angelic Brothers have wisely elected not to continue the conversation, from verse nine.

Genesis speaks of the Adamic family that was stolen from Jehovah, by the Satan. Likewise, Jesus spoke of a "vineyard" that was stolen from his Father. (Mk 12:1-12)

In verse 11, the Angelic Brothers reveal that those thieves have been executed, and the property has been returned to the legitimate family head. Later, the Shulamites will be appointed as the vineyard's "overseers." But . . . Solomon heads the harvest.

This husband of the multitude (בבעל המון) literally; "in-husband-of the-multitude."

Many translators don't like translating *Baal Hamon*. So, they don't. They prefer to treat this Hebrew word like a location, or a place name. There is a big problem, however: like the city of "Shulam," the city of "Baal Hamon" doesn't exist. There is no such place as "Baal Hamon."

The divine author is forcing you to come to terms with His metaphorical speech. Follow the thought: the Hebrew word *baw-al* (#H1166 בעל) means "to be master; be husband." The Hebrew word *haw-mone* (#H1995 המון) means "mob, crowd, company, multitude." Solomon had 1,000 wives, the Heavenly Solomon: 432,000 wives (144,000 full-wives and 288,000 half-wives)—a multitude.

The wealth of Solomon is his family, which includes his wives. "Now the weight of gold that came to Solomon in one year was six hundred threescore and six [666] talents of gold." –*1Ki 10:14* But why would holy text bother to include such a detailed number? Why 666?

Six is a man's number, but 666 symbolizes mankind in total. Ps 2:2 highlights "666" arrogance, and the inevitability of human rule.

Human rebellion began in *Genesis*, when the Satan turned mankind away from Jehovah. (Ge 3:13) Both Eve and Adam decided God's counsel should take a backseat to theirs.

God, however, decided to let Adam's unborn children make their own choice: "and before him shall be gathered all the nations: and he shall separate them one from another, as the shepherd separateth the sheep from the goats." –*Mt 25:32*

Taking back God's wealth (His family) will be a long-awaited vindication. Like David, Jehovah will retrieve His family, as described at 1Sa 30:1-20.

to those given to him (לנטרים) literally; "to-ones-being-overseers."

It's difficult, in English, to separate the "keepers" from the "overseers." Solomon's full-wives prefigured those who rule from Heaven, "Overseers." Solomon's half-wives (concubines) prefigured the earth's "keepers."

Both categories of Solomon's wives will have divine positions of leadership (wives and concubines) since, "those given to him" are surrounded by ongoing references to 1,000, translated from *aleph* (אלף).

It hasn't been mentioned before, but there is more than one way to translate *aleph* (אלף). Aleph also contains the idea of "boss, overseer, head one." Verse 13 will introduce the word "keepers" (מקשיבים). The "overseers" and "keepers," however, appear to be separate groups, prefigured at 1Ch 27:1-15.

Hebrew poetry loves progressive word pictures. The Hebrew word used in this verse *naw-tar* (#H5201 נטר) means "to guard, to cherish, oversee." Since verse 11's rare word (נטר) contains the Hebrew letter *tet* (ט) it conveys the additional idea of "nursing, or caring for children."

This takes us back to her early origins, at So 1:7, where the Earthly Shunemite resists the requests to be a hired nurse to outsiders.

Finally, she is where she wants to be. She is nursing Solomon's children. Note her lilting, but regal, satisfaction in the following verse—verse 12.

12 [HEAVENLY SHULAMITE:] My vineyard is mine. Before me is the 1,000. . . to you Solomon. 200, goes to those tending his FRUIT.	כרמי שלי לפני האלף לך שלמה ומאתים לנטרים את־פריו:

MEDITATE ON THIS TEXT WHILE LISTENING TO DEMO 812

12 *the 1,000, to you* (האלף לך) literally; "the-thousand to-you."

When this Shulamite states "My vineyard is mine." she continues to assert her authority as a full-wife. And she has a seal to prove it!

Again, "vineyard" equals family.

Yet, why would such an intelligent, capable woman concern herself with a tribute to her husband? Because, proper reverence of his authority aligns family health. Jehovah asked His wife, ancient Israel, to deliver a tithe. She didn't.

The Shulamite is a better wife than ancient Israel. This is the beginning of a *new* family with more care for the family unit than for herself. By giving Solomon 1,000 (1,000= אלף or authority) she is both giving him the leaders of the earth (Zion), and acknowledging his authority over her children.

There is a saying: "To keep a wife's feet on the ground put more responsibilities on her shoulders." The Heavenly Solomon appreciates his wife, because of her motives.

The ancient matriarch, Sarah, set the tone for our family by giving her brother-husband a "1,000." Her "1,000" was also taken from a king of the earth—a symbolic "keeper" or "tender."

"And unto Sarah he said, Behold, I have given thy brother a thousand pieces of silver. Behold, it is for thee a covering of the eyes to all that are with thee. And in respect of all thou art righted. And Abraham prayed unto God. And God healed Abimelech, and his wife, and his maid-servants. And they bare children." –*Ge 20:16-17*

Like the Shulamite, Sarah's husband was also her brother. (Ge 20:12) She too was a "sister bride." The Heavenly Shulamite, however, is greater than Sarah.

and 200 (ומאתים) literally; "and-two-hundreds."

"Two" implies potential kingdom badness, but also potential kingdom goodness. The heavenly overseer (the Shulamite) was giving earth's keepers a chance to make good, with *new* behaviors. "And thou, son of man, say unto the house of Israel: Thus ye speak, saying, Our transgressions and our sins are upon us, and we pine away in them; how then can we live?'" –*Ezk 33:10* The *new* Earthly Brothers are better than the ancient Jewish Brothers, but they are not out of danger.

The Satan will be released after the 1,000-year (millennial) reign. "And I saw an angel coming down out of Heaven, having the key of the abyss and a great chain in his hand. And he laid hold on the dragon, the old serpent, which is the Devil and Satan, and bound him for a thousand years, and cast him into the abyss, and shut [it], and sealed [it] over him, that he should deceive the nations no more, until the thousand years should be finished: after this he must be loosed for a little time." –*Re 20:1-3*

What are you doing to prepare your children for this event? Question: How many will the Satan dupe, at the end of the 1,000-year (millennial) reign? Answer: As many as the sands of the sea. (Re 20:8)

NUMERICS: *vineyard* (כרם) literally; "vineyard." Vineyard equals family. This is the final of nine uses. At the *remez* level, the number nine hints at lactation. It takes nine months for a mother's milk to come in. Therefore, the final stage, before family life begins.

The fruitage of the Heavenly Shulamite's vineyard has "come in." "Whereas thou hast been forsaken and hated, so that no man passed through thee, I will make thee an eternal excellency, a joy of many generations. Thou shalt also suck the milk of the nations, and shalt suck the breast of kings; and thou shalt know that I, Jehovah, am thy Saviour, and thy Redeemer, the Mighty One of Jacob. For brass I will bring gold, and for iron I will bring silver, and for wood brass, and for stones iron. I will also make thy officers peace, and thine exactors righteousness." *–Is 60:15-17*

NUMERICS: *Solomon* (שלמה) literally; "exuding peace, achieving abundance." This is the final of five uses. At the *remez* level, five portends judgment with a potential for salvation. It means a great multitude, which no man could number, out of every nation and of [all] tribes and peoples and tongues, standing before the throne and before the Lamb, arrayed in white robes, and palms in their hands; and they cry with a great voice, saying, Salvation unto our God who sitteth on the throne, and unto the Lamb.'" *–Re 7:9-10*

NUMERICS: *FRUIT* (פריו) literally; "FRUIT." This is the final of three uses. At the *remez* level, the number three means, life everlasting. On the third day, God created the seed-within-the-seed; recursive life; life in perpetuity. "And he showed me a river of water of life, bright as crystal, proceeding out of the throne of God and of the Lamb, in the midst of the street thereof. And on this side of the river and on that was the tree of life, bearing twelve [manner of] fruits, yielding its fruit every month: and the leaves of the tree were for the healing of the nations." –*Re 22:1-2* The "fruit" described here, brings everlasting life to their children on earth.

13 [HEAVENLY SHULAMITE:] Those dwelling in the gardens, friends, keepers, let me hear your voice.	היושבת בגנים חברים מקשיבים לקולך השמיעיני:

MEDITATE ON THIS TEXT WHILE LISTENING TO DEMO 813

13 *Those dwelling in the gardens* (היושבת בגנים) literally; "the-one-dwelling in-the-gardens."

Genesis speaks of a single garden, within Eden. In this time period, however, garden has become plural.[38] The Shulamite will multiply gardens until the entire becomes a garden.

Who are the "keepers?" Not everyone will go to Heaven with our Messiah.[39] Adam was the original "keeper" of earth's Garden of Eden. (Ge 2:15) The 288,000 earthly concubines will be the new "keepers" of the earthly gardens. (Re 2:7; Ps 115:16)[40] In this verse, Jehovah's original plan, for Adam's descendants to live on a paradise earth, has been restored.

Like Adam, these concubines will be given custodial custody over the vineyards ("Earthly Brothers").[41] Like perfect Adam, they too will be above all the creatures of the earth, but a little lower than the angels.

The Shulamite has already given Solomon her earthly leaders as concubines. Solomon will make the rules that emanate (like veins / מוֹצָא So 8:10) from the Jerusalem Above, throughout Zion, then throughout the world. (Re 21:27)

let me hear your voice (לְקוֹלֵךְ הַשְׁמִיעִינִי) literally; "to-voice-of-you let-hear-me."

The commentary at So 8:6 contains a quote from Pearl S. Buck. The same warning could be made to someone who overestimates what a mate can do for them. A marriage mate is not enough!

I will slightly revise Ms. Buck's quote to demonstrate: A wife's lack of emotional security is due, I believe, to their isolation from an extended family unit. No two people—no husband and wife—can provide enough emotional security for a family. Both need to feel themselves as one, with a world of kinfolk, varieties in age, and temperament, yet connected through family bond.

This new Shulamite is also a mother. She is the mother of the Earthly Brothers, and she is securing a deal for her children (the Earthly Brother class). "And the Spirit and the bride say, Come. And he that heareth, let him say, Come. And he that is athirst, let him come: he that will, let him take the water of life freely." *–Re 22:17*

With Jehovah, silence is insufficient. Vows of intent must literally come out of your mouth, as spoken words. What's in your heart, must agree with what crosses your lips. (Nu 30:2) When this Heavenly Shulamite announces "let me hear your voice," she is publicly demonstrating, to her Father, her children's level of commitment.

The ability to count blessings is a math that few families master. The Shulamite is teaching her children that their appreciation must be vocalized. There is no such thing as silent gratitude. Unexpressed gratitude is called, "ingratitude."

14 [HEAVENLY SHULAMITE:] Come away, my beloved, and be like a gazelle, or like a young stag, on the spice-laden mountains.

ברח | דודי ודמה־לך לצבי או לעפר האילים על הרי בשמים:

MEDITATE ON THIS TEXT WHILE LISTENING TO DEMO 814

14 Come away (ברח) literally; "come-away."

Armageddon is over. "The Lord's Model Prayer" has been answered. "Let your kingdom come. Let your will take place, as in Heaven, also upon earth." This gazelle (Solomon) moves quickly throughout his kingdom.

The Heavenly Shulamite, however, is now interested in his quick return to her. He is her husband. But, dozens of new problems are born every morning you wake up. The way your family handles those problems reveals your family's strengths and weaknesses. There is a new focus in this kingdom—family.

NUMERICS: beloved (דוֹד) literally; "family love, beloved." This is the final of 40 uses. At the *remez* level, the number 40 describes re-birth. For Hebrews, pregnancy is expressed in weeks—40 weeks. "Beloved" hints at family love—but which family? The Heavenly Shulamite's Father is Jehovah and her mother is "the woman." "'Marvel not that I said unto thee, 'Ye must be born anew.' The wind bloweth where it will, and thou hearest the voice thereof, but knowest not whence it cometh, and whither it goeth: so is every one that is born of the Spirit.' Nicodemus answered and said unto him, 'How can these things be?' Jesus answered and said unto him, 'Art thou the teacher of Israel, and understandest not these things? Verily, verily, I say unto thee, We speak that which we know, and bear witness of that which we have seen; and ye receive not our witness. If I told you earthly things and ye believe not, how shall ye believe if I tell you heavenly things?'" – *Joh 3:7-12*

Let me end the chapter with this story: At the warm surface, in the fresh air, a little wave was playing among his friends. In the distance, the little wave heard excitement. In the distance, he saw older waves collapsing on shore.

In a panic of sudden recognition, the little wave began churning about, crying to the others, "Go back! What will become of us? What will become of me? We're headed for the rocks, where waves die!"

Beneath him, grandfather undertow whispered, "Calm down. You're more than a wave. You're part of a great ocean."

If there is one lesson to be learned from ancient Israel, it's this: if you will let your life be directed by God, He will bring you through everything—even death.

SUMMARY

Husbands: You have just finished eight chapters, and not once will you find Solomon reminding his Shulamite of her subordinate position. Instead, he showers her with compliments, rewards her with new responsibilities, and encourages her with gratitude. Are the husbands in your neighborood this magnanimous? Whose example do you prefer? (Koran 4:19)

If only modern husbands were as committed to the growth of their wives' as Solomon was. Husbands might discover worthwhile wisdom they never knew existed. Marital growth presents many hidden pathways to God, previously unknown. Every wife is an undiscovered gateway to God.

Women may attend the same religious meeting that we men do, but they attend for slightly different reasons, and draw slightly different conclusions. That's why we must serve our women tea. It gives us a chance to see Heaven from their side of the table.

The incompatibilities that God put between man and woman are like a cosmic joke that resolves the puzzle separating man and God.

No one has all the answers to relationship success, but our women do have something in common with God. Like God, women listen to some very undeserved requests. There is no magic arrangement of words that will compel God to answer your prayer. Like women, God prefers a personal relationship.

I know I am making a broad generalization, but most husbands become frauds after only a few years of marriage. Don't overestimate your deeds. History shows that stupid men continuously overestimate their gestures. Historians claim that, on the way to his beheading, King Louis the 14th was heard to lament, "Has God forgotten all I have done for Him?"

"The garment is the grace, the beauty, the embellishment of the body. So too are wives to their husbands, as their husbands are to them." –*Koran 2:187*

Good Muslims see marriage as a vehicle for deeper insights. "And among His signs is this, that He has created for you mates from among yourselves, that you may dwell in tranquility with them; and He has put love and mercy between you. Verily in that are signs for those who reflect." –*Koran 30:21*

Mohammed instructed his followers well. "The best of you are they who behave best to their wives." Are you seeking a meaningful relationship with God? Then, include Him, thank Him, honor Him, and show your gratitude, by being kind to His crazy daughter—your wife.

Tonight, somewhere, a daughter of God will cry from a broken heart. Her girlish dreams of a husband who would love her is fading away. Her children are growing numb, because they anticipate another family squabble. They fear their family is dying.

Somewhere, a son of God is secluding himself, feeling useless, and unappreciated. Maybe that's you. Maybe you never anticipated a family with so many problems. Maybe you never fathomed you could make everyone so unhappy.

Don't be that man.

The best thing Solomon taught Israel had nothing to do with wisdom. It was the deep, empathetic love that he spread throughout his kingdom. Everyone knew they were in his prayers. Everyone knew he cared about them.

Be this man.

HOLY TEXT SOURCES

For original Hebrew text, I used the Hebrew *Leningrad Codex*. The original *Leningrad Codex* was copied (from a much older Hebrew text) around 1010 A.D. The *Leningrad Codex* belongs to a group of Hebrew texts called the Masoretic texts. The Masoretes were very careful to preserve the accuracy of holy text. The Masoretes even noted the unusual formations, and spellings. Not a letter was lost.

Since the *Septuagint* predates the *Leningrad Codex* by 1100 years, why not use the *Septuagint*? Because the *Septuagint* is Greek. As a foreign translation, it's a mere shadow of the original Hebrew, from which it was taken.

Both manuscripts were produced by exemplary Jewish scholars. The *Septuagint* is a Jewish-produced, Greek document, while the *Leningrad Codex* is a Jewish-produced, Hebrew document. When Jewish scholars translate holy text for foreigners, they do so at the *peshat* level (for simple minds). Quoting from the *Septuagint* limits yourself to the lowest level of understanding. Which language would you choose, to understand the mind of God? (Am 4:13)

English speaking Bible readers often overlook how *Song of Songs* came to us. The *Song of Songs* is part of the five *megillot* which includes, *Esther, Ruth, Ecclesiastes, Song of Songs* and *Lamentations*—in no particular order. This hints that these scrolls (books) should be read together. They are related. So, this is the beginning of the "Hidden Series" from the *megillot*. It's my intention to translate each of these sacred books into English, from Hebrew—not Greek—*never!*

Let me address the deliberate, non-traditional, methods I have employed. The vowel indicators were added by the Ben Asher family. The original Hebrew scrolls had no vowel indicators and used a 22-letter alphabet, with no spaces between words. That being said, let me list some of the methods recent Jewish scribes used to "fix" God's holy text.

(1) Scribes added five additional ending letters, or sofeets, to show where a word ends. Notice, however, that when scribes began inserting spaces, between words, they did not discard their invented "sofeets."
(2) Some scribes decided to revise God's superscripts (introductions) to discourage "schisms" (Christianity). (Ps 20)
(3) Scribes added vowel indicators to assist with pronunciation. This helpful tool began to bog down, however, when so many vowel symbols began to duplicate sounds and guess at original pronunciations. To make matters worse, cantillation marks were added and brought hopeless complexity to simple holy text. Oh, yeah, have you read about the new vowel indicators?
(4) It's possible that Masoretic scribes made some letters extra-large, or extra-small. It's quite possible, however, that these were part of the original text.
(5) Some scribes decided to add tagims to some letters, showing further significance and depth to some words. Tagims were not part of the original text.
(6) Some Hebrew scribes decided to remove God's personal name from their translations, to save foreigners (non-Hebrews) from mispronouncing by non-pronouncing.

    On and on it goes. I have spared you many other needless details, but you get the idea. Any subject can be made so complicated that the average person just gives up. This brings me back to my original point: the original Hebrew manuscripts employed a simple, 22 letter, alphabet. That's what I have chosen, for simplicity's sake. Too often, well meaning religious adherents "fix" what God should, if only He knew better. So, I give you the simple Hebrew. Decide for yourself.
    In the English, however, I CAPITALIZED all words identified by the definite direct object marker (את). It's such a simple solution I am horrified that this has never been done before. In Hebrew, את is never translated. It can't be

translated, because it's not a word. Rather, it's an indicator. It indicates that the following word is important. So, aren't you curious which words God thought was important? Well, I was. So, I put the words that follow את in all CAPS. For the first time (in English) you can see what Hebrews have known for centuries.

For scholars, I have used *Strong's* numbering system, which facilitates research and referencing. You will first encounter this system in the "Key Words" section. The first word you will encounter will be "Angry" (#H2734 חרנ). The #H2734 is the corresponding *Strong's* number.

There are eight chapters. The first four chapters focus on the Shunemite's earthly life. The last four chapters focus on her transformation into a Heavenly Shulamite. If you have timed the reading of the *Song of Songs*, you know this book can be read in less than 20 minutes. There are exactly 2,050 Hebrew words. There are 49 words found only in *Song of Songs*, and no other Bible book. There are 20 Hebrew words that God has designated as important (as indicated with, את).

The infinite absolute is never used. The *vov* (ו) consecutive is completely absent. Many seeming incongruities exist with masculine forms of verbs. Pronouns and suffixes often appear, rather than expected feminine forms. None of this should be surprising, considering that *men* becoming part of a *bride class* is difficult to convey in any language.

If you have counted the range of Hebrew words in the *Song of Songs*, you know there are just over 100. Anyone can learn 100 words. Whoever wants to see the deeper things, it's within reach. Regular people, such as yourself, can learn enough Hebrew to read and understand *Song of Songs*—in the original Hebrew, in less than a year.

This book does not advocate any specific religious interpretation. It was not funded, sponsored, or initiated by any religious organization. Simply put: this is a translation with commentary that explains why, and how, something was translated. I will leave it to the religious community to make their own applications.

KEY WORDS

*The 20 Words that God designated as important with, את (definite direct object marker), are: their-vineyards (1:6); kids-of-you (1:8); love (2:7); faces-of-you (2:14); voice-of-you (2:14); whom-she-loves (3:1); whom-she-loves (3:2); whom-she-loves (3:3); whom-she-loves (3:4); she-love (3:5); cloak-of-me (5:3); feet-of-me (5:3); wrap-of-me (5:7); beloved-of-me (5:8); beloved-of-me (7:13); the-love (8:4); the-love (8:7); all-of (8:7); the-vineyard (8:11); fruit-of-him (8:12).

Angry (displeasure; fierce; furious; wrathful) (#H2734 חרנ) (one time: 1:6)

Angry (disrespect; contempt; despised; shamed) (#H937 בוז) (three times: 8:1; 8:7; 8:7)

Apple (apple; blow; breathe; kindle) (#H8598 תפוח) (five times: 2:3; 2:5; 4:16; 7:8; 8:5)

Arise (rising; resurrect; ascending) (#H6965 קום) (four times: 2:10; 2:13; 3:2; 7:8)

Arouse (watcher; angel; guard of Heavenly Jerusalem) (#H5892 עיר) (five times: 2:7; 3:2; 3:3; 3:5; 8:4)

Awake (to be made naked; exposed to ridicule; revoke citizenship; deemed wicked; punished) (#H5783 עור) (seven times: 2:7; 3:5; 4:16; 5:2; 5:11; 8:4; 8:5)

Black (early dawn; dark part of the morning; early at a task) (#H7835 שחר) (four times: 1:5; 1:6; 5:7; 5:11)

Come (abide; depart; enter) (#H935 בּוֹא) (six times: 2:8; 4:8; 4:16; 4:16; 5:1)

Curtain (to drape; hanging; grieving) (#H3407 ירע) (one time: 1:5)

Daughter (female child; apple branch) (#H1323 בת) (12 times: 1:5; 2:2; 2:7; 3:5; 3:10; 3:11; 5:8; 5:16; 6:9; 7:1; 7:4; 8:4)

Find (appear; attain; acquire; meet; presence; meet) (#H4672 מצא) (eight times: 3:1; 3:2; 3:3; 3:4; 5:6; 5:7; 5:8; 8:1)

*FRUIT (reward; reached for; plucked) (#H6529 פרי) (three times: 2:3; *8:11; *8:12)

Incense (turn into fragrance by fire; incense; kindle) (#H6999 קטר) (one time: 3:6)

Jerusalem (two hills; foundation of peace) (#H3389 ירוּשלמ) (eight times: 1:5; 2:7; 3:5; 3:10; 5:8; 5:16; 6:4; 8:4)

Kiss (catch fire; inflame; kindle) (#H5401 נשׁק) (three times: 1:2; 1:2; 8:1)

*LOVE [Godly] (superlative love; godly affection; godly attraction; principled desire) (#H160 אהבה) (17 times: 1:3; 1:4; 1:7; 2:4; 2:5; *2:7; *3:1; *3:2; *3:3; *3:4; *3:5; 3:10; 5:8; 7:6; *8:4; *8:7; 8:7)

*LOVE [Family] (beloved; affectionate love; boiling; legal relation) (#H1730 דוֹד) (40 times: 1:2; 1:4; 1:13; 1:14; 1:16; 2:3; 2:8; 2:9; 2:10; 2:16; 2:17; 4:10; 4:10; 4:10; 4:16; 5:1; 5:2; 5:4; 5:5; 5:6; 5:6; *5:8; 5:9; 5:9; 5:9; 5:9; 5:10; 5:16; 6:1; 6:1; 6:2; 6:3; 6:3; 7:10; 7:11; 7:12; *7:13; 7:14; 8:5; 8:14)

Love / masculine [Pastoral] (shepherd; pastor; caretaking partner) (#H7473 רעי) (10 times: 1:8; 1:9 (feminine); 1:15 (feminine); 2:2 (feminine); 2:10 (feminine); 2:13 (feminine); 4:1 (feminine); 4:7 (feminine); 5:16; 6:4 (feminine))

Name (nomenclature; conspicuous position; current title) (#H8034 שם) (two times: 1:3; 7:13)

Pleading (to seven; repeat a declaration; prophetic times brought to full; swear) (#H7650 שבע) (five times: 2:7; 3:5; 5:8; 5:9; 8:4)

Search (striving; enquiring; seeking) (#H1245 בקש) (five times: 3:1; 3:1; 3:2; 5:6; 6:1)

Seat (UNCERTAIN; from chariot: covering; saddle) (#H4817 מרכב) (one time: 3:10)

See (behold, see, lo) (#H2009 הנה) (nine times: 1:15; 1:15; 1:16; 2:8; 2:9; 2:11; 3:7; 4:1; 4:1)

Sister (sister) (#H269 אחות) (seven times: 4:9; 4:10; 4:12; 5:1; 5:2; 8:8; 8:8)

Solomon (exuding peace; achieving abundance) (#H8010 שלמה) (five times: 1:5; 3:9; 3:11; 8:11; 8:12)

Song (rhythm, beat, strike, play with fingers; instrumental [not vocal]) (#H2167 זמר) (one time: 2:12)

Sun (generator of inner and outer life) (#H8121 שמש) (one time: 1:6)

Sun's radiation (heat; warmth of raised woman) (#H2535 חמל) (one time: 6:10)

Twig (bough; shoot) (#H5577 סנסן) (one time: 7:9)

Vine (bending; twining) (#H1612 גפן) (four times: 2:13; 6:11; 7:9; 7:13)

***VINEYARD (given through noble birth)** (#H3754 כרם) (nine times: *1:6; 1:6; 1:14; 2:15; 2:15; 7:13; 8:11; *8:11; 8:12)

Wine (effervesce; fermenting) (#H3196 יין) (six times: 1:2; 1:4; 4:10; 5:1; 7:10; 8:2)

MAIN CHARACTERS

You may need to refererence this section (Main Characters) throughout your read, since *Song of Songs* is so densely packed with prophetic types. This section provides the scriptural citations that defines each type.

Every character, in *Song of Songs*, is a multiplicity of persons, under one label. How does the Bible's divine author create one character to span many generations? As Da 2:32-44 demonstrates, God forces one prophetic type to take on the multi-generational objectives of all its predecessors. There have been many Kings of the North, and many Kings of the South, for instance.

In the case of Daniel's prophetic statue, it encapsulates, Babylon, Medo-Persia, Greece, Rome, and the Anglo-American dual powers compose this single entity. (Da 2:32-44) The same method is used for the characters in *Song of Songs*.

The divine author has done this throughout holy text, with messiahs, kings, beasts, dragons, and trees. This is one of Jehovah's signature means of prophetic communication. Even if real names are used (such as Solomon), the characters in the story are metaphorical representations. In other words, the characters in *Song of Songs* are composite characters.

For Jews, the Solomon entity would include, Solomon, the shepherd, and the Solomon-like messiah who will lead them into a messianic age. For Christians, the Solomon entity would include, Solomon, the shepherd, earthly Jesus, and the resurrected Jesus. For Muslims, the Solomon entity would include, Solomon, the shepherd, Jesus, Muhammad, and the Solomon-like Mahdi who will lead believers into Paridise.

Like the picture of the Shulamite on the cover of this book, many persons (144,000) form one composite Shulamite. So, if your goal is to use these descriptions to prove an actual physical characteristic of the Shulamite, stop it! Neither the Shunemite, nor the Shulamite, is a Cushite. (So 1:5)

Scholars, such as Thorlief Boman makes this point better than me. "In one Old Testament book, the *Song of Solomon*, we apparently have extensive descriptions of human appearance; these descriptions, which we designate by the Arabic word *wasf*, show immediately with their grotesque images, however, that there are no descriptions in our sense of the word. If we proceed from the knowledge we have attained that the Israelite considers persons in order to discover their qualities, it's not very difficult to understand the peculiar images in these descriptive images. In the form of a simple riddle, easy to solve, the *wasf* describes the dominant and admirable qualities of two [or more] principal persons, particularly the bride or fiancée."[42]

There are two aspects to Solomon, two aspects to the Shulamite, two aspects to the Brothers, and two aspects to the kingdom. The Father's kingdom is described at Joh 3:5 and Jos 5:13-14. The Messiah's kingdom is described at Col 1:13-14 and Re 3:21. Understanding the method behind the distinction will help to reveal their place in prophecy.

HEAVENLY SOLOMON:

Both Solomon's cared deeply for the kingdom promised to Abraham. (Gal 3:29) The legitimate, and final shepherd was prophesied, at Ge 3:15.

Earthly Solomon was wise enough to put kingdom interests first. According to the New Testament, Jesus was, "something more than Solomon." (Mt 12:42; Ro 16:20)

According to Islam, the death of Solomon was a lesson to be learned. (Koran, sura 34 (Saba), ayah 14) Solomon was a king, prophet, and shepherd of God's servants. Solomon remains one of the most commemorated holy figures in Islam. Muslim tradition still maintains David, Solomon, and Dhul-Qarnayan, as the three greatest monarchs of all time. Muslims still await a Solomon-like messiah (Mahdi).

It will be difficult for Westerners to identify the "shepherd" (in *Song of Songs*) without using Hebrew. What Westerners call, the book of "*Ecclesiastes*," Hebrews call *Qo-he-leth*. *Qo-he-leth* (קהלה) is a "shepherd" of people. So, it's easy for a Hebrew to identify Solomon the "shepherd."

Hebrew poetry loves progressive word pictures. The shepherd/Solomon/Jesus are all the same entity. "And further, because the Preacher was wise, he still taught the people knowledge; yea, he pondered, and sought out, [and] set in order many proverbs. The Preacher sought to find out acceptable words, and that which was written uprightly, [even] words of truth. The words of the wise are as goads; and as nails well fastened are [the words of] the masters of assemblies, [which] are given from *one shepherd*." *–Ec 12:9-11* The final words, cited in *Ecclesiastes*, calls Solomon the "one shepherd." Is calling Solomon a "shepherd" so difficult to grasp?

Hebrew poetry loves progressive word pictures. In this strange, prophetic song, each character takes on many identities. Notice how the Shulamite is described as a "mare" and a "lily." (So 1:9; 2:1) At So 2:9 and 8:14 Solomon is described as a "gazelle" and a "husband." (So 8:11,14)

So, there is no need for the Shunemite to reject Solomon for the "shepherd." Solomon *is* the "shepherd." Solomon will have many descriptions, just as the Shulamite will have many descriptions.[43] (Zec 13:7; Heb 13:20)

The Earthly Solomon's prayerful request to become a good *shepherd* impressed the God of Israel ("give to your servant an obedient heart to judge your people, to discern between good and bad"). In many respects Solomon's rule (as long as he was a good *shepherd*) was a small-scale pattern of the future Messiah's reign. Solomon's name (from a root meaning "peace") fits the "Millennial" Jesus, or the "Prince of Peace." (Is 9:5-6)

In this commentary, the Heavenly Solomon's main focus is keeping his promise to re-gather "the seed of Abraham" and shepherd them with the assistance of his 144,000 joint rulers—the bride class, brides selected by his Father. (Mt 20:23; Re 21:9-10, 22-24; 1Ch 22:1-19; 1Ch 23-26)

Jesus could be described as the uniting force behind the fulfillment of Ezk 37:16-19, by reuniting Heaven and earth. (Joh 17:20-21)

HEAVENLY SHULAMITE:

The first hint that God separated his favored people into two separate groups, appears at Ge 28:12. There, Jacob saw "angels" going up from earth, to Heaven, then coming down from Heaven, to earth. Humans dwelling in Heaven, however, was a concept unknown to Israelites . . . until the arrival of Jesus.

Jacob added clarification when he prophesied that Ephraim would have greater numbers than Manasseh, at Ge 48:13-20. This foreshadowed Manasseh's smaller numbers would rule from Heaven. For example: Note that God removed Ephraim from the tribes listed in Heaven, at Re 7:5-8.

Although these two groups are described extensively in *Song of Songs*, Isaiah provided further information in less poetic language. (Is 66:18-22)

Jesus taught extensively on this heavenly class, who would be purchased with his blood. (Lk 10:20; Lk 12:32) This "little flock" of Manasseh was not to be confused with Joh 10:16. Jesus, himself, provided further details clarifying those two groups in *Song of Songs*. (compare Re 19:7-9; Re 21:9; Re 22:17; and So 8:4-5)

Apostle Paul had no problem understanding the existence of these two groups. Paul reminded the Earthly Brothers who their true mother was: the Heavenly Shulamite. (Gal 4:21-31)

As you have been taught, there are two resurrections. (Re 20:4-5) Because of their special duties, these 144,000 rulers, the Manasseh class had to be resurrected first. (1Th 4:16-17)

The book of *Revelation* provides marching orders for the Heavenly Shulamites (a.k.a. known as the Manasseh class), from the lips of Jesus: "He that overcometh, I will give to him to sit down with me in my throne, as I also overcame, and sat down with my Father in his throne." –*Re 3:21*

Jesus was describing his Shulamite bride (a.k.a. known as the Manasseh class). The legal feature of this wedding ceremony involves bringing the bride from her earthly home to her husband's heavenly home. (Mt 1:24; Re 21:2-9)

She will be assigned maidservants who resided on earth before the death of Jesus—also known as the 288,000. (2Sa 24:9; 1Ch 27:1) These future administrators will be called "concubines," as opposed to a wife. A Hebrew husband pays for a wife—not a concubine (a.k.a. half-wife). They died prior to the arrival of Jesus/Solomon.

So, the blood of Jesus has yet to pay for these future concubines. (compare 1Th 4:16 & Heb 11:13) In fact, these "concubines" will not be resurrected as citizens, since entry into the New Israel requires subjection to the king of New Israel—whom they have yet to meet. (Gal 6:15-16)

Just as Sarah had a foreign hand maiden, Rachel had a foreign hand maiden, Leah had a foreign hand maiden, the Shulamites will have foreign earthly hand maidens, exactly 288,000—two for each Shulamite.

The Heavenly Shulamite entity is composed of former Shunemites who were prepared for their heavenly duties. These 144,000 were discussed many years before, at Is 65:17 (compare Is 65:17, Ps 45:10, and Ge 41:51).

In *Song of Songs* it's easy to know when the Heavenly Shulamite is speaking, because she speaks from Heaven. The Heavenly Shulamite will engage in activities that the Earthly Shunemite can't. Sitting at the serving table will take place in

Heaven. (So 1:12) Their verdant bed is in Heaven. (So 1:16) Notice that in verses So 1:10-11 one woman has earrings and the other does not. Who has earrings and who doesn't? So, it can't be the same woman. One is a Heavenly Shulamite and the other is an Earthly Shunemite.

EARTHLY SHUNEMITE:

When *Song of Songs* was written (approx 1,000 B.C.E.), there was no concept of humans graduating to Heaven. At that time, an Israelite's concept of "ascendance" would be living atop Zion, in the king's palace.

So, the average Israelite would know the Shunemite was Abishag. With such a well documented story, in the *First Book of Kings*, what better fit was possible? Abishag was what the dying King David needed, but, as far as Solomon was concerned, not quite what Israel needed.

Abishag was a Shunemite. She was taken from Shunem to the city of David, Zion. (1Ki 8:1) Her village, Shunem, was located in the tribe of Issachar, about 15 miles southwest of the sea of Galilee, or about 55 miles north of Jerusalem.

By contrast, there was no such place as Shulam (or Salem)—on earth. Shulam is not listed in *Strong's* concordance, *Young's* concordance, or *Encyclopedia Judaica*. Shulam exists only in Heaven—as a symbolic city of peace (the Jeru-salem above). (Gal 4:26; Heb 7:1-2)

Abishag served as a human metaphor, a human bridge who witnessed the conclusion of David's Zion, and the beginning of Solomon's Jerusalem. (2Sa 5:7-10; 1Ki 3:1) Abishag could say that one day she looked out her window and saw a Temple . . . where there was nothing before. Today's Abishag class will see a much greater marvel.

Abishag's brief story is so full of startling and bizarre facts that we are left to wonder why God would provide such unusual details. (1Ki 1:1-4; 2:17-22) In fact, the Abishag story makes no sense, until we insert it into *Song of Songs*.

There, we discover that (as a matter of Hebrew law) Solomon inherited David's wives. Otherwise, Solomon would have no legal claim to Abishag. In *Song of Songs* we are introduced to a new problem for Abishag: Solomon was choosing wives for political advantages, while she was wasting away in Zion—without children.

Only one of David's wives, however, is young; only one still has her youthful beauty; only one is a virgin (who had not known a man); only one would Solomon kill for. When Adonijah colluded with Bathsheba for Abishag, Solomon quickly put him to death. How attached (legally and emotionally) was Solomon to Abishag? If Abishag was not a legitimate wife, she would be free to marry Adonijah, or whoever Abishag chose. (So 1:7) But, every royal wife (wife and half-wife) had royal duties. (Pr 31)

Do not, however, confuse the Shunemite with the 288,000 earthly concubines, described at So 4:8; 6:6, 8, 9; 7:13; 8:7, 11-13. They too have a place in the messianic kingdom, but they are not heavenly rulers. Those future concubines will be Millinial Administrators.

In this song, the Heavenly Solomon never dialogues with the Earthly Shunemite, until her resurrection, at So 5:2-4. Given our times, why would the Earthly Shunemites claim that they receive no direct communication with God? Why doesn't God dialogue with the Shunemites? Because, she is our sister, not our mother. She has a unique assignment to care for her brother's vineyard, but not a vineyard of her own. (So 1:6) The Shulamite, however, has a vineyard of her own. (So 8:12; Gal 4:26)

When the Israelites were in Babylonian captivity, God left a very cryptic message for the Babylonian king, Belshazzar. Eventually, Daniel was dispatched to interpret the cryptic writing, but not until the Persians had already entered the gates. Until that moment, Daniel was in the dark. Like an Earthly Shunemite, Daniel didn't know what was about to unfold.

Paul was a symbolic Shunemite (who hoped to become a Shulamite). He said: "Brethren, I could not myself yet to have laid hold: but one thing [I do], forgetting the things which are before, I press on toward the goal unto the prize of the high calling of God in Christ Jesus," –Phlp 3:13-14

There is no shame that God's people don't know every hidden matter of God. It has always been so. Jesus wasn't embarrassed when he admitted he didn't know the "day nor the hour." (Mt 24:36) Muhammad wasn't embarrassed when he confessed that neither he, nor anyone else, knew about his ancestors beyond al-Nather bin Kinaneh. (Halabieh I, pg 36)

Why doesn't our God dialogue with today's Earthly Shunemites? They are like Daniel, waiting in Babylon. For them, holy text will have to suffice.

What's the point of a prophet, unless they intercede in behalf of the innocent? At least the Earthly Shunemite is painfully aware of the implications of the appointed time, spoken of in Re 11:18, ". . . thy wrath came, and the time of the dead to be judged, and [the time] to give their reward to thy servants."

The Shunemite may not be a prophet, but she makes four intercessions. (So 2:7; 3:5; 5:8; 8:4) She intercedes for those who have yet to make it to safety. (Re 6:11; 18:20) The Earthly Shunemite is Abishag (before Jesus) and the Earthly Shunemite class (after Jesus) who are waiting for the world-to-come—the "Israel of God." (Gal 6:15-16)

HEAVENLY BROTHERS:

After the Earthly Shunemite is resurrected, she lingers between Heaven and earth. Jesus, himself, lingered forty days before ascending to Heaven. (Lk 24:51) Only then, did his Angelic Brothers (angels) take him away to Heaven. (Ac 1:1-11)

Likewise, the Shulamite's new Angelic Brothers will escort her into Heaven—after a period of time. These are her new brothers. Heavenly Brothers are uncles to the Earthly Brothers, since they are brothers of our eternal father (Jesus) and our mother (the Jerusalem Above).

The prophet Ezekiel described how Jehovah would put new flesh on those with an earthly resurrection. (Ezk 37:3-6) That passage applies to Earthly Brothers—not Heavenly. Flesh cannot reside in Heaven. Likewise, before the Earthly Shunemite can ascend to Heaven (as a Shulamite), her "wrap" of flesh must be removed. That removal service will be performed by her Heavenly Brothers. (So 5:7; Is 53:10)

Heavenly angels support the Heavenly Solomon and his family. Angels announced the conception and birth of Jesus; they ministered to Jesus after his forty-day fast; they strengthened Jesus when he prayed in the Garden of Gethsemane; they announced the resurrection of Jesus, and escorted him to Heaven. (2Sa 24:16; Ps 34:7)

"Are they not all ministering spirits, sent forth to do service for the sake of them that shall inherit salvation?" *–Heb 1:14*

EARTHLY BROTHERS:

Earthly Brothers seek God, but they are naïve. The naïve have no strength against evil. "He that trusteth in his own heart is a fool. *–Pr 28:26*

Ephraim represented the Earthly Brother class. Jeroboam, an Ephraimite, was the first king of the ten-tribe nation. Ephraim was the greatest of the ten tribes, in terms of population. But, their Temple was invalid. (1Ki 12:27-28) Jesus described the ten-tribes' fraud politely at Joh 4:22.

Simply put: the God we worship doesn't like naïve people, because they endanger His children. (Is 5:13; Jer 4:22) If the entire book of *Proverbs* can't convince an Earthly Brother of God's disgust for stupidity, nothing can.

Earthly Brothers seek God, but they can't go to Heaven. (Ac 24:15) The nearest they can get to Heaven is, earthly Zion. (Is 24:23; Jer 3:14; Mic 4:2)

No ancient Jew was ever promised, or expected, a heavenly life. (Ezk 37:3-6) That was a wild and outrageous teaching of Jesus. Holy text never offers a heavenly hope . . . until Jesus arrived.[44] Think about it: no matter how faithful Adam would have been, he could never graduate to Heaven. Going to Heaven was a "Jesus" teaching. It simply does not exist in *Torah*.[45] (Is 11:6-9; 35:5-7)

Just because 144,000 designated followers of Jesus go to Heaven, doesn't mean God's original plan for a paradise earth went away. "The righteous shall inherit the land, And dwell therein for ever." *–Ps 37:29*

The Earthly Brother class was typified when Jacob prophesied Ephraim would have greater numbers. (Ge 48:14-19) That was fulfilled at Re 7:9, when the Ephraim Class was described as a great crowd, which no man could number.

Faithful Ephraimites have grabbed the "fringe" of the Manasseh class. (Jos 22:9) That marked the time period when the "jealousy" of the Ephraimites (Earthly Brothers) would disappear. (Is 11:13)

Ancient Israel was put to death in 70 A.D. At that time, the Earthly Shunemite's Earthly Brothers became the Messiah's "other sheep." (Joh 10:16)

Michael Ben Zehabe
Author; Guest Speaker; Educator: and All-Around-Really-Nice-Guy

Michael Ben Zehabe has written *Semitic Tales, a commentary on Jonah, The Meaning of Hebrew Letters, Ruth: a woman's guide to husband material,* and has an upcoming release, *a commentary on Esther.* Mr. Ben Zehabe has also written curriculum for educators who teach Hebrew. His syndicated column, "Plug In To The Universe," is for an audience with no previous knowledge of Hebrew, but wonder how it influences their spirituality. He has been a guest speaker at various organizations; a guest on radio; appeared on television; and written extensively on the holy language.

If you book guest speakers and want your Youth Group; Married Couples; or Singles Group to get back to basics, ask about his one-hour seminars. If you own a Bridal Shop and would like to sell this book as a wedding gift, go to wholesale at: www.benzehabe.com

Stay In Touch:

Book Stores: In-store seminars and book signings (Sarah Levy: info@benzehabe.com
Media Interviews: Television; Radio; and Journalists (Jonathan Friedman: benzehabe@gmail.com)
LinkedIn: www.linkedin.com/in/Michael-ben-zehabe-31aa0942
Tumblr: www.michael-ben-zehabe-blog.tumblr.com
Pintrest: www.pintrest.com/benzehabe
Web Page: www.benzehabe.com

ENDNOTES

[1] "This song is the most difficult book in the Bible to interpret and has received more different kinds of interpretation than any other." Rev. Arnold B. Rhodes, *The Mighty Acts of God*, Geneva Press, KY, 2000 pg 208

[2] *The New Jerusalem Bible*, Doubleday, New York, 1999.

[3] www.champagnepierremorlet.com, "The Vineyards," 2011

[4] O. Schroeder, *ZAW* 34 (1914), pg 69f; L. Duerr, *Sellin-Festschrift* (Leipzig, 1927), pg 37-48.

[5] Michael Ben Zehabe, *The Meaning of Hebrew Letters*, Shema Publishing, Los Angeles, 2011. (www.benzehabe.com)

[6] "For verily I say unto you, Till Heaven and earth pass away, one jot or one tittle shall in no wise pass away from the law, till all things be accomplished." –*Mt 5:18* "And he came to Nazareth, where he had been brought up: and he entered, as his custom was, into the synagogue on the sabbath day, and stood up to read. 17 And there was delivered unto him the book of the prophet Isaiah. And he opened the book, and found the place where it was written, 18 The Spirit of the Lord is upon me, Because he anointed me to preach good tidings to the poor: He hath sent me to proclaim release to the captives, And recovering of sight to the blind, To set at liberty them that are bruised, 19 To proclaim the acceptable year of the Lord. 20 And he closed the book, and gave it back to the attendant, and sat down: and the eyes of all in the synagogue were fastened on him." –*Lk 4:16-20* "And when we were all fallen to the earth, I heard a voice saying unto me in the Hebrew language, Saul, Saul, why persecutest thou me?'" –*Ac 26:14*

[7] E. Von Dobschutz, 'Zeit und Raum," *Journal of Biblical Literature*, XLI (1922), 212 ff.

[8] "The *Song of Solomon* is a difficult and mysterious book." William Walshamttow, *Twenty-Four Practical Sermons*, Wells Gardner, Darton & Co, London, 1899, pg 145.

[9] *Theological Wordbook of the Old Testament,* edited by R. L. Harris, 1980, Vol. 2, p. 586.

[10] Joseph Epstein, *Divorced in America*, E. P. Dutton, New York, 1974.

[11] "Of all the Bible's chapters, none is more surprising and pagan than the *Song of Solomon.*" John Updike, *More Matter: Essays and Criticism*, Ballantine Books, New York, 1999

[12] "The Apostolic history shows us that many of the old church fathers were leaning toward this view [earthly 1,000-year reign]. So for example Corinthes, who is thought to have been a contemporary of the Apostle John, believed that Christ would have an earthly reign lasting a thousand years with his seat in Jerusalem. Papias in the middle of the second century holds the same view. Likewise, Justin Martyr (about 150 C.E.) says that the majority of the Christians at his time were looking forward to an earthly kingdom." William Masselink, *Reformed Perspectives Magazine*, "The History of Chiliasm," Vol 10, Nu 12 3-22-08.

[13] In the early church Theodore of Mopsuestia (ca. 350–428) took a stand for a literal understanding of the *Song of Songs*, suggesting that it should be read in its plain sense as an erotic song. In time, his view was rejected as heresy by the Second Council of Constantinople in A.D. 553

[14] Michael Ben Zehabe, *The Meaning of Hebrew Letters*, Shema Publishing, Los Angeles, 2011. (www.benzehabe.com)

[15] Reprint requests for his research is available at: Robert M. Rose, MD, Department of Medicine, 720 Harrison Av., #604, Boston, MA 02118

[16] *Ancient Near Eastern Texts,* edited by J. Pritchard, 1974, pg. 280

[17] If you think one king (Jesus), 144,000 underkings (the Bride Class), and 288,000 administrators sounds intrusive, compare their numbers (**432,001**) with the current number of politicians serving in 2023: **over 30 million**, according to Wikipedia. Few and efficient describes the world-to-come. https://en.wikipedia.org/wiki/List_of_legislatures_by_number_of_members

[18] "Those who oppose the teaching of a literal one-thousand year reign of Christ upon earth are in direct opposition to the Word of God!" Jack Van Impe (Television Evangelist), *Revelation Revealed,* pg 233, 1987

[19] David Ian Miller, *SFGate.com,* "Finding My Religion," 11-14-05

[20] Michael Ben Zehabe, *RUTH: a woman's guide to husband material*, 2023, Shema Publishing Company, www.benzehabe.com

[21] Michelle Flythe, *Greater Good,* "The Biology of Happiness," summer, 05

[22] Saadia, a medieval Jewish commentator, said the *Song of Songs* is like a book for which the key has been lost.

[23] Uriel Simon, *Jonah*, The Jewish Publication Society, pg 22, 1999.

²⁴ "The millinial rule of the Messiah will restore mankind to perfection." Dr. David Jeremiah (Television Evangelist), *Turning Point*, www.davidjeremiah.org

²⁵ Over 100 years ago, the noted Old Testament scholar Franz Delitzsch remarked, "The Song is the most obscure book of the Old Testament. Whatever principle of interpretation one may adopt, there always remains a number of inexplicable passages, and just such as, if we understood them, would help to solve the mystery. And yet the interpretation of a book presupposes from the beginning that the interpreter has mastered the idea of the whole. It has thus become an ungrateful task; for however successful the interpreter may be in the separate parts, yet he will be thanked for his work only when the conception as a whole which he has decided upon is approved of."

²⁶ Chrissie Long, *Tico Times.net*, "Elderly Abandonment Peaks During Holiday Season," 12-14-10

²⁷ Judi Culbertson, *The New York Times*, "Some Elderly and Handicapped Being Abandoned," 11-1-81

²⁸ Stan Tenen, *Meru Foundation eTorus*, Number 52, December 2010, pg 3

²⁹ Stan Tenen, www.meru.org/dinisgorilla.html

³⁰ *Watch Tower*, 6-15-09, pg 23, pp 15

³¹ Josephus, *The Jewish War*, III, 516, 517 (x, 8)

³² Isadore Twersky, *A Maimonides Reader*, Library of Jewish Studies, 1972, pg 447.

³³ "Any solution to understanding the *Song of Songs* must first be settled at the hermeneutical level. What hermeneutical

principles are valid for dealing with this literary genre of ancient love poetry? Is there sufficient warrant for departing from a grammatical-historical-contextual hermeneutic?" J. Paul Tanner, *Bibliotheca Sacra* 154: 613 (1997): "The History of Interpretation of the Song of Songs," pg 23

[34] Uriel Simon, *Jonah*, The Jewish Publication Society, pg 22, 1999.

[35] Michael Ben Zehabe, *The Meaning of Hebrew Letters*, Shema Publishing, Los Angeles, 2011, pg 90 and 26. (www.benzehabe.com)

[36] Regarding So 8:1-2, E.P. Eddrup made the following observation: "This, though the most brief, is perhaps the most difficult of any of the portions of Song of Solomon." E.P. Eddrup, *The Old Testament*, Society for Promoting Christian Knowledge, New York, 1896.

[37] Josephus, *The Wars of the Jews,* Book 6, Chpt 4.

[38] In the second century C.E., Irenaeus distinguished paradise from Heaven. In *Against Heresies*, it was written that "only those deemed worthy would inherit a home in Heaven, while others would enjoy paradise." Islam also seeks, "Paradise."

[39] Many provincial thinking Christians forget much of the world does not connect death with living in Heaven. Certainly the Jews were surprised to hear Jesus speak of this new concept of going to "Heaven." Buddhists and Hindus do not share this Christian hope of Heaven. Islam shares a view similar to the early Jews. "Jannah" is the Islamic conception of the resurrection. The Arabic word "jannah" is a shortened version meaning "garden." According to Islamic eschatology, after death, you will reside in the grave until the appointed resurrection on Yawm-al-Qiyamah. Muslims believe your resurrected life will be in accordance with your deeds in your

former life. "Paradise" itself is frequently described in the Koran. The highest level of Paradise is Firdaus, which is where the prophets, the martyrs, the most truthful, and pious people will dwell.

[40] John Calvin's exposition of that part of the Lord's Prayer all but adopts the minority postmillennial position but Calvin, and later Charles Spurgeon, were remarkably inconsistent on eschatological matters. Spurgeon delivered a sermon on Psalm 72 explicitly defending the form of absolute postmillennialism held by the minority camp today, but on other occasions he defended premillennialism. John Calvin, *Institutes of the Christian Religion*, 2:190, Eerdmans, Grand Rapids, 1981.

[41] "The most striking point in the eschatology of the ancient church is the widely current and very prominent chiliasm [1,000-year reign], or the doctrine of a visible reign of Christ in glory on earth with the risen saints for a thousand years." Philip Schaff, LLD, *The Creeds of Christendom*, Harper & Brothers pub., NY, pg 299, 1877.

[42] Thorlief Boman, *Hebrew Thought Compared with Greek*, W. W. Norton & Company, Inc., New York, 1970, pg 77.

[43] As Erich Auerbach points out in his essay "Figura," typological (figural) interpretation as *figura rerum* they were a prefiguration of Christ." Eric Auerbach, "Figura," pp 53-57.

[44] "The Judaistic features of Chiliasm [mellinnial reign] can be readily seen by an examination of the Apocalyptic writings of the Jews. The genesis of this doctrine may be found in these writings which are generally dated in the pre-Christian period." "This is exactly the position of the Premillennialists of today. Christ's Messianic kingdom comes first and after that the kingdom of God. That the Chialiasts have incorporated a part of ancient Jewish eschatology in their scheme of the future is very evident. A general survey of the Jewish writings

is all that is necessary to establish this fact." William Masselink, *Reformed Perspectives Magazine*, "The History of Chiliasm," Vol 10, Nu 12, 3-22-08.

[45] Modern theologians such as Chuck Smith, founder of Calvary Chapel mega churches states, "The rapture of the Church will occur first, followed by a literal seven-year period of Great Tribulation, followed by the second coming of Jesus Christ, and then finally a literal thousand-year reign of Jesus Christ on earth called the Millennial Kingdom." Chuck Smith, *Calvary Chapel Doctrine and Distinctives*, "The Rapture of The Church," The Word For Today, 1993.

www.ingramcontent.com/pod-product-compliance
Lightning Source LLC
Chambersburg PA
CBHW050528300426
44113CB00012B/1999